Tanami

Also by Kieran Kelly

Hard Country Hard Men – In the footsteps of Gregory

Kieran Kelly
Tanami

On foot across Australia's desert heart

MACMILLAN
Pan Macmillan Australia

First published 2003 in Macmillan by Pan Macmillan Australia Pty Limited
St Martins Tower, 31 Market Street, Sydney

National Library of Australia
cataloguing-in-publication data:

Kelly, Kieran, 1952– .
Tanami: On foot across Australia's desert heart.

ISBN 0 7329 1188 5.

1. Gregory, Augustus Charles, Sir, 1819–1905 – Journeys – Australia.
2. Stuart, John McDouall, 1815–1866 – Journeys – Australia.
3. Warburton, Peter Egerton, 1813–1889 – Journeys – Australia.
4. Terry, Michael, 1899–1981 – Journeys – Australia.
5. Kelly, Kieran, 1952– – Journeys.
6. Tanami Desert (N.T.) – Discovery and exploration.
7. Tanami Desert (N.T.) – Description and travel.
8. Australia – Discovery and exploration.
I. Title

919.429104

Typeset in 13/15pt Bembo by Midland Typesetters
Printed in Australia by McPherson's Printing Group
Cartographic art by Laurie Whiddon, Map Illustrations
Internal photographs: Kieran Kelly & Andrew Harper
Michael Terry's photograph of Thomson's Rockhole
courtesy of the National Library of Australia

To Bert Hingley,
literary mentor

This is really a crazy idea. It probably won't work but that will be interesting, too. You have to motivate yourself with challenges. That's how you know you're still alive. Once you start doing only what you've already proven you can do, you're on the road to death.

Jerry Seinfeld
The New York Times
September 2002

CONTENTS

LIST OF MAPS

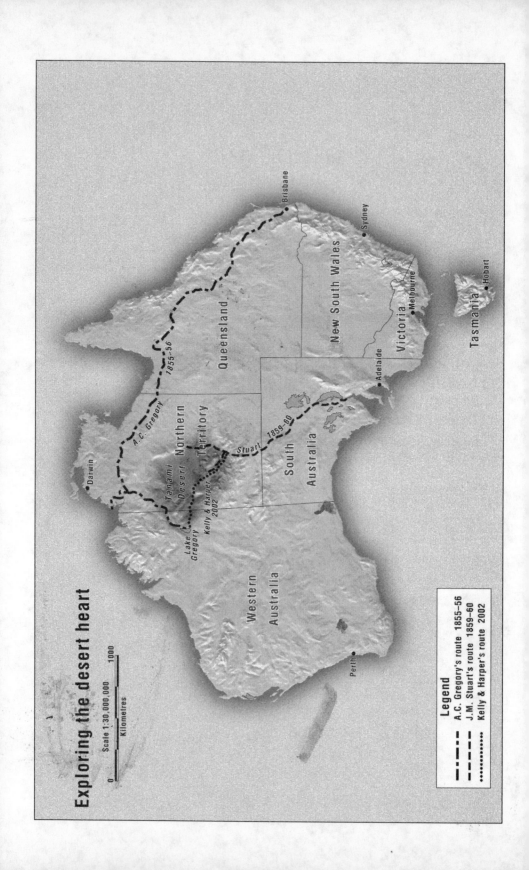

Exploring the desert heart

Scale 1:30,000,000

0 ___ Kilometres ___ 1000

Legend

— · — A.C. Gregory's route 1855–56

— — — J.M. Stuart's route 1859–60

· · · · · Kelly & Harper's route 2002

Darwin

Tamami Desert

Northern Territory

A.C. Gregory

1855–56

Queensland

Brisbane

Sydney

New South Wales

Melbourne

Victoria

Tasmania

Hobart

Adelaide

Stuart

1859–60

South Australia

Western Australia

Perth

Lake Gregory

Kelly & Harper 2002

INTRODUCTION

Stuart's furthest point west:
What am I doing here?

The last time white men had stood on this ridge, they were dying – their bodies ripped by scurvy and weakened by starvation rations. Their horses were perishing from lack of water. They were beaten. It was a sobering thought, and as I looked across to my travelling companion I took a long drink from my water bottle. The water was warm, but I didn't care. Andrew looked around at our grim surroundings. When the explorer John McDouall Stuart reached this lonely spot in 1860, not far from the centre of Australia, he felt life slipping through his grasp. Beyond rescue, his group faced a desperate scramble back through the wilderness to a tiny waterhole on dying horses. It would take more than great horsemanship; he needed luck now. Stuart realised that his horses and men had only a day before the harsh desert consumed them. It was a frightening place. I took another mouthful of water. It was almost hot, but I had never tasted anything as good.

In front of us was a wall – a wall not built by man, but by nature; a wall of dense spinifex and acacia. The late afternoon heat boiled out of the scrub. There was no sign of water, no sign of life, not even native animals. It was a brutal landscape. Sweat ran down my backbone like a river. My shirt was soaked. Our pack camels looked forlornly at the dense bush that hemmed us in.

'How're we going to get through this?' I asked Andrew, whose desert experience had provided all the answers so far. 'It's no wonder Stuart turned back here.'

'We'll just have to pick our way through it,' he replied. 'But there'll be a lot of weaving around and it won't be easy.' Andrew looked as battered as I felt: bare arms in his sleeveless shirt burned from the sun and legs black from spinifex resin. He took a long swig from his canteen.

'What would you do in this situation in other deserts?' I asked.

He took a moment to reply. 'Well, it never gets this dense in the Simpson or Gibson deserts. You can always walk around the spinifex and mulga down there. This sure is thick. I've no idea how far we'll have to go before the country breaks, either. It might be like this all the way to Thomson's Rockhole. It's going to be slow.'

'Scrub traps the heat, doesn't it?' he added.

I had never experienced anything like it. This was the dry season, the cool time of year in northern Australia, but the desert surface was so hot I could feel it through the soles of my boots. We were walking northwest, straight into the afternoon sun which burned through my shirt. I turned up my collar for protection. Waves of heat billowed out of the spinifex. Sweat running down my face dripped off my chin and I wiped it on a shirt sleeve caked in dirt. I had been wearing the same clothes for nearly a fortnight.

We stood catching our breath, two men and five camels attempting to cross the Tanami Desert on foot. Andrew broke the silence. 'So this is where Stuart got to?' he asked, looking around thoughtfully. 'How accurate is your fix?'

'I took his position from the map Stuart drew when he

came back from his trip, then I transferred it to the modern topographical map,' I replied.

I looked at Stuart's map as I had done many times in recent weeks. It was a copy of the nineteenth-century original, showing Stuart's attempt to penetrate the Tanami Desert. His line of march stopped abruptly in the middle of the map. On the modern map in my other hand, a thin pencil line stretched up from the southeast to the point where we now stood. Sweat fell in fat drops on the maps and ran down the creases. A circled cross on the map marked our location. Beside the cross, I had written the words: *John McDouall Stuart. Furthest point west 1860.*

'If we're out, it's only marginal. I couldn't find his original sketchbooks. They seem to have disappeared. The probable error is less than a kilometre, but keep in mind he was fixing his position with a sextant, so I won't vouch for the original map,' I said.

'Well, I think you're right. This ridge would've been burned in Stuart's time, with a lot less scrub. He'd have had a pretty good look at the country ahead from up here and he'd have realised how hopeless it was. He wouldn't have camped here, though, on top of the ridge.' Andrew looked despairingly at the dense mulga.

'There would've been nothing here for his horses to eat. I think he would've gone back down to the plain, where there's some grass,' he added. 'I think we should do the same.'

The dense scrub pressed in on us, emphasising the oppressive heat. This was no desert vista. The thickets of sun-withered, thorny vegetation blocked any view. I had seen wider aspects in Sydney's back lanes.

'Imagine dying of thirst in a place like this, beyond any help,' I said. Andrew just shook his head. It didn't bear thinking about. We turned and headed back the way we had come, back down off the ridge, as the sun dipped towards the horizon. The pressure from the relentless heat eased momentarily.

The camels crashed through the mulga: mobile, scrub-clearing leviathans mounted with packsaddles and water jerrycans. The temperature began to drop and a slight breeze cooled the sweat on our bodies. Silence and stillness shrouded the Tanami.

We camped at the top of the long plain just below the line of scrub. It was late in the afternoon of 26 July 2002. It had been a difficult day, but the first part of our journey was over.

We had hit our first target. The ridge above where we sat was the furthest point reached by the gutsy little Scotsman John McDouall Stuart in his 1860 pack-horse trip into the Tanami Desert. Desperate to pioneer a transcontinental route, he risked everything. Nevertheless, on this, his first attempt, he would be denied. Despite his boundless courage and keen bush skills, the Tanami battered him so badly he threw in the towel. A stubborn, determined man, oblivious of personal hardship, Stuart made his decision to retreat with great regret and only when death was the other option. This decision, taken where our tiny campfire now burned, saved his life and those of his men and horses. He lived to explore another day and in doing so wrote himself into Australian history. We now faced the same choice: would we turn back as Stuart had done, or would we keep going deeper into the desert?

'I don't know if it's the end of the beginning or the beginning of the end,' I said to Andrew that evening as we sat on our swags. 'But it feels like we've achieved something.'

'We're just getting warmed up,' he replied.

In my 50th year I was sitting beneath a lonely ridge in an ancient desert, a desert devoid of water and blasted by a pitiless sun. Far from home, wife and family, my only companions were five camels and a man, eleven years my junior, whom I hardly knew. We were attempting a journey on foot that had defeated not only Stuart but also his contemporary, Augustus Gregory, the greatest explorer to saddle a horse in Australia. Many experts said it was impossible, that we were mad to try. How did this strange turn of events come about? What was I doing there, a businessman more at home in Sydney's glass towers? I shook my head in wonder and turned back the clock two years.

CHAPTER 1

A crazy idea

'This looks interesting,' Prue said. My wife was sitting at the kitchen table one Saturday morning, flicking through the pages of *Outback* magazine. 'Someone has just walked across Australia on his own, with three camels. On his own! Gee, that's dangerous.'

She threw the magazine over to me. I looked at the cover. It was the February 2000 issue, with four mounted horsemen on the front. Inside were photographs showing a man in a sleeveless shirt and a white hat seated on a ridge overlooking red desert country, his gaze fixed on three loaded pack camels off in the middle distance. His name was Andrew Harper.

I sat reading the article in the brief interlude between finishing breakfast and driving the children to rowing training and tennis practice. The sound of Catherine's clarinet wafted in from the lounge room. My youngest daughter was practising scales and melodies.

The story riveted me. Andrew Harper had walked from south of Exmouth Gulf on the Indian Ocean to Rockhampton on the other side of the country, the article said. In eight months, he travelled almost 5000 kilometres from coast to coast, following his compass and the Tropic of Capricorn. Alone, except for Mac, a kelpie, and three camels, he had crossed some of the harshest deserts in the world, seeing few roads or people. He had no back-up vehicles or support. Why did he do it? *I really don't know, it just seems an obvious thing to do. I know that if I never attempted it, I would be forever frustrated. If there are reasons why I shouldn't attempt the journey, I guess they'll occur while I'm out there,* the article quoted him as saying before he set out.

With a cup of tea in hand, I picked up the story again later that afternoon. I got out a decent atlas and traced the route of Harper's astonishing adventure. 'Bugger me! That's really a long way. Right across the guts of Australia,' I said to Prue. 'I'm going to write to this bloke and invite him to dinner.'

'Whatever for?' she asked, surprised.

It was a spur-of-the-moment thing, prompted by the sight of the fully laden pack camels in the photos that accompanied the article. The story had given me the germ of an idea. 'I'd like to meet him. I think what he did was amazing.'

'What are you planning?' She looked suspiciously at the atlas, open next to the magazine article.

'Nothing. And don't give me that look. I'd like to hear how he planned it and organised it, why he chose camels and not horses, and why he went on his own; particularly, why he went on his own. It's so bloody dangerous and it's such a long way.'

'I hope you're not planning to disappear into the desert with a bunch of camels?' my long-suffering wife said.

'No, of course not,' I said. Not immediately, anyway, I thought.

However, there was a small matter I was concealing from my wife.

In 1856 the peerless Australian explorer, Augustus Gregory, led three men and eleven horses in a lightning, lightweight dash from a depot camp to the headwaters of the Victoria River in today's Northern Territory. He hoped the river would lead him to central Australia, but the waterway petered out and he found instead a red desert hell, which we know today as the Tanami Desert. He was the first European to see this fearsome wasteland near the present-day Lajamanu Aboriginal community. Undeterred, he retreated and travelled west into Western Australia and then trekked down the side of the desert until he reached a large salt lake. The lake he discovered was thereafter shown on maps as Gregory's Salt Sea. Today it's called Lake Gregory. Climbing a nearby mountain, which he named Mt Wilson, he looked towards central Australia and speculated that there was no water to be found there. To continue into the Tanami would destroy his men and his horses, he wrote.

Four years later, John McDouall Stuart pushed into the Tanami from the other side – the eastern side. Like Gregory, he used pack and riding horses. Stuart tried to reach Gregory's lake or the Victoria River but was also beaten back, speculating that there was no water and to continue would mean death.

Drawn indelibly on maps of Australia are two lines reaching out towards each other, across a sea of sand. No one has ever joined them. This gap had intrigued me since I was a high school history student. Why had both explorers chosen to turn back where they did? What was the country like, beyond their chosen points of return? What would have happened to them, and their men and animals, had they kept going and not retreated? Why had no one since tried to join the two points?

I had presumed for over 30 years that it hadn't been done because it *couldn't* be done. Now, I wasn't so sure. All these thoughts tumbled around in my head as I sat in the sun that Saturday afternoon, looking at the photographs of the camels and the desert and studying Andrew Harper's route in the atlas. 'God, that's a long way,' I kept saying to myself. For now, my thoughts remained my own, but a plan was forming.

Tilly, our dog, barked to announce Andrew's arrival. It was evening, Easter Saturday 2000. A Toyota four-wheel drive was parked in the driveway. The thicket of radio and satellite telephone antennae on the bullbar signalled that this wasn't a city visitor. Andrew bent down and soothed the dog, like a person long used to handling animals. First impressions: he was clean-cut, a bit shorter than me and a lot younger. Face tanned by the sun, fit-looking, firm handshake. That was a good start. Over a roast dinner, he copped a grilling.

'Why'd you go on your own?' was my first question.

'It's much easier to do these things by yourself. You don't have to worry about conflicting personalities and keeping everyone happy. Also, you don't need as many camels, so it's easier to manage.'

'Didn't you get lonely?' Prue asked.

'Not really. There was always plenty to look at, and I'm pretty happy with my own company.'

'Weren't you scared? What would have happened if you got hurt?' she asked.

'I had a satellite phone on one of my camels, so I could always call for help,' Andrew said.

'It breaks every rule in the book, though. Ever since I was a kid I was told you should never go into remote places by yourself,' I said.

'That's true, but I've spent a lot of time out in the desert and I'm experienced with camels. I think I've got a good appreciation of the risks. I felt in more danger driving here this evening,' he said with a laugh.

Andrew clearly wasn't someone who felt totally at ease in

cities, but an eccentric recluse he was not. As the evening progressed and we continued to ply him with questions, I learned that he was an intelligent, quietly spoken person who loved the solitude of the Australian deserts and the challenge of walking across them. I couldn't wait to ask Prue what she thought of him – her instinct for character was infallible.

We sat enthralled as he talked about his first trips taking tourists across the Gibson and Simpson deserts with Rex Ellis, the pioneering South Australian camel operator. Andrew learned the business by providing his labour cheaply. Ultimately, Andrew bought the Outback Camel Company from Ellis and went into business for himself. He developed a model of tourists walking, rather than riding the camels, and taking very long trips, up to 30 days. His clients were clearly not average tourists. Our girls were starting to drift away from the dinner table, as teenagers do, but Hilary couldn't help but ask, 'Don't camels bite and spit?'

Andrew laughed. 'Well, they've never bitten or spat on me,' he said. 'They wouldn't be game.'

'Why don't you ride the camels, instead of walking?' Amelia asked.

'We always provide a couple of riding camels for guests on the trips who get too tired to walk, but the more riding camels you take, the fewer you have to carry food and water. Personally, I get a bit bored riding. While I still can, I prefer to walk.' This fitted perfectly with my philosophy that one way to see Australia is in a four-wheel drive, but a better way is on the back of a horse, exposed to the environment. The most effective experience, although the toughest, is on foot.

Although our lives were very different – Andrew challenged the deserts, while I sat behind a desk – I sensed a kindred spirit. I finally got around to the question I had been bursting to ask all night. 'So, you've done the Gibson, the Simpson, the Nullarbor and the Sturt Stony Desert – why not the Tanami?' The question seemed to surprise him.

'The Tanami, that's an interesting one. I don't know much about it. It's a long way north, way above the Tropic of Capricorn, so it'd be difficult to organise trips up there. From what I've heard, it's very flat and very dry. It'd be hot, too, up in the tropics. I've never heard of anyone walking across it. I don't even know if any four-wheel-drive tracks go across it.'

'So, it would be impossible to take horses across it?' I asked.

'My word. Even today, with all our modern technology, you couldn't get horses across most of the deserts I've crossed, and I think the Tanami wouldn't be any different.'

'But it should be possible to walk across it?' I asked.

Andrew thought for a while before replying. 'Ummm, it's possible to walk across *any* desert with camels, though, as I said, as far as I know, no one's walked right across the Tanami.'

We pounded Andrew with questions all night but he never blinked. His courtesy and patience were apparent long before the evening had finished. As we shook hands and said goodbye, I gave him a copy of my book, *Hard Country Hard Men*, which deals with the life and explorations of Augustus Gregory.

'Thanks. I'll read it out in the desert.' He threw the book into the Toyota and drove off.

'So what'd you think?' I asked Prue, who was cleaning up in the kitchen.

'He's a nice bloke. Different than you'd expect from someone who makes a living hauling camels around the outback. Very courteous and thoughtful, very well educated, I'd say. Didn't grow up in the bush. I bet he went away to boarding school,' she said.

'How can you tell that?' I asked, surprised.

'By the way he speaks; he doesn't have the country accent that you have.'

'Thanks a lot. People can't tell I come from the bush,' I said, laughing.

'Not much!' she said.

'There's certainly an interesting story there. I wonder what his family does?'

After everything was packed away and the children had disappeared to bed, I pulled out the atlas and a pair of dividers. One point of the dividers I placed on Central Mt Stuart in the Northern Territory, where Stuart had begun his push into the Tanami. I stretched them out and placed the other point on Lake Gregory – the scale read 720 kilometres. Prue was closing the curtains and looking over my shoulder.

'It's 720 kilometres from Mt Stuart to Lake Gregory. You could walk that in seven weeks,' I said.

'Yes, but why would you want to?' She sat down heavily in a chair. 'What are you cooking up? Come on, tell me. I'm not getting up 'til you tell me what's on your mind.'

My plan was a simple one. Two men, half a dozen camels, using Gregory's and Stuart's maps to establish the starting and finishing points. Food and water on the camels. Walk all the way.

Prue sat looking at me with her mouth open as I outlined my plan. 'You can't be serious,' she said.

'Yes, I am. I think it can be done,' I said. I had completed three expeditions in the Northern Territory, retracing parts of the route of Gregory's North Australian Expedition, one with pack horses and two on foot. We'd had this conversation before.

'There's one small problem: you don't know Andrew that well. You've only met him once and you don't know if he would want to do it. You'd have to get the time off work. And it's very dangerous. You've got a family to think about, you know.'

'I agree with everything you say, but all those things can be solved.'

'Is there any water out there?'

'No, probably not. But you heard him, it could be carried on the camels.'

Prue looked upset. 'What if the camels take off? What if you can't keep up with him? He's eleven years younger than you. And what if something happens to him? *You* can't manage the camels! Have you ever *seen* a camel?'

'I've seen pictures of them in books. They're brown.'

'This isn't funny,' she said as she walked away.

'Anyway, don't worry about it, it's just a crazy idea. Nothing'll come of it,' I said to my wife's retreating back. She was right about one thing: I had to convince Andrew first. How to do it? I decided that direct action was the best approach.

Over the following months, I mapped out a potential route that followed Stuart's journey out into the desert, then went straight across the central Tanami, crossing the border at Wilson's Cave bore and then went south and west to Lake Gregory. I photocopied Gregory's and Stuart's maps and made a rough trace of them on the modern maps I planned to send to Andrew. I estimated the amounts of food and water required, and wrote lists of all the issues that would have to be resolved: transport of camels to and from the expedition, likely navigational problems, safety, rescue, communications and cost. The last one was the big one. Previous experience had shown me that there would be no sponsors for something like this in Australia. We would be funding it out of our own pockets. It would be expensive.

In August, I rang Andrew at his home in Deniliquin and pitched the idea to him. He didn't say anything as I outlined my proposal. When I had finished, I held my breath, expecting that he would rubbish the idea. After all, we had only met the once.

'That explains why you were so curious about the Tanami,' he said.

'Are you interested?' I asked. There was silence on the line.

'I'd have to think about it. I've got some reservations. It won't be easy and it won't be cheap,' he said, prophetically.

We talked at length about some of the problems. A big one for both of us was taking time away from our respective small businesses. There would have to be sacrifices. For me, there was also the time away from my family. This was always hard. Andrew also saw a shortage of camel feed – trees and shrubs – as being possibly a bigger problem than the lack of water.

'We could carry enough water for ourselves, and in an emergency top-up the camels out of our supplies,' he said. 'Anyway, they could probably do the whole journey on one good drink of water at Mt Stuart, as long as the feed's good enough. If the feed's sparse or we strike a lot of burned country, we'd be in trouble.'

One of the myths about camels is that they don't need water. Like all mammals, they need water and will die without it. It's how they get water that makes them unique. They have evolved a mechanism of dual stomachs for extracting water from the shrubs and trees on which they feed. They strip the tree of greenery, chew it, send it down into one stomach, bring it up, chew it, and send it down again. Three or four turns of this extracts up to 90 per cent of the moisture in the plant before it's finally sent down into the second stomach and digested.

Andrew seemed particularly intrigued by the opportunity to do something that hadn't been done before – to walk across a part of Australia that had defied earlier attempts. The idea of finding out what would have happened to both Gregory's and Stuart's expeditions if they had kept going also intrigued him. Nevertheless, and not unexpectedly, he wouldn't commit there and then, on the phone.

'Send me all the material and I'll let you know,' he said.

A month went by, then two, and as the rest of Sydney wound up for the Sydney Olympics 2000 party, I became increasingly restless. 'I wonder why he hasn't called,' I said to Prue. 'Maybe he's just not interested.'

Finally, he rang.

'Hi, it's Andrew. Sorry it's taken so long, but I've been out in the Simpson Desert and only got back to Birdsville last week. I thought a lot about your proposal while I was out there, and I'd like to give it a try.'

I jumped out of my chair with excitement.

'But I couldn't do it next year, or even the year after. It would probably be three years before my business would be sufficiently established to be able to run without me during the busy season. Can you wait that long?'

My heart sank. That's 2003. I'd be 51 years old. I felt the stab of time slipping away. But if that's the best he can do, I thought, then I'll just have to wait. We agreed to stay in touch.

The delay had some advantages. It was a great relief to Prue, who figured that the longer the postponement, the less chance there was that it would happen. While I, too, felt that something planned for three years in the future had little chance of eventuating, it gave me something to look forward to as I went off to work each day. More importantly, it gave me plenty of time to research and plan the trip.

The first job was to find out more about Stuart. Much had been written about the man traditionally anointed as Australia's greatest land explorer. As Sydney was gearing up for the Olympics, I learned that John McDouall Stuart was born in Dysart, on the north side of the Firth of Forth opposite Edinburgh, Scotland. Educated as a civil engineer at the Scottish Naval and

Military Academy, he sailed for South Australia in 1839, aged 23 years. He was neither an imposing figure nor the stuff of legend. Standing only 168 centimetres and weighing less than 54 kilograms, he was shorter than my teenage daughters and lighter than most of the saddles that Andrew and I would one day heave on to our camels. Described by a fellow passenger on the *Indus* as 'delicate', Stuart twice vomited blood on the journey to Adelaide.

'How's the research going?' Catherine would inevitably ask, wandering into my home office on her way to bed. The office was crammed with reference books, navigational instruments and maps.

'Well, it looks like Stuart may have had a duodenal ulcer or tuberculosis, as he was vomiting blood during the voyage to Australia. Not a bright start for a rugged man of action.'

'Yuk,' was her considered reply.

I explained that there were further reasons why Stuart was at a disadvantage compared to Gus Gregory. Gregory was four years younger than Stuart, and by his early twenties was already a seasoned Australian explorer.

'Is that important?' Catherine asked.

'I think so. Gregory grew up in Australia in the deserts east of Perth. I'll be very surprised if we don't find that he was a better bushman than Stuart. And Gregory wasn't from the military, so he wasn't in it for the fame. Exploration was his day job.'

'Sounds very interesting,' she said, rolling her eyes and giving me a hug.

By 1844, Stuart had gained sufficient experience to be included in Charles Sturt's expedition to the centre of Australia. This expedition revealed Sturt's bull-headed, death-or-glory approach to exploration. This never-say-die mentality, pushing on even when common sense said 'go back', was obvious in Stuart's later attack on the Tanami. Sturt's expedition almost reached the centre of Australia; he came closer than any previous European. This was little consolation to James Poole (Sturt's friend and second in command), who died on the expedition from a combination of scurvy and exhaustion.

Sturt's expedition, while brave, showed much that was wrong with British military attitudes to the Australian out-back and how to penetrate it. It was burdened with too much gear loaded on slow-moving bullock drays. It attempted to move live food supplies – flocks of sheep – across the country. In the desert that Sturt was trying to penetrate, there was never enough water for men, let alone a vast herd of thirsty mammals. Most importantly, it showed the typical willingness of English officers such as Sturt to risk the lives of their men in the pursuit of glory. Sturt either completely misunderstood scurvy or completely disregarded it. Captain James Cook had shown 74 years earlier how to keep men alive and healthy on long exploring trips. Gus Gregory, only a decade after Sturt, would emulate Cook's example. Sturt chose to ignore the impact of this dreadful disease. Both Sturt and Stuart were so stricken with scurvy that Stuart lost the use of his limbs and was virtually bedridden for a year following this initial explor-ing foray. While Stuart would ultimately jettison much of Sturt's inappropriate exploration technique, a disregard for scurvy and a willingness to expose both himself and his men to extraordinary privation would become hallmarks of his expeditions.

Despite the hardships of this first journey a fire had been lit in Stuart. During a speech he made in Adelaide on the expedition's return, he said that people would be mistaken in believing that journeys *through the scorching deserts of the north were unrelieved by any agreeable change. This was a mistake. They had all along the pleasure which enlightened men know how to appreciate of admitting the stupendous works of nature.* Over the next sixteen years, Stuart led three expeditions into those scorching deserts north of Adelaide, surveying, exploring and seeking arable grazing land, and probing ever closer to the mythical Australian centre.

The Olympics came and went, and my life took a jolt. For me the Games left a terrible legacy. I had floated a small publishing company on the stock market in May 2000, and by December of that year it was struggling to survive. Crushed between the worst advertising market in two decades and the shattering decline in share-market values following the collapse of the Internet bubble, I suddenly had no time to think of exploration.

In January 2001, as Australia returned to work with a post-Olympics hangover, Bernadette Brennan, my very capable marketing manager, told me that not one of our major advertising clients had re-signed for 2001. They had spent all their money during the Olympics and there was nothing left for the following year. It was the low point of my commercial life. I wondered how we would get through the year. Between us, we decided to remake the company, taking it away from low-margin publishing into higher-margin marketing. It took all the experience I had gained from over twenty years of dealing with public companies. Every day was a crisis, and I would drag myself home in the evening and just sit and stare at the wall. I was exhausted.

In late April, as our battle for corporate survival continued, Cheryl, our receptionist, put a call through: 'Kieran, a Mr Harper for you.'

I didn't immediately recognise the name and, thinking it was a disgruntled shareholder, I picked up the phone with about as much enthusiasm as I would a tiger snake.

'G'day, Kieran. It's Andrew Harper from Deniliquin,' a cheerful voice said.

'Hello, mate,' I said, relieved at the prospect of a conversation on a subject other than business. 'What can I do for you?' He was in town and wanted a meeting tomorrow morning. He only had an hour.

I hadn't seen or heard from Andrew for six months, but he was unmistakable when he walked into the coffee shop on George Street – the suntan, shorts and big Blundstone boots certainly set him apart from me and the other suits. The words from Henry Lawson's poem floated into my mind: *There was a man from Ironbark who came to Sydney town . . .*

He got straight down to business.

'I've been thinking about your proposal and I've read your book. I'm interested in trying this Tanami trip. Are you still keen?' He put on the table the proposal I had sent him the previous August.

I told him that I was still keen, but that the last six months had been such a nightmare that I'd hardly thought about it. I hadn't finished the research and I hadn't done any training. I asked if he was still tied up until 2003.

'Yes, I think we should do it in June or July 2003. That's the coolest time of the year, and it gives me plenty of time to organise my schedule of guided trips.'

Andrew certainly planned well in advance. He was proposing a date more than two years away. I told him I'd probably be dead by then, the way things were going with work.

He laughed and we got down to the practical realities. One big issue was cost. Andrew agreed to provide six camels and all the equipment. I would have to pick up the bulk of the other costs.

'We'd have to hire a truck to transport the camels. The only place I could do this is Melbourne and we'd need it for two months. I'd have to go down and pick it up and drive to the Northern Territory. Fuel would be expensive. The camels would have to be trucked from Morgan in South Australia to Central Mt Stuart in the Northern Territory, then picked up in Western Australia at the end of the trip and trucked back to Morgan via Alice Springs,' he said.

This was a huge logistical feat covering over 7000 kilometres. I said I would work out a budget and then we would talk about the most sensitive issue – the split of the cash costs. We agreed it was hopeless trying to get sponsorship – both of us had begged in the past and I was certainly not going to do it again.

Andrew combined enthusiasm for the idea with a regard for the logistical hurdles we would have to overcome to make it a reality. His thoughtful approach to problems was business-like and encouraged me that I had chosen the right man for the job. We were both attempting to run businesses in trying circumstances. I began to understand how he thought. He had spoken to Rex Ellis, his former boss, about the Tanami. It sounded forbidding, although no one he knew had been to the places we planned to visit. 'Hot, flat and monotonous,' was how Ellis described the region after numerous trips up and down the Tanami track, the only serviceable road through the desert.

Andrew and I shook hands on George Street. 'I'm sorry I can't do it any earlier but that's the first window I've got,' he said loudly, over the buses. 'We could do it outside the tourist season, in May or September, but the heat would be a killer.'

Suppressing my disappointment, I agreed to wait and do the trip in the winter – the dry season – of 2003. We went our separate ways – me back to the office and Andrew back to the bush.

'How was Andrew?' Prue asked when I arrived home from work.

I told her that he was keen to go but couldn't do anything for another two years.

'Oh, well. Maybe it's all for the best. Anything can happen in that time,' she said. I detected a sigh of relief.

Despite the proposed trip being two years distant, I began, in my spare time, the painstaking business of transferring Stuart's and Gregory's exploration routes on to modern topographical maps.

The maps required for the journey, six in all, were purchased from the Lands Department in Sydney. When I spread them out end to end in the lounge room at home, they went from one wall to the other – a picture of desert bleakness.

'There's not much detail on any of these maps,' I said, looking at the large patches of white and the lines indicating rolling sandhills.

'Show me where the water is,' Prue said.

'I can't, it's on the back of the camels,' I replied.

Working up modern expedition maps involves taking photocopies of the microfilmed explorer's maps in the Mitchell Library, tracing these often faint maps on to tissue paper, scanning the traced image into a computer and enhancing the image with Photoshop. The maps are usually annotated in copperplate handwriting, which can be difficult to read until the image is enhanced.

The scanned image is then transferred on to a modern topographical map by superimposing the computer image over the map. This is difficult, as an adjustment has to be made for the difference between magnetic declination (the difference between true north and magnetic north) in the nineteenth century and declination in our own century. I always keep the explorer's journals handy as a reference and, in Gregory's case, his painstakingly accurate sketchbooks. These were compiled while he rode along, using a compass mounted on his saddle. This unique design was well known in the nineteenth century as the Gregory patent compass.

I carefully plotted Stuart's route northwest from Central Mt Stuart on to the modern maps and used a set of dividers to convert the latitude and longitude of his furthest point west from the 1860 map on to the modern one. It was exacting work, and tiring on the eyes. By November, working sporadically, I had finished Stuart's map, nailing his turn-back point to within a kilometre. It was marked with a small ⊕ . This would be our first target.

Then Andrew dropped his bombshell. It was mid-December 2001. It had been one of the toughest years of my life, but we had survived. With the company now in good shape, I had resigned to allow the marketing manager a shot at the top job while I headed back into merchant banking. I was looking forward to taking a break with Prue and the girls at Mollymook on the NSW south coast.

Prue handed me the phone after dinner.

'It's Andrew Harper.'

I guessed that he was ringing to say that, for some reason, he was withdrawing from the expedition. I had been expecting it for the past year. In some ways it would be a relief, as at least one avenue would then be definitely closed off.

'Change of plans. How would you like to do this trip in June 2002?'

I was dumbfounded. For a minute, I said nothing. 'That's only six months away.'

I saw Prue flinch and stop what she was doing. Andrew explained that he was closing his business temporarily from June 2002 while the imbroglio over insurance for tourist operators was sorted out. He had become yet another victim of the Australian insurance mess.

I had a million questions rattling around in my head. 'Can it be organised in that time? What about the permits, would we be able to get them?' I stammered. This had genuinely taken me by surprise. The permits were to cross Aboriginal land. Gaining them can be a difficult and time-consuming process.

'Yes, I think we can do it in that time. There's a lot to do, but I'll go if you will,' he said.

One of the big problems I saw straightaway was fitness training. I hadn't even started, and I had originally planned to give myself a twelve-month window to get physically ready.

'I'll have to talk to the family. I'll call you back,' I said.

Prue had gleaned the essence of the phone conversation and didn't say anything when I first sat back down at the table.

'Well, that's given us something to think about, hasn't it?' she finally said. I opened my mouth to speak. She held up her hand. 'Don't even ask the question. I won't stop you going if you really want to. I think you're mad, but I won't stop you going.'

N
W ✦ E
S

After the children were in bed, Prue and I had the first of many conversations about the expedition. All of them would be variations on a single theme.

'I don't know why you set yourself these impossible tasks. You're making life so hard for yourself. It's hard enough already. Most men are happy just to go off to work. I know you're not, but can't you set goals that aren't so difficult?'

I struggled to explain. 'I need something extra. Just working all the time isn't enough for me. And I think if most blokes were honest with themselves, they'd like more from life than just work.'

The majority of modern men attempt to juggle work and family and there is precious little time for anything else, especially for self, for things of the male spirit. In attempting to juggle all three, they seldom do justice to any. The spirit often suffers the most. Neglect of the inner man is one reason why so many men are unhappy and, possibly, why some die so young.

'Working stimulates my mind, and it's necessary in order to pay the bills and support the family. But there's a part of me that's not challenged, and I *need* that challenge. I need to set a difficult task for myself, almost like a test. It has to be mentally challenging and physically demanding. And yes, it's got to be dangerous. It's not interesting, otherwise. I just can't get that sort of challenge in the office,' I said.

'But you could die out there.'

'Possibly, but unlikely,' I said. 'We take most of the risk out of it with the planning.'

'But you can't take out *all* the risks.'

'No, but therein lies the challenge.'

I was trying to explain to my wife the needs that have whispered to men down the centuries. As modern men age, their service behind a desk wearies them and life can be a chore. You can give up and accept that, and just go through the motions, or you can set a challenge, a test that asks: 'Am I still alive? Am I still growing, still developing and still learning?' It was this need for a test of will, a test of mind, body and spirit, that was drawing me to the desert. It seemed that the ancient Australian wilderness was calling me for a trial.

'I can't really explain it. I'm not sure I really understand it myself. But I bet Andrew knows what I'm talking about. There's absolutely no reason for what he's done, other than the sheer exhilaration of the challenge.'

'Yes, but he hasn't got a family.'

I felt I understood what Andrew had done. Like him, I craved the adventure; the heart-pumping, sinew-stretching and sweat-inducing excitement. The conflict between my obligations to my family and my burning wish to cross the desert caused me great inner turmoil, which ended up staying with me for the entire expedition. The night of Andrew's call, I couldn't give Prue a satisfactory answer, but I had never neglected my family and wasn't going to start now.

'It seems irrational . . . unnecessarily difficult,' Prue said.

'Maybe that's the point.'

'Anyway, you've provided very well for us and never stopped me doing anything I want to do, so I'm not going to stop you doing this,' she said.

CHAPTER 2

Making it happen: In search of the dancing hare

From that point on I pushed the pedal to the metal and kept it there for the next seven months. We had committed to making the trip; now we had to make it happen and it was all up to us. There would be no outside assistance. We split the work: I would tackle the permits and organise the food; Andrew would organise the truck and the fuel.

The first job was to obtain the permits. The Cental Land Council, based in Alice Springs, controls entry to the areas we wished to visit between Mt Stuart and the Western Australian border. The council represents all Aboriginal people living in the cental Australian region – the entire bottom half of the Northern Territory – about 780,000 square kilometres. This is roughly the combined size of France and Switzerland.

Aboriginal land is privately owned and, like all other land-owners in Australia, Aboriginal people have the right to refuse others permission to cross the 600 kilometres between Mt Stuart and the border. If they didn't give us a permit, we weren't going anywhere. On the other side of the border, the Western Australian Department of Indigenous Affairs controlled access to the Balgo permit area, which covered Lake Gregory. A permit would be required to go there, too.

I downloaded the permit application forms from the Internet. From the questions, it was clear that they anticipated four-wheel-drive incursions into the bush. There were no boxes to tick for unsupported travellers on foot with camels.

I spent many nights preparing the applications, explaining who we were, how we were planning to travel and what we were trying to achieve. I stressed that the expedition wasn't commercial and that we were funding it out of our own pockets. I agreed to the most sensitive requirements – not to visit sacred sites or remove artefacts – signed the applications, and finally sent them off in February 2002 along with detailed maps showing our planned route.

Five months before we leave . . . that should be plenty of time, I thought.

As part of the permit applications, I had been required to include detailed accounts of Andrew's and my backgrounds. Andrew emailed me his CV from Deniliquin, and I read it with great interest. Prue's hunch was correct – Andrew was educated at Melbourne Grammar. Grammar is the prestigious boys' boarding school in Melbourne, alma mater to the sons of Victoria's politicians, squatters and industrial titans. He had also worked for Rupert Murdoch, Australia's most powerful industrialist, as overseer on Boonoke Station. Boonoke, Murdoch's merino sheep stud in southern New South Wales, is regarded as one of Australia's finest.

'How did he end up in tourism, in the camel business?' Prue asked.

Andrew's CV didn't say. His first job out of school was jackarooing on Kelso Station in Queensland and then in southern New South Wales, before he went to Boonoke in the late 1980s. By the mid-1990s, he was in the camel business. How he got into the Simpson Desert in 1995, and what happened in the intervening years, was a mystery. It's like his life stopped for a while.

'There must be a story there,' I said.

'Well, you'll find out if you spend five weeks in the desert with him,' Prue replied.

No, I had definite opinions about that. 'I'm not going to sit out there and ask him to tell me his life story. I wouldn't like him interrogating me, so I've got to show him the same respect,' I explained. I'd been in the bush enough to know that one of the most precious things among men is privacy.

Prue did have a point, though. I knew virtually nothing about Andrew. He had shown in his trans-Australia walk that he was happy to tackle the wilderness alone, and his business required him to adapt to the needs of large, diverse and in-experienced groups in the bush. How would he respond to just one other person? How would he react in a crisis? Was he moody? What if he got sick of either me or the trip and wanted to quit half-way? I felt queasy just thinking about it.

My next challenge was to get fit. After Andrew gave the expedition the green light, I started walking. Everywhere. Before work, after work, on the weekends. I had a bit of a head start. Earlier that year with my brother Damien, I had traced Augustus Gregory's route from his forward base camp at Depot Creek back to the Wickham River. Dropped in by helicopter, we undertook a gruelling backpack trip through the ruggedly beautiful gorge country that was first explored by Gregory in 1856. Still, that had been only eight days and 100 kilometres; the challenge now was on a different scale.

Central to my training was a soft-sand program at Manly Beach. The two-kilometre return journey in bare feet, test-ing quadriceps and calf muscles and stretching hamstrings, would be the key to my fitness program. For many years, a daily one-kilometre swim had been compulsory, and I kept this up to maintain my upper body strength for lifting heavy gear. To increase this strength, I started weekend kayaking on Sydney Harbour and gradually pumped up the distances.

For Prue, this was a difficult time. Wives in these situations shoulder a heavy load, as they aren't going on the adventure, aren't involved in the turmoil of organisation and sometimes struggle to understand the motivation. Their minds are free to imagine the worst. Once she had accepted the trip as a reality, my back being injured became a constant fear.

'You've already had one lot of spinal surgery. I just hope this doesn't wreck your back, or that you don't end up in the middle of nowhere and can't move,' she said one night. Andrew had told us about the heavy saddles, weighing around 60 kilograms apiece, which had to be lifted on and off the camels each day along with the rest of the gear. He had also mentioned that some people had trouble lifting the jerrycans, which weigh around 24 kilograms each when full of water, two at a time on to the racks on the saddles.

'Well, the camel is sitting down when you load him, so you don't lift the saddle all that high, and it's a two-man lift, so that shouldn't be too bad. If the jerrycans are too heavy, I'll put 'em on one at a time,' I said.

Prue didn't seem convinced. To be honest, neither was I. I'd have to walk the same speed as a man eleven years my junior who spent his every waking moment walking, while I spent every waking moment sitting. Furthermore, to begin constant heavy lifting every day, when I had no history of it, was asking for trouble. I hoped that the swimming and kayaking would get me through.

Lying in bed one night I thought that Prue was asleep until she said suddenly, 'What about snakes?'

'What about them?'

'Are there snakes in the Tanami?'

'Of course. There are snakes everywhere in Australia.'

'What sort?'

'Mulga snakes and death adders.'

'Are they poisonous?'

'What d'you think?'

'What're you going to do if you get bitten?'

Silence. 'Go to sleep.'

'Well, what are you going to do?'

'Put a pressure bandage on, but I won't get bitten by a snake. I've got more chance of being hit by a bus or a meteor out there than I have of being bitten by a snake.'

While I respected snakes, I didn't fear them. One day many years ago, a brown snake had slithered into our family's farm kitchen, while we were having lunch. Apprising itself of the situation, it quickly decamped to the bathroom before taking up residence on the veranda. It was coaxed out of there before a gentle tap on the head with a shovel despatched it to the great beyond. It was huge; when I held it by the tail at full stretch, its head was still on the ground.

'What're you going to do with it?' one of my young brothers had asked.

There was only one thing to do. I retrieved a dinner plate from the kitchen, curled the snake up on it and placed it in the kerosene fridge so that its head poked out from among the lettuces. My mother shrieked the next time she went to get something from the fridge. I'd never seen her move so quickly. We thought it was a hell of a joke.

With the passing of the years came a growing appreciation that snakes are native animals and inevitably, when encountered, are heading the other way. I have left them alone and they have always left me alone. As long as some basic rules are followed, I regard them as being part of the landscape and no threat to humans.

In the Tanami, we could encounter a couple of special snakes. Native to the region is the mulga snake, *Pseudechis australis.* It's a big, cantankerous snake, with a strike-and-chew defensive mechanism that gets plenty of venom into its victims. Known colloquially as the king brown (it's a member of the black snake family), it feeds on mammals, frogs and other reptiles. While it's immune to the bite of other snakes, its venom is deadly to its brothers. The desert death adder (*Acanthophis pyrrhus*) is a smaller, superbly camouflaged snake, with a thick body and a twitching lure on the end of its rat-like tail to attract prey. It uses a strike-and-release defensive mechanism, but its long fangs and toxic venom mean it's a feared reptile. It's nocturnal and difficult to see when resting during the day. This one bothered me, as it hides under sand or leaf litter and waits for something to alight near it. It would be most unfortunate to place your hand carelessly on the ground near this critter. We would probably not see either of these types of snakes during the trip, but if we *were* to step on one with bare feet or find one in the food box or, worse, our swags, it would be goodbye and Godspeed.

Truthfully, I couldn't allay my wife's fears about these characters. The mulga snake has a higher venom yield than the Indian cobra or the American eastern diamondback rattlesnake. Other than to assure her that the risk was minimal, there was nothing I could do. Snakes remained a sore point with Prue until I left for Alice Springs, while I regarded a personality clash with Andrew as a greater threat to the success of the expedition.

N
W ✦ E
S

Andrew did the final costings, and after my initial shock at the price of diesel fuel in outback Australia, we arrived, after some horse-trading, at the split that each of us would have to bear. The contract was a verbal handshake over the phone. It wouldn't stand up in court, but it's the most binding of all agreements between honourable men.

I did a provisioning budget based on my previous experience of bushwalking and horse riding, allowing one kilogram of food each per day. It was based on dried food: oatmeal for breakfast, dry biscuits with cheese and beef jerky for lunch, and freeze-dried meals with pasta and rice for dinner. Staples such as sugar, salt and pepper were included. The schedule called for a 47-day trip averaging twenty kilometres a day and assuming a rest day every seven days. The only luxuries were dried fruits, such as sultanas, dates and apricots. I planned to use Alpenaire and Back Country dried foods, brands I had used before which, though expensive, had proved reliable. Contingencies for speed of walking and consumption of food and water were built in. The total weight of food was 94 kilograms. I costed it and sent my list off to Andrew.

He called in mid-March. 'Thanks for all that. I've a few comments. You've been too tough on the food. Remember, we're not carrying the food ourselves; we've got camels, so we can take a few luxuries.'

'Such as?' I asked.

'Well, apples. I'd budget for an apple a day each, a muesli bar a day each, some UHT milk, some vegetables, jam, peanut butter – stuff like that.'

'If you say so, but you're really talking about some weight. I'll do it again,' I said.

'One other thing.' He was about to flatten me. 'I've checked your route maps and distance calculations and it won't take anything like 47 days. We'll average better than twenty kilometres a day and we won't be stopping for rest days. Unless something really goes wrong, we walk every day. I reckon it'll take about 35 days non-stop.'

I told him he was a slave driver and suggested – hopefully – that the camels would need a spell. A non-stop trek of that length would kill horses, I said.

'That's the point of the trip – these aren't horses. We won't be asking them to work that hard, as the country is flat, there aren't many sandhills and it's the cool time of the year. Never-theless, we'll have a limited amount of water, so we can't afford to just sit around in the desert letting the camels get thirsty. We have to keep moving.'

Prue found me in my office staring at the wall. 'What's wrong?' she asked.

'Thirty-five days non-stop, that's what's wrong,' I replied.

'You're kidding?'

'No, he reckons we'll do 750 kilometres non-stop in 35 days. Reckons we'll do better than twenty kilometres a day. That'll be beyond me,' I said. Memories of a 22-kilometre forced march across the stony, spinifex plains south of Wick-ham Gorge in the Northern Territory in 2000 came flooding back. The journey, with my brother Mike, retracing yet another part of Gregory's route and carrying a backpack full of water, was a killer. I couldn't do that day after day.

'You'd better ring him back and tell him,' Prue said. I decided to sleep on it. With any challenge, especially some-thing requiring detailed organisation and logistics, the hardest thing is to stay positive and to flex and bend as circumstances change in the run-up to the jumping-off point. Andrew's comment had rocked me, but I tried to stay positive. I upped my training, from two laps of Manly on the sand to four laps, then to six laps. By the time of the expedition, I was doing ten kilometres in the soft sand. On weekends, I had a well-grooved fifteen-kilometre walk around the harbour sandwiched between driving the children to their myriad sporting events. Starting with light weights, usually bricks, in my backpack, I gradually increased my training weight as the weeks went by.

I took heart when Andrew put his sword in the sand and gave me a date – we planned to leave Central Mt Stuart on 13 July.

There were some animals in the Tanami I was happy to avoid, such as our reptilian friends; however, there was one I was especially keen to see. It's one of Australia's most beautiful, yet saddest animals, and we would be walking right through its homeland. The mala, *Lagorchestes hirsutus* (*Lagorchestes*: from the Greek word *lagos* – hare; *orchestes* – dancer), is a wallaby that bounds through the scrub like a kangaroo or hare. Unlike a kangaroo, though, it would almost fit in your pocket, even when fully grown. With its big ears and friendly face, it epitomises everything that city people love about Australian marsupials. The Central Australian Expedition 2002, the name with which we had christened our adventure, adopted the mala as its mascot.

Mala were once common throughout the western deserts, including the Great Sandy, Gibson, Great Victoria and Tanami deserts. Throughout this range they were important to Aboriginal people as a food source and are still a cultural and mythological icon. Mala declined rapidly following European settlement, as they were forced to compete with exotic herbivores such as sheep, cattle, rabbits and camels. Changes in the vegetation as Aboriginal people ceased their traditional burning patterns, and the introduction of predators, especially cats and foxes, also put pressure on the animal. By 1991, the mala was extinct in the wild.

Fortunately, a breeding program at the Parks & Wildlife Commission of the Northern Territory in Alice Springs was successful, enabling researchers to build an electric-fenced mala enclosure on the Lander River in the Tanami, about 500 kilometres northwest of Alice Springs. By 1992, there were about 150 mala in the 'paddock' and another 50 in the Alice Springs colony.

Over the years, numerous attempts were made to reintroduce mala bred in the mala paddock into the wild. Sadly, all of these animals disappeared, devastated by cats and foxes. In the early 1990s, it appeared that the Tanami was unsafe for wild mala. I couldn't find out what had happened since, and hoped that Andrew and I might find the 'dancing hare' surviving outside the protective fence.

As March came to a close, no approval had come for our permits and I really started to work the phones. Kathy Satour, who had been handling the permit applications for the Central Land Council, left suddenly in March and I turned to a senior lawyer at the council, Michael Prowse, who said he would look into the matter. Prowse was genuinely helpful, but admitted he could do little until another permit officer was appointed in the third week of April. I was duly told by the new permit officer, Marah Edwards, that the Tanami communities wouldn't be prepared to rubber-stamp our application; detailed letters would have to be sent out to the community groups and they would have the final say.

Persistence and many phone calls to Western Australia finally paid off and the permit for Lake Gregory came through in the last week of April. One down and one to go.

6000 km trek ends in tears for an adventurer and his camels

The headline sprawled across page three of the *Sydney Morning Herald* on 29 May 2002. Stories of camels don't normally engender broad column inches in the bible of Sydney's northern suburbs. Mr Chris Richards (28) had set out with eleven pack camels to walk the Dingo Fence from Ceduna in South Australia to Longreach. Deserted by his companions on the first day, Richards abandoned the expedition shortly afterwards and shot his camels. It was a sobering reminder of just how badly things can go wrong.

The expedition had been a showpiece for the Year of the

Outback, which seemed to lay the blame on the camels: '. . . if they smell a stranger they bite and kick out, doing their best to maim you. They're not friendly beasts,' Rob Comerford, a spokesman for the event, was quoted as saying.

I showed Prue the article. She was surprisingly composed.

'I don't think it's all that relevant. Andrew's very experienced with camels – they're his livelihood. And given all the planning that's gone into your trip, I don't see this happening,' she said, reading the story carefully. 'And you never leave anything to chance.' Her support was reassuring, but three days later the *Herald* did a follow-up:

Tempests that sank adventurer and his ships of the desert

A long story detailing the minutiae of the failed journey and the inevitable criticism ran in a prominent position. Reading the story on a Saturday morning, I felt for the poor bloke. 'Imagine seeing your failure splashed all over the Sydney papers. He'll carry this around with him for the rest of his life,' I said to the family.

The Chris Richards story really rattled me. Failure was one thing; being publicly torn limb from limb by the press was another matter entirely. The embarrassment for my family was something I wouldn't contemplate. Tossing and turning sleeplessly one night after the stories appeared, I got up, dressed and went to my study. I switched on the light – 2 am. I opened one of the folders holding the notes and plans I had prepared for the expedition. I tried to pinpoint anything I'd missed.

Picking up a pen, I drew up a table.

These six factors are the key ingredients in the success of any remote-region expedition. Even with all these items ticked, an expedition may fail; if they aren't ticked, it will *definitely* fail. I was convinced that we had the first five covered; it was number six that still bothered me.

EXPEDITION LOGISTICS THE BIG SIX	
1. Water	4. Navigation
2. Food	5. Safety/communications
3. Transport, i.e. camels	6. Teamwork/leadership

'What will Andrew be like? Could we work as a team?' I asked myself, staring out into the night at the lights glittering on the harbour. I didn't have the faintest idea of the answer. I knew little about Andrew other than what I had read in *Outback* magazine and what I had learned in our few meetings. How would he react under pressure? What sort of person was he? I imagined being stuck in the desert for five weeks with someone I hated. There was no one to ask. We had no mutual acquaintances; the orbits of our lives had never crossed before now. I opened *Outback* magazine and read again the stories of Andrew's Capricorn Expedition.

There *is* someone I could ask, I suddenly realised.

The next morning I phoned Paul Myers, the editor of *Outback*, whom I knew quite well, and who knew about our planned trip. Myers is a straight-shooting media veteran whose frankness I could rely on. He had commissioned the articles and photographs from Andrew.

'Well, I don't know him all that well, but he was a pleasure to deal with,' Myers said.

'How do you think we'll get on?'

'I don't think you'll have much trouble with Andrew. I found him very personable. You're both pretty easygoing, so I think you'll get on fine,' he replied.

'He certainly seems to be very experienced,' I said.

'Yes, he's got the track record. Well, you *both* have. He doesn't have the background in the historical stuff that you have, but he's proven he can go out there and do it. At least you both know what you're letting yourselves in for,' Myers observed.

'I suppose so, but Andrew has never crossed the Tanami.'

'No, but he's crossed just about every other desert in Australia. It can't be that different and he's obviously very experienced with camels,' Myers said.

'How do you think he'll react in a crisis? Do you think he'll do his nut and start cursing and carrying on?' I asked.

'I don't know,' he replied. 'You won't know until you get out there. I'd be surprised if he carried on like that, but that's one of the risks you'll have to take, I suppose.'

The other big question was whether Andrew would get sick of the trip and quit half-way through, but no one could answer that question other than Andrew.

My conversation with Paul Myers was one of the most important I had before the expedition began. He gave me at least some of the comfort I sought. If he had found Andrew difficult or was wary of him in any way, I would have pulled out. The risk was just too great. At least now we had a chance that the teamwork and leadership demands of 'the Big Six' would be met.

As May rolled on, I still hadn't heard from the Central Land Council. It was four months since I had submitted the application and I was starting to panic. I called Michael Prowse in Alice Springs.

'We're having some trouble with this application, I have to be honest,' he said. 'We've never had an application to go to these very remote areas – most people stick to the roads.'

'Well, as I said in the application, we've given very firm undertakings to avoid any sacred sites or other important places.'

'But that's the point – how can the old people tell you

what sites to avoid? They don't know what's out there. They'd like to go and have a look, too, but the logistics of organising it are too great. Also, they don't want you going out there with four-wheel drives and helicopters, leaving a mess.'

'Michael, we're not taking any support crews or four-wheel drives – it's just us and six camels. All the rubbish gets packed out on the backs of the camels. The only things we'll leave behind are our footprints, and they won't last beyond the next wet.'

'What about helicopters and film crews?' he asked.

'No helicopters, no film crews; just me and Andrew and the camels,' I replied.

I spent over an hour telling him about Andrew's experience in crossing Australia – trips for which he had been issued permits by the Central Land Council. I explained the history of Gregory's and Stuart's attempts to penetrate the Tanami and told him of my experiences following Gregory's journey through the Victoria River country in northern Australia, both on horseback and on foot. These journeys had required permits from the Northern Land Council and there had been no problems. He listened patiently and politely, and asked me to put down everything we had discussed in a briefing paper.

'I'm not sure we understood exactly what you were trying to achieve,' he said, as he hung up.

It was a very late night, but by morning I had a briefing paper completed and on the fax machine to Alice Springs. I had done all I could. I was resigned. Our fate was now in the hands of people I had never met. It was a lonely time. Andrew had left for the desert in early May, the start of the tourist season. He wouldn't be available until early June, so there was no one to bounce ideas off or simply to talk to about the myriad organisational trials that still remained. My poor wife copped all the moaning. Many times I asked her, 'What am I doing this for?' She didn't really know.

Nevertheless, the work went on. I read everything I could find about the area we were to penetrate. A significant obstacle was the lack of written material. The libraries in Sydney had plenty on the other Australian deserts, particularly the Simpson, but little on the Tanami. Nor did the Internet yield anything much. I regaled my family with my small discoveries about this mysterious area plonked in the middle of the Northern Territory and extending to Lake Gregory in Western Australia.

'Catherine, did you know that the Tanami Desert covers an area of 184,500 square kilometres, about the combined size of England and Scotland or the American state of Oklahoma? It's the third-largest desert in Australia behind the Great Victoria and Great Sandy, and it's larger than the Gibson and Simpson deserts.'

'That's great, Dad, really interesting. Get a life.'

'The rainfall's about 300 millimetres a year, compared to Sydney's 1200 millimetres.'

'Fascinating, Dad. I've always wanted to know how much rain falls in central Australia,' came the less-than-enthusiastic response.

'This will really help you in your life one day.'

'I'm sure.'

I chased her around my desk.

Many Australians of my generation had their first look at deserts in the David Lean film, *Lawrence of Arabia*. A half-mad Peter O'Toole, burnoose flying in the wind as he careened down a sand dune on an out-of-control camel, left me with an impression that deserts are beaches without any water. The rolling sand dune and the palm-fringed oasis are what I imagined deserts to be. The Tanami Desert is different. It's flat in the east and gives way to sand ridges and stony escarpments in the west. The few photos I found showed a sea of scrub. Dense mulga thickets spread wherever the camera pointed, and where the scrub receded, spinifex triumphed. Too much, rather than too little, vegetation seemed the problem, and for the first time I wondered whether the scrub would form an impenetrable barrier, impossible to push the camels through. Looking around in the breathless quiet of the Mitchell Library as the lunchtime sun filtered down through the central skylight, the Tanami seemed a foreign and faraway place.

After Gregory's and Stuart's tussle with the region, Colonel Peter Egerton Warburton tried to reach Lake Gregory from Alice Springs. He couldn't find it and was beaten back into the desert, barely making it to the Western Australian coast. Nathanial 'Bluey' Buchanan made the first successful crossing of the Tanami in 1896. Riding a camel, he crossed from Tennant Creek to Halls Creek. So terrified of the area was Buchanan's guide that the explorer handcuffed him to his saddle's stirrup iron and the unfortunate Aborigine had no choice but to comply.

It was Michael Terry, however, whose name appeared most. This resourceful gold prospector took the first vehicles into the area in 1928 and revisited it many times. At a time years before any roads were built, this was a feat. In his book *Hidden Wealth and Hiding People*, I read for the first time of Thomson's Rockhole, a large natural granite well buried deep in a remote part of the eastern Tanami. Jack Keyser, Terry's young offsider, was photographed sitting on the lip of the granite well, dangling his legs into the void. It became a mission of mine to find the rockhole and for one of us to be photographed in the same position to see how things had changed. A copy of the Keyser photograph and the relevant parts of Terry's book went into the growing stash of material I was packing for the journey. In all my reading, I could find no evidence that anyone had ever crossed the Tanami on foot; this was our challenge.

My brief to Michael Prowse obviously had some effect, for on 15 May, Marah Edwards from the Central Land Council phoned to say that a permit to enter the region of the Central Desert Aboriginal Land Trust had been granted. I let out a huge sigh of relief. We were good to go, from Mt Stuart all the way to Lake Gregory. I couldn't share my elation with Andrew, as he was out with camels somewhere west of Birdsville. I opened a bottle of champagne with Prue and we toasted the last hurdle to the expedition.

I lay on my back looking at the ceiling. It was the first week in July. The expedition was upon us and my tired brain went over everything one more time to see if I had missed anything. Food, permits, maps, water, camels, trucking, fuel, safety, communications, resupply, first aid, maps, boots, clothing. On and on it went into the night, as I mentally ticked the boxes. What had I missed? What were the critical ingredients needed for us to succeed where Chris Richards had failed? How could we differentiate ourselves? Could I take luck out of it and reduce it to experience and careful planning? And the big questions: had I done enough training? Could I keep up? Could I lift the weights? Inevitably as I lay there tossing and turning the question would come: Why am I doing this?

I had pushed the training program up during June, exercising at every possible opportunity. At Manly, I was doing ten laps in the soft sand and bathing my feet in the ocean between each set. In the past, the salt water had helped to toughen the soles of my feet. I had done several 32-kilometre hikes from Palm Beach to Manly carrying a 25-kilogram pack. However, I needed a test. I wanted to know how I was going. I phoned an old mate, Barrie Rhodes, and suggested a walk in the national park south of Sydney. The coastal track beginning at Bundeena has plenty of ups and downs and a killer finish straight up the Otford escarpment. Barrie is a career soldier who experienced Northern Ireland tours with the British paratroopers. He was my age and superfit, so this would be a good guide.

A Friday night saw us set off with fully loaded packs under a starlit sky on the two-day walk. Barrie left me for dead. Try as I might, I couldn't put any pressure on him. As we came up the escarpment, a long, steep cliff coming out of the sea, on the second day, he left me behind. I had no trouble doing the climb, but with the heavy backpack on, I couldn't get close to his speed. While I did a monotonous plod, he nearly ran up the trail.

'It was humbling; I can't even keep up with a guy my own age,' I said to Prue, who drove down to Otford to pick us up. She found us at the edge of the escarpment, looking out to sea.

'Don't forget, you won't have to carry a pack on your trip,' she replied.

'I know, but Andrew's a decade younger than me and Barrie, so it doesn't look great,' I said. Indeed, when I thought of the consequences of not being able to keep up, it was very sobering.

Much time was spent stockpiling provisions for the expedition. Meat was a problem. We needed a supply of meat that would last for six weeks in temperatures up to 40°C with no refrigeration. I decided to take beef jerky as one of the protein staples. Jerky (from the Peruvian word *charqui*, meaning flesh) is raw meat cut into thin slices, then salted and air-dried. It is eaten raw, and if correctly prepared, it will last years. It was once a vital food source on many Australian expeditions, a lightweight source of portable protein. Explorers' journals are full of accounts of bullocks, camels and horses being slaughtered and their meat jerked. The fresh meat was usually hung over bushes to dry, sometimes with a smoky fire underneath to keep away the flies. I found a butcher's shop, Springbok Delights, in Chatswood which supplied three kilograms of jerky in cyro-vacced packets. The jerky was prepared in the South African manner and is known there as Biltong, a softer, spicier item than the Australian version. Outdoor Agencies, a Sydney importer, sold me 70 freeze-dried meals, consisting of both single and double serves. A menu that included Thai chicken curry, beef and pasta hotpot and lamb fettuccine meant that we would eat to a standard undreamed of by Gregory and Stuart, who were sustained primarily by dried beef and damper. Our food came as powder in a packet, but technology had advanced to such an extent that these packets would provide wholesome evening meals, simply by adding boiling water. And they never spoiled, no matter what the temperature. The menu was organised so that we would have only one repeat meal over the entire journey. The firm was shocked at the size of the order.

'We've never had an order this big. Most people use our products for short trips of about a week. We've never heard of anyone trying to live on this food for that long,' Ben Ryan, its Sydney manager, said.

'But there's no reason why they can't?' I asked.

'No, absolutely not. The meals are balanced, with adequate nutrition, but it'll be an interesting test. These packs have never been carried on camels and we've not provisioned a desert expedition before. Our meals are made up with mountaineers and cold-climate bushwalkers in mind,' he said.

The Alpenaire and Backcountry meals, the premium brands handled by the company, arrived in their airtight packets and were boxed with the jerky and freighted to the TNT depot in Alice Springs. I had agonised over how to get all the food and equipment to Alice and finally decided on road freight as the least risky method. The boxes were despatched to Alice with two weeks to spare.

My brother Damien, who had hiked with me down Depot Creek in 2001, wasn't a great fan of dried food after living on it for a week. The 'brown muck' he had called it. 'It's the monotony of it that got to me, and that was only after a week. It all started to taste the same. I don't know how you'll be able to face it after five weeks. You'll be eating your boots!'

He came up with some light, helpful suggestions, such as Deb mashed potato powder and Surprise dried peas. I later followed his advice and added an onion or a carrot where possible to the evening meal.

The final list of provisions included, in addition to the basics, tinned fruit, dried prunes, dried tomatoes, powdered fruit juices, packet fruit juices and muesli, which Andrew assured me he couldn't live without. The total weight of food, even with the luxuries, was about 109 kilograms, only a quarter of the water burden of 484 kilograms. Even in Sydney, during the planning, it was obvious what the most important commodity carried would be.

The powdered fruit juices, Prue's idea and her parting gift to the expedition, were to be a godsend beyond anything we could have imagined. In the not-too-distant future, under many a dusty bloodwood tree, after a scorching dry stage, two tired cameleers would pour those drinks down their parched throats and make a toast to 'Mrs Kelly'. And this from a person who hated camping!

With a week to go, I was sure that I had everything covered. But it was never going to be completely smooth sailing, no matter how thorough the planning. Fate intervened when TNT, the road freight company, rang to say they had lost all the dried food. I had sent two boxes to Alice Springs, one containing food and the other equipment. The equipment box, which was sent last, arrived on time; however, the box containing the dried food vanished. I went on the warpath. At one stage, I believe that every executive at TNT, senior and junior, was looking for that box.

With two days to go, I had to accept that it was gone. Flex and bend, improvise as circumstances change, I told myself. Roll with the punches. However, this was an insoluble problem. It takes two weeks to dry beef and make jerky – I had two days. Gone was the cornerstone of my lunch-halt food ration. The 70 freeze-dried meals would have to be replaced, but I couldn't go back and ask Ben Ryan for another supply of Alpenaire and Backcountry meals. He had gone to considerable trouble to think up a varied menu at a reasonable price. I was simply too embarrassed to admit to him that I had lost the lot even before I had left Sydney. Instead, I phoned Paddy Pallin, the large camping goods store. Yes, they could replace the dried food, but it would take all the stock on their shelves and they couldn't give me the variety and lines that I had previously worked out so pain-stakingly with Ben. On the Paddy Pallin schedule, we would be eating the same meal up to five times! I was incandescent with rage that all my careful provisioning plans had been wrecked. Moreover, I was humiliated. The provisioning, a vital area of an expedition, which Andrew had entrusted to me, was in chaos. Before we had even left, I had crashed headlong into the first hurdle. I immediately felt at a dis-advantage and cursed the freight company.

I summoned up the courage to phone Andrew on the evening of Tuesday, 9 July. I had been on the phone all day to TNT employees in Sydney, Adelaide and Alice Springs. He was in the truck crossing the South Australian border on his way from Deniliquin to Morgan to collect the camels. It was too late to turn back. We were committed.

'You want the good news or the bad news?' I said.

There was a significant pause. 'Well, give me the good news,' he replied.

'There is none.'

'Well, what's the bad news?' Andrew's voice sounded a long way away.

'I've spoken to the freight company and all the dried food is missing.'

'*What?* Oh, no!'

'Yeah, so here's the alternative. I buy more dried food in Sydney and take it with me on the plane. Bloody expensive, have to pay full retail at somewhere like Paddy Pallin, and no time to get a good variety. Alternatively, and just in case it turns up in the next two days, I wait until the last minute and buy it in Alice Springs.'

'No, you won't get it in Alice. None of the camping places stock it. What about the jerky?'

'No good here. I have to order it a couple of weeks in advance. Can't get it in Alice, I suppose?'

'Don't know,' Andrew replied.

We decided to continue with the expedition and, as a worse case, fall back on packaged pasta meals and rice; adequate, but a purgatory of monotony. With the jerky gone, I was stumped as to how to provision the midday meal. 'Hope for the best, but plan for the worst, 'cause the worst is probably what you'll get' is the motto I adopt in business, and I approached this expedition in the same way. However, the prospect of a national freight company losing all our dried food without trace had never occurred to me. This frustrating dilemma exposed an important side of Andrew's character – he took setbacks very calmly. I hardly noticed it at the time, because I was so stressed out, but his ability to roll with the punches would become critical to the success of our trip. He sailed over this first hurdle with considerably more composure than me.

I took my girls to see the film *Bend it Like Beckham* after I got off the phone to Andrew. I needed to relax. Hilary, in particular, loved this moral tale about an Anglo-Indian girl trying to play professional soccer. The papers that day had been full of Lleyton Hewitt's win at Wimbledon, which had enthralled my tennis-mad wife, so the family was bubbling as we drove home from Cremorne across the Spit Bridge. However, I couldn't match their mood. 'So ends one of the worst days of my life,' my journal for Tuesday, 9 July, recorded.

Two days later, I was on the plane to Alice Springs.

On the plane, I read *The Heroic Journey of John McDouall Stuart*, Ian Mudie's study of the explorer. As usual, the story gave me a feeling of unease. And surprise. As a schoolboy, I'd been told that Stuart was the greatest explorer to mount a horse in Australia, a man of indomitable willpower, perseverance and courage – the Napoleon of explorers.

Much of this is true, but he is a more complicated character than the stick man sketched in school history books. A broken engagement to the cousin of his friend William Russell was possibly the critical factor that drove him on to the ship to Australia and may explain his subsequent solitary life in the bush devoid of female company. His tiny physique may have left him with a dogged passion to prove himself worthy in the company of other men. He would not be the first small man to suffer this affliction. His enthusiasm for whisky may have been a sign of his torment. Uncharitably, one of Sturt's exploring party referred to him as 'this mushroom' and dismissed him as a drunkard.

Stuart led his first major expedition in 1858, fourteen years after his ordeal with Sturt. It would set the pattern for all that followed. He left Oratunga Station in South Australia in mid-May with two pack horses and four riding horses to tackle the arid regions northwest of Lake Torrens. He rode with two companions and took no navigational instruments other than a compass. He packed food for only four weeks, although he planned to be out for six. Taking less food than the journey would require was the opposite of good expedition practice. Given the shoeless condition of many of his horses as the trip progressed, it also appears he was woefully under-provisioned for horseshoes as well.

By the time he reached the present site of Coober Pedy, he had been out for two months, twice as long as he had provisions for. He was 600 kilometres from his starting point

– about three weeks' ride – and his horses were lame. Did he retreat? Not likely. In late July, Stuart baked the last of the flour into damper. He had to make four weeks' supply of food last for over ten weeks, but they were still a long way from Oratunga. The damper was stored in the packbags and doled out each day in tiny portions. His Aboriginal guide had fled and starvation loomed. Still, he didn't turn back.

He rode south, arriving at Maryvale Station on the Great Australian Bight in the third week of August. Starving, and in pain from the onset of scurvy, he had nevertheless survived. It was a magnificent achievement. Without a sextant or chronometer for finding longitude, he had ridden almost 1700 kilometres through arid country largely devoid of features, using only a compass to guide him to a place he had never seen. So was set a pattern of superb bushmanship, uncanny dead-reckoning navigation, persistence and courage, combined with an ability to extract the last inch from a failing horse.

Less acknowledged by historians is Stuart's lack of fore-sight and planning, and his complete disregard for his own physical privations or those of his men and horses. He had embarked on the expedition under-provisioned and ran out of food. He took a month's food and stayed out thirteen weeks. During the last month, he and his remaining companion shared a kilogram of damper per day. On the last three to four days of the trip, they had no food at all. Had Maryvale Station not been manned, they would have died.

To place himself in harm's way was Stuart's right as an explorer; to place his men and horses in harm's way, with reckless disregard for adequate provisioning or essentials such as horse-shoes, set a precedent that would plague all his expeditions. My study of his journals had convinced me that while he was ulti-mately successful, there wasn't one expedition led by Stuart where his men didn't return reduced to skeletons by starvation and scurvy, and riding horses broken down from thirst and work.

At the tail end of this trip, as Stuart rode towards the settled districts, he spent a night at Arkaba Station. Years later, Robert Bruce, the station's overseer, left an eyewitness account of the tyro explorer's celebrations with Angus G., a stockman. Like me, Bruce seemed to struggle with the contradictions of the man:

> *Stuart was a Scotchman, he was not over communicative, even to his friends . . . Under the influence of Angus' whisky, however, the little man's tongue became loosened, first on exploring, and then on convivial matters, and the two friends were soon singing 'Willie brewed a pack o' maut' and shortly afterwards, with clasped hands, 'Auld Lang Syne.' They then became boastful anent their pedigrees, and as Stuart proudly claimed to have descended from the royal Stuart, while Angus G was equally proud of a cateran ancestor, to wit the famous Rob Roy McGregor, why neither could crow much above the other. As I had my hands full of work I didna wait to feenish the whusky, but left the two Scots to dae it. Anyhow, baith had sair heads the morn.*

I laughed on reading this. Having a sore head in the morning is a very Australian response to celebration.

> *Everyone has a besetting weakness of some sort or other, and little Stuart's was too great a craving for the blood of bold John Barleycorn, and so drank as much of it as he could. But, to give Stuart his due, he had the pluck of a giant in his puny frame, coupled with a prudence and good judgement that eminently fitted him for the leadership of men. The success of his exploring journeys abundantly proves this, for travelling in the most difficult and dangerous regions on the world's surface, when as yet untracked and in the burning months of summer, he*

*surmounted difficulties and privations undreamed of by
those who are ignorant of the interior of Australia; and,
though solely dependent on horses for his means of transit,
always brought his followers safely back.*

This bush synopsis, rich in Scots' brogue, is a revealing insight
into Stuart the man, but 'prudence and good judgement' were
not words I associated with Stuart.

Stuart was soon back in the saddle and into the bush. By late
1859, while surveying grazing runs and gold prospecting, he
had probed towards the northern tip of Lake Eyre – he was
now only 800 kilometres from the fabled centre of Australia.
Drawn on by its proximity, he appears to have decided almost
on a whim to try for the centre and, if possible, the northwest
coast somewhere near the mouth of the Victoria River,
recently explored by Gregory. In 1860, he began another
expedition, the first serious attempt by a European to cross
Australia from south to north. It was this expedition that
intrigued me. Despite what appeared to be a lack of planning
and with only two other men and thirteen horses, he set off to
ride across Australia.

What sort of bloke would do that? He must have been a
bit nuts, I had thought many times since first reading this
account. With that number of horses, there was no way he
could carry enough supplies. Nevertheless, Stuart intrigued me.

On 2 March 1860, Stuart set off on his memorable journey. With him were Bill Kekwick, a knockabout 38-year-old
Englishman who had been out with Stuart on previous
explorations, and Ben Head, an eighteen-year-old who, despite
his tender years, had already been out on brief exploring
forays. Head was everything Stuart was not. Half Stuart's age,
at 1.8 metres, he towered over the diminutive Scot and,

weighing 115 kilograms, was a giant of a man. What a sight Head would have made sitting in the saddle next to his leader. This disparity in physique and Stuart's obstinacy would have almost fatal consequences for Head.

True to form, the expedition was grossly undermanned, under-horsed and badly provisioned. Stuart was reported to be planning a four-month foray. To get to the northwest coast and back from Chambers Creek – a distance of 3800 kilometres – was impossible in this time frame. Using pack horses, I would have allowed six months at the minimum. Taking only seven riding and six pack horses, he set himself a hopeless task. No list of his provisions survives, but given that two pack horses would have been required for expedition equipment such as horseshoes, shoeing tools, navigational instruments, gunpowder and shot, it appears he only had four pack horses for food, with no tag-along horses.

The human body exhausts its store of ascorbic acid – vitamin C – in about six weeks, less if the body is subject to physical stress or abused by excessive alcohol consumption. After that, scurvy rips the body to shreds. Stuart was planning to be out at least four months, and given his history, this would be exceeded, so in the absence of vital anti-scorbutics, such as lime juice, he was guaranteeing a dose of this potentially fatal affliction to every member of his party. There is no evidence that he provided lime juice for the expedition. Indeed, it is improbable that this commodity would have been available at a remote outpost like Chambers Creek.

Despite the small number of horses, it would be a major job for three men to undertake the labours of tending gear and animals, keeping watch, writing journals, performing sextant sights, cooking food and keeping shoes on the horses. As the party rode north into the wilderness beyond Lake Eyre, fame and a £2000 prize beckoned. This expedition, poorly provisioned and eschewing planning for inspiration and per- severance, was never going to succeed. Nevertheless, despite his own shortcomings and the ruthless country he faced, Stuart nearly pulled it off.

If Gregory's gift to Australian exploration was egalitarianism, careful stewardship of his men's health, extraordinarily accurate navigation, and meticulous, almost corporate planning, Stuart's bequest was a whimsical 'She'll be right, mate' attitude. He may have even invented the term.

As my plane flew high over the red heart of Australia, I looked out at the red sandhills of the Simpson Desert, visible in the clear winter air. This was the country that had turned Sturt and Stuart back on their expedition together. As if to mock me, an advertisement for TNT – *Faster, more reliable* – played on the in-flight movie screen. I continued reading so that I didn't have to watch it. As Stuart knew, scurvy is a punctual affliction, but it arrived early, in the second week of April 1860, only a month into the journey. Head reported later that their *weekly* ration was 2.3 kilograms of flour baked into damper, 57 grams of jerked beef, fourteen grams of tea and a stick of tobacco. This hardly seems enough to sustain life and is a pittance considering that I budgeted for Andrew and me to eat about a kilogram of food each per *day*. Apparently, they had no fruit, green vegetables or lime juice. Their bodies had exhausted their store of vitamin C and they would now pay the price. Stuart recorded in his journal southwest of today's Alice Springs: *Our hands are very bad . . . indications of the scurvy are beginning to show themselves upon us.*

A fortnight later, with no thought of turning back despite the encroaching illness, he overtook the achievements of his mentor, Charles Sturt, and became the first white man to see central Australia. Raising the Union Jack on Central Mt Sturt, he claimed the middle of Australia for the British Crown. (The name was later changed to Central Mt Stuart in his honour.)

Mt Stuart, a place that had occupied a large space in my boyhood dreaming, but which I had never seen, in a part of Australia I had only read about, was the planned starting point of our journey. *I do not like the appearance of the country to the north for finding water; it seems to be sandy*, Stuart wrote. He then headed west into the Tanami Desert hoping for better conditions.

Sitting on the plane, enjoying a cold beer and looking at the desert, I was excited by the prospect of seeing central Australia, seeing what the little Scotsman had seen, walking where he had ridden and finding out what sort of person he had really been.

CHAPTER 3

**Tea and scones in the Tanami:
The expedition gets under way**

The sun came up behind Mt Esther as we stood around the campfire knocking off the remains of a billy of tea. It was cold – -3°C overnight – so jackets were on and hands were warming over the fire.

'Well, I'm off. Should be back by midday. Anyway, you'll be able to see me from here walking along the ridge.' I pointed to the long spur that I planned to climb to get to the volcanic plug that capped Mt Esther. It was a stunning red finger of stone pointing into the blue sky.

Slinging a two-litre Macpac water bladder over my shoulder, I checked that my map case and compass were in place and set off, walking east through the lightly timbered scrub.

Recent days had been a blur. Andrew's longtime friend, Trevor Shiell, had met me at Alice Springs airport along with the Northern Territory identity, Ted Egan. I was soon settled into a motel where I began packing the food into boxes for the journey north. Andrew arrived in Alice from South Australia at the same time. Seeing the big truck parked in the busy street next morning, with a cattle crate on top and a sign on the back, **CENTRAL AUSTRALIAN EXPEDITION 2002**, jolted me. Andrew climbed down from the cab.

'This is really going to happen,' I said, after we shook hands.

'Guess so. Too late to pull out now,' he said, smiling.

I climbed on to the back of the truck, then up the side of the stock crate. Neatly stacked inside the crate were camel saddles, carrying racks, grey plastic gear boxes, green metal 'camel-proof' boxes, spare drums of fuel for the truck's journey north and the all-important water jerrycans – 24 in all – arranged in orderly rows. The organisation was impressive.

'There's nothing slipshod about the way Andrew organises things, is there?' I said to Trevor as I climbed down from the truck. Andrew was walking around the vehicle checking that everything was shipshape after the drive from Melbourne.

'No, certainly not. You'll find him a very organised, methodical person – but you *have* to be organised where you're going,' he replied. Trevor had been arranging resupply for Andrew's camel journeys for many years, a job that took him into some of the remotest parts of Australia. The space where the camels would sit was empty, as they had been unloaded at the Frontier Camel Farm, just outside of town.

'Will you get six camels in there?' I asked, pointing doubtfully at the small space.

'No. There was only room for five. I had to leave one behind, so we won't have a spare. Never mind, they'll organise themselves to use the available space. Plenty of room,' Andrew said. 'So, let's go and meet the humps.'

'Humps' was, I guessed correctly, Andrew's affectionate term for his charges. When we were in the desert, he would occasionally refer to the whole string of them as 'the water tanker'.

As I began the steep climb up the side of the Mt Esther spur, my mind went back to my first meeting with the camels just three days before.

They stood in a huddle in the middle of a dusty yard at the Frontier Camel Farm. Heads up, all were staring in different directions, their halters with lead ropes dragging on the ground. Two had traditional nose pegs. They were huge. I followed Andrew into the yard.

'Now, the first thing they'll do is come over and smell you, and try to work out who you are. Don't be alarmed,' Andrew said.

Sure enough, a long-legged camel walked over and sized me up before gently lowering his snout into the crown of my hat. He left it there for awhile before lifting his head and peering off into the distance. He appeared to have no interest in me. 'That's TC, which stands for Tall Camel. He's the oldest camel in the string, more than twenty years and getting towards the end of his career, but he's very experienced. He walked across Australia with me and will be the lead camel on this trip,' Andrew said.

In turn, I met the other animals: 'Cooper, he's an over-grown teenager and the one who'll lead the others astray. Former Monaro driver, former ratbag, but a strong camel. He'll be number two. Sang is usually a lead camel, but on this trip he'll have the number three spot. I find him the most aggressive. If any of them were going to strike someone, it would probably be him, but he never has.'

'Not yet, anyway. He's probably been saving it up for me,' I said. Andrew laughed.

'Number four in the string will be Char.' He patted the animal's side. 'He's the smallest and youngest of the group, and the least aggressive. We won't hear "boo" out of this camel for the whole trip. All the sensitive gear goes on him – the sextant, satellite phone, and solar panels and batteries.'

Char peered timidly out at me from behind his larger mates. He had an 'I'll do anything I can to please' look about him. In the coming weeks, I would become very fond of this animal. That, however, was in the future. Now, standing in that hot, dusty yard, I was overwhelmed.

They all looked the same to me. I asked Andrew how he could tell them apart. No two horses ever look the same, but all these camels looked like they were punched from the same mould.

'What about this one? D'you think *he* looks different?' he asked.

We came to the last camel. 'Say hello to Morgan.' Before us stood a massive camel, broad-shouldered and heavily muscled in the chest and legs. He had a regal air. His lordship's feet were the size of dinner plates, his neck thick with coiled muscle.

'Why's he so much bigger than the others?' I asked.

'He was cut late, so he was a fully grown bull before his meeting with the vet. All the others were gelded much earlier,' Andrew explained. 'He's got almost perfect confirmation for a pack camel and is definitely the strongest of the bunch.' It was obvious that Morgan was something of a favourite.

'Because he's so like a bull camel, his position is at the back, the last in line, where a bull would be in the wild. The biggest and strongest go at the back. They don't lead; they drive the mob in front of them.'

'Like a wild stallion,' I ventured.

'Exactly,' Andrew said.

'Come on, Morg – say hello.' He grabbed the animal's lead rope, one end of which trailed along the ground making him easy to catch; the other end was tied to the halter. The animal opened wide his mouth and let out a ferocious roar – it went on and on and on, then changed tone to a moan and a series of honks. He then closed his mouth and began chewing vigorously.

'He sounds like he's in pain,' I said, shocked. I had for the first time heard the song of the desert, celebrated in literature going back thousands of years.

'No, that's just Morgan saying g'day. He's the noisiest of the camels, but very gentle and unaggressive; he would never strike. He's a great favourite with all the guests on my tours,

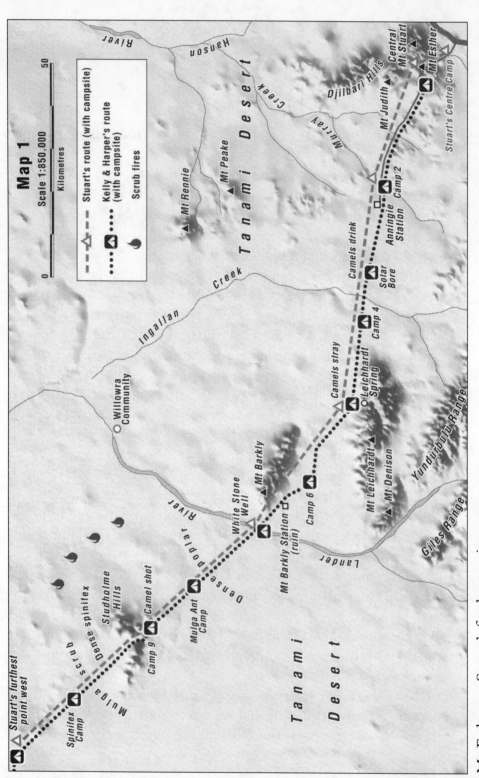

Mt Esther to Stuart's furthest point west

probably because he makes a lot of noise but never does anything.' I would quickly adapt to the camels' song, which became part of my day, but it was frightening when heard for the first time coming from deep within a towering, imperial camel still convinced that he is an entire male.

Morgan, I would learn later, like TC, had walked across Australia with Andrew and was guaranteed a very comfortable retirement when his working days were done.

I was immediately struck by how calm the camels were. A mob of horses in a similar situation with strangers in the yards will often mill around nervously, or at least move away. Contrary to popular belief, they didn't smell. Their woolly coats didn't seem to give off any sort of odour. They trailed lead ropes off their halters as they wandered around the yard. I shook my head in amazement. To leave horses roaming in a yard with lead ropes dangling was to guarantee their destruction. Unlike horses, these camels were big – and scary.

As we prepared to leave Alice, TNT in Sydney phoned to say they had found the missing food box and I could pick it up at the local depot. 'Don't know when it arrived, mate. Just found it sitting on the loading dock yesterday,' the manager said. The truant box, battered and forlorn but otherwise intact, was retrieved from the depot.

'Do you know where it's been?' I asked.

'No idea, mate. It just turned up here,' the manager said.

Because of a rushed and very expensive purchase of dried food from Paddy Pallin on the way to Sydney airport, I now had twice as much as I needed. I was overjoyed, however, to recover the jerky, my gaiters and the Nalgene water containers, which were irreplaceable in Alice Springs. I frantically packed up the surplus food and sent it back to Sydney.

Although it was no comfort at the time, TNT graciously refunded all the freight costs on my return from the expedition.

Scrambling over broken red rock, I climbed the last twenty metres of Mt Esther. The view from the top should scare any city dweller new to central Australia – it certainly scared me! Here was the burning, glowing gut of our country laid bare. To the east, the barren dome of Central Mt Stuart dominated the skyline. *Took Kekwick and the flag, and went to the top of the mount, but found it to be much higher and more difficult of ascent than I anticipated. After a deal of labour, slips and knocks, we at last arrived on the top.* This was where Stuart raised his flag and claimed central Australia for the British Empire. *Built a large cone of stones, in the centre of which I placed a pole with the British flag nailed to it. Near the top of the cone I placed a small bottle in which there is a slip of paper, with our signatures to it stating by whom it was raised.* Here he had written, *We then gave three hearty cheers for the flag, the emblem of civil and religious liberty, and may it be a sign to the natives that the dawn of liberty, civilisation and Christianity is about to break upon them.* Civilisation had arrived in central Australia and did break over its inhabitants like a tidal wave. I pondered on its supposed benefits long and hard while I stood there.

I hope from the top of Central Mt Stuart to find something good to the northwest, the little Scotsman wrote. I looked to the northwest. It was a smooth vista of dry scrub and heat haze. No good looking out there, mate, I thought. To the north of my position atop Mt Esther was the outline of the rugged Djilbari hills, flanked by Mt Judith sticking up out of the desert like a bottle. It was hard to think of it as anything other than desolate, but beautiful nonetheless. There wasn't a sign of water anywhere. Not even a strip of greenery to suggest a watercourse.

For the first time I got a good look at what we were taking on, for it was the west and north that were most terrifying. *The view to the north is over a large plain of gums, mulga and spinifex* . . . Despite the passage of time, nothing had changed. Almost due west over a sea of flat scrub and barren red plain, Mt Leichhardt dominated the view. The second-highest mountain in the Northern Territory, it would draw any traveller to the area looking for water. It had drawn Stuart and we would shortly follow. I reckoned on about five days to reach it. North of Mt Leichhardt, I tried to follow our route and could just make out Mt Barkly, almost swallowed up in the mirage. The whole area looked as if it had never seen rain.

'That's what this desert is, it's a beast. How did Stuart have the guts to tackle this? I would've taken one look and gone back to Adelaide, sat on the porch and had a whisky,' I said to myself. After reading of Stuart's struggle with the drink, I saluted his pluck. Out there somewhere north of the mirage, Stuart had lost his arm wrestle with the beast and was beaten back. We'll need our fair share of pluck, too, I thought.

My musings were uninterrupted by other human voices. I could see from my eyrie where Stuart had camped on the bone-dry Hanson River. A couple of kilometres away was the geographic centre of Australia and I took a bearing to it. To the west, about two kilometres away, I could see our camp and the truck, impossibly tiny in the scrub. Save for the *tinkle, tinkle, tinkle* of the camel bells drifting faintly in the hot, still air, the silence was complete.

'Just in time. I'm ready to start packing the food,' Andrew said, when I arrived back at the camp. He had spread out a large tarpaulin and all the expedition food was arranged on it. In neat rows were the jerky, pasta and rice; in another row, the tinned fruit; in another, the dried bread, dried biscuits, jam and Vegemite. All in order, nothing left to chance. I recorded each item, including its weight, in the trip journal as Andrew carefully packed them into the rectangular grey boxes. He gave me a running commentary.

'These grey boxes are reasonably waterproof and dust-proof, but they aren't camel-proof, so we have to stop the camels rolling on them at all costs. The really valuable stuff goes in the two green metal camel-proof boxes.' He indicated two boxes on either side of the line of saddles. As each box was filled, it was labelled on the outside.

'Two of the boxes will be "lunchboxes". We'll live out of those, and they always have to be accessible. We'll top them up each night from the other storage food boxes with everything we'll need for the following day.'

I was learning about Andrew. He had supervised the loading of the camels the previous day in Alice. Enlisted in the cause were Trevor Shiell, John Wilkinson, an experienced bushman friend of Andrew's, plus obliging staff of the Frontier Camel Farm. However, there was no doubt that Andrew was in charge. Getting camels into the confined space of a cage on the back of a flatbed truck wasn't easy, but Andrew explained exactly how he wanted it done and began loading with a surprising minimum of fuss. He never lost his composure when the animals declined to walk on, when people got in the road, or when ropes weren't tied just so. He talked calmly to the camels and, while firm with them, never struck them or swore at them. Loading horses on to floats is a great test of a person's character, and getting a camel on to a truck is no different. I was impressed with Andrew's performance. There's some leadership skills there, I thought to myself.

Unloading had been no different. We had selected the campsite at Mt Esther for its plentiful camel feed and prox-imity to Mt Stuart. This was the closest we could get the heavily laden truck to the mountain's base, about fourteen kilometres from the Stuart Highway, the main north–south trunk road in central Australia.

The camels came tumbling off the truck and were quickly

caught and tied to shrubs and trees. I immediately saw the wisdom of the long lead rope trailing behind the bounding animals. Then came the gear. Saddles came off and were placed in a row – and not just in any order. They were placed in a line according to the order in which the camels that would carry them would stand in the string. Next to each saddle were placed the racks, which would soon be tied on. Next to each rack were placed the food boxes or jerrycans that would go in that rack. When all was unloaded, we had three lines of equipment stretched out on the red desert sand. Even the shovel had a place – on the off side of Morgan, the rear camel. Our individual water bottles were strapped on the off side of TC, the front camel, while the rifle and cameras were strapped on his near side. Andrew's swag was on the top of the front saddle with the shotgun; my swag was on top of the third saddle. The two all-important billycans also were tied either side of the third saddle. Andrew quietly supervised the equipment unloading which soon produced order out of potential chaos. With only minor variations, this order remained set in stone for the entire journey. If I wanted to find something, even in the middle of the night, there would be no doubt where it would be. 'A place for everything and everything in its place.' Those stale old words suddenly had new meaning for me.

Trevor and John, while experienced in the ways of camels and the bush, accepted Andrew's directions without hesitation. This was a second tick in the box for Andrew. Australian men in the bush don't easily accept direction, and it's only accepted cheerfully when the person giving the directions has earned their respect. Authority works differently when administered in the bush from the way it does in the glass towers of Sydney and Melbourne. Outback authority cannot be imposed from above.

With the gear packed in boxes, Andrew set me the task of tying the racks to the saddles with a series of half-hitches. There is no leather strapping in a camel packsaddle; everything is tied on by rope. Over 50 metres of rope tie the wooden frame to the pads, the racks to the frame, and then the gear to the racks. The girth and breastplate are made of webbing secured to the saddle by rope. The crupper is made of rope.

Last to go on were the all-important 'quart pots'. A combination cup and billycan of spun steel, these small versatile vessels served as drinking mugs, containers for boiling water and myriad other camp chores.

'Well, that's done. Now let's give the boys a test run,' Andrew said, standing back and looking at the orderly row of saddles, now mounted with racks. Packed food boxes and water-filled jerrycans were organised alongside each saddle.

I went with John Wilkinson to bring the camels in. We found them in a thicket near the camp. 'First thing you do is take the hobbles off and attach them to the halter,' he told me. 'Try to work from the back of the animal's feet, so that if he lashes out he won't catch you.' I watched while holding the halter rope of TC, the lead camel.

'Next we take the second camel in line, young Cooper, and tie him to TC. Come here, Coop. Ultimately, we end up with a line of camels like a locomotive pulling a string of carriages.' John threaded Cooper's long lead rope around TC's neck and deftly attached it with a neat bowline. His years of stock work showed in the confident way he handled the camels and in his efficiency of movement.

'Now, *you* try it,' he said.

I caught Sang, third in the string, relieved him of his hobbles, led him behind Cooper, taking care to stay away from that animal's hind legs, threw Sang's lead rope around Cooper's neck, and tied it off at the shoulder with a quick-release, safety bowline.

'What sort of a knot's that?' John asked.

'Snap bowline,' I replied. 'Just pull on the tail of the rope and it falls apart – quick-release, but it will never come undone. Use it with horses when they pull back.'

'Andrew uses a fixed bowline and if the camel gets caught up, you just cut the rope.' He pulled from his belt a finely honed, open-blade knife. 'You don't want to be around camels trying to get a knot undone if they're thrashing about. Too much risk you'll get caught up in a rope and dragged, or worse. You should get one of these.' John handed me the knife. 'No decent cameleer is without one.' I wasn't convinced and handed him back the knife. It was razor sharp.

When we arrived back at the camp, Andrew took TC and led him down the row of saddles until he reached the front of the queue. Pulling lightly on the lead rope, he said, '*Hoosh*, TC. *Hoosh*, mate.' The camel let out a loud moan and dropped to its front knees before working its back legs underneath its body and flopping down. It then shuffled around, getting comfort-able. Andrew then led in Cooper, pausing to examine the knot I had tied in Sang's lead rope, which was around Cooper's neck. It passed unremarked. With the five camels seated next to their saddles, the thick saddlecloths were thrown on each animal's back and we moved to the saddles. 'We start at the back and move forward,' he said, walking towards Morgan. 'You take the back of the saddle and I'll work the front.'

The camel saddles had surprised me the first time I saw them. About 1.2 metres long and a metre high, they were tradi-tional Afghan packsaddles unchanged in design from the first examples brought to Australia in the nineteenth century. They consist of two long pads stuffed with straw, which fit either side of the hump. Holding the pads together and giving the saddle its shape is the *cuttah,* a timber wishbone fitting on the outside of the pads. At the back, a lighter wishbone made of hardwood keeps the rear of the pads in place. Down the outside of the pads, parallel to the ground, run three hardwood ribs against which the boxes rest. The *cuttah*, rear wishbone and timber ribs form a frame imposed over the top of the pads. Attached to the *cuttah* is a breastplate, which goes around the camel's chest to stop the saddle slipping back. From the rear of the saddle runs a rope

Camel packsaddle and rack, Mt Esther, Northern Territory

crupper, which is slid under the camel's tail to stop the saddle sliding forward. The saddle unloaded weighs about 60 kilograms.

Andrew moved to the front of the saddle, bent down and put a hand under each pad, waiting for me to do the same at the back. I immediately saw a problem. I'm partially paralysed in the left hand, a result of surgery on my cervical spine, and I had about as much chance of getting the fingers of my left hand under the heavy pads of the camel saddle as I would have of pushing wet spaghetti under a house brick. I improvised. Sliding my right hand under the right pad I used my left hand to grab the hardwood ribs on the saddle's left side. Planting my right boot as close as I could to my right hand, I drove down with my right leg while at the same time lifting with my right arm. I used my left arm only for balance, doing all the lifting with my right. The saddle was a dead weight, but it came up and cleared the camel's hump and was on.

'Try to lift the saddle by the pads,' Andrew said. 'If you lift by the frame, you leave the pads behind.' Andrew's advice, while logical, was unfortunately not an option for me, but at least I knew we could get the saddle on. We wrestled the next two saddles on and then came to Cooper. Like all the camels, he started to bellow and roar as I walked up to him. Suddenly, and to my considerable shock, he swung his head around, opened his mouth and displayed his fangs, letting out a furious bellow. I was looking straight down his gullet at the bony, ripple-board, grinding surface on the roof of his mouth. Unfortunately, at the time he swung around with mouth gaping open, he had a gob full of partly digested acacia leaves, which sprayed all over my almost-clean shirt. I looked at the globs of green goo all over my chest.

'Well, you're part-way towards being a cameleer now,' John Wilkinson laughed, as he walked past. 'Just wait until you're in the bush and there's no water to wash it off.' There were black spots dancing in front of my eyes which, when I took off my sunglasses, I saw were gobs of green spew. This was the origin of the infamous camel 'spit'.

I staggered through the afternoon, Andrew showing me how to pass the girth under the camel and attach the hobbles while the animal was seated. He showed me how to tie on the jerrycans and food boxes, and how to strap on the swags.

'How'd you know where to put everything?' I asked, exasperated.

'There's only one place for everything and it goes in the same place each trip. I then know straight away if something's missing,' he said.

When they were fully loaded, with girths and breastplates knotted and cruppers attached, Andrew stood the camels up and roped them together again, end to end. Everything was surprisingly compact, neat and orderly. He walked up and down the row, checking ropes, tightening girths, screwing down lids on jerrycans, making sure that everything was secure. After a detailed inspection, he seemed happy and the animals were hooshed down once more. The gear came off, in precisely the same order it went on – we did everything in reverse. All was confusion to me that first day and I couldn't imagine that in the weeks ahead this routine would become second nature.

It had been a long day. As the sun set way off in the west, turning Mt Esther from red to purple, I cooked dinner, giving everyone, including Andrew, their first taste of dried food, which everyone seemed to enjoy.

The conversation turned back to camels. I'd heard stories about their phenomenal memory – about how a camel that's been beaten by a person will never forget, and if it meets its tormentor again, even years later, it will attack him.

'How do they attack?' I asked.

'Usually they get hold of a limb, an arm or a leg – you saw how long their fangs are. Then they'll toss him back and forth, throw him on the ground and fall on him with their front knees. People have been killed that way,' John said. 'A kick from a camel is also lethal; it's so quick you could never get out of the way.'

'Sometimes they fall on the person, crushing him with their pedestal,' Andrew added. The pedestal is a bony extension of the animal's chest, running down between its front legs. 'You would get the entire weight of the camel dropping on you.' I tried to imagine what that would be like – the weight of a small car dropping on your chest.

As I banked the fire before turning in, John was finishing his tea.

'I don't know how I'll handle these camels . . . they're sure different from horses, especially the way they share their half-digested breakfast with you,' I said.

He laughed. 'You'll find they're the only thing for out here. You'll swear by them by the time you come back, and you're going out with someone who really understands them,' he said.

'He's that good with camels, is he?'

'My word. He's a thorough-going bushman. You'll learn a lot from Andrew. He's very steady.'

This was a big statement. John, in his 81st year, was an Australian army veteran and fourth-generation Australian. As a boy he worked on Mt Riddock Station, in the remote Harts Range near Alice Springs. Since World War II, he has spent his life managing sheep and cattle stations. Men like him are usually sparing in their praise and seldom recognise bushmanship in those younger than themselves. To be called 'steady' in the bush was high praise indeed!

'You're doing well to be still coming out here and doing camel trips and lifting the weights. You should be coming with us,' I said.

'I'd love to, but I'm starting to struggle with the walking. I couldn't keep up with Andrew. I'd need a riding camel for the afternoons.'

'Good walker, is he?' I asked, already guessing the answer.

'Yes. Very strong.' Not what I wanted to hear. 'This bloke must have *some* weaknesses,' I thought.

'I hope *I* can keep up with him,' I said.

'You'll be right,' he said, with a twinkle in his eye. 'You may be a cob now, but you'll be a cameleer at the end of this.' He threw the dregs of his tea into the sand and disappeared into the night.

As I lay in my swag, looking up at the night sky, Scorpius with its luminous red star Antares – the heart of the Scorpion – wheeled overhead. This was the view I would see every night in the coming weeks. I don't think I have ever felt more alone. With the brooding presence of Mt Esther blocking out the eastern sky, I felt a long way from my family and all that was familiar. Tomorrow I would begin a journey with a stranger, relying on unfamiliar animals who seemed determined to live up to their dangerous reputation. I decided that

I didn't like camels much. In the morning, I would take the first of the 750,000 steps required to get me to Western Australia. It was impossible not to believe that I was facing the toughest test of my life.

I drifted into an uneasy sleep, wondering what a cob was.

On the morning of Tuesday, 16 July, in the centre of Australia it was 3°C at sunrise. After a hurried breakfast, Andrew, John, Trevor and I toiled all morning in ordered, though feverish, activity to load the camels and get under way. At 11.23 am, after numerous last-minute adjustments, photographs and goodbyes, the Central Australian Expedition 2002 left its first campsite under the brow of Mt Esther. The great adventure had begun.

'Just stand in front of him and block him. He won't walk over you,' Andrew said.

The camels were supposed to follow in obedient, single file. Andrew led the stately TC, but Cooper, the unreformed bovver boy, second in line, decided he should go to the front. Crashing past TC, he tried to take the lead. I grabbed his halter rope and stood my ground. He walked right up to me, the brim of my hat just touching his long neck. Another step and he would walk right over me. I took off my hat and waved it in front of his face as Andrew had instructed. He stopped. His bony pedestal was level with my head. I looked up. He was looking over me, ahead down the dusty track. I put a hand on his chest and pushed. He stepped back. I felt fear, but I didn't dare show it to the camels. Andrew led them on.

'*Oodoo*, boys. *Oodoo*. Steady, TC. Steady, Cooper. *Oodoo*, boys.' Andrew continually talked to the animals, trying to get them to settle into single file and not walk around each other. He would pull them up when they got into too much of a muddle. *Oodoo* is probably a corruption of the Afghan word for 'stop'.

We headed west, following Stuart's track towards Mt Leichhardt. John and Trevor went in the opposite direction. We could see the dust plume from the truck as it headed towards the Stuart Highway, Alice Springs and a hot shower. That first step on a long journey is usually the hardest to take, but I was so involved in helping to lead the camels, ensuring that they didn't walk over the top of each other, and in checking the loads, that I didn't think about it until we were already several kilometres down the road.

Several hours later, the camels had settled, walking in a tidy single file with a cadence that would govern our lives for the next five weeks. I was surprised by how well they were travelling. I'd expected biting, kicking and bolting. I reminded Andrew that when Augustus Gregory left Depot Creek heading for the desert, all the pack horses bolted into the bush and it took him all day to round them up again. Andrew reminded me, as he would do on many occasions, that these weren't horses.

'So far, so good, anyway,' he said. Frequently, he would hand me the lead rope attached to TC's halter and walk around behind the string checking each saddle and its load. He didn't miss a thing.

We settled into the camels' rhythm – Andrew leading, me walking alongside the string watching the loads. The books were right; camels do walk majestically, with long, even strides, the loads high on top of their humps swinging easily in time with their gait. That gait, the result of their long, swinging stride, produced only a muffled thud as the broad, soft pads connected with the ground. The sound of a team of working camels is a melodic one: the creak of the saddles, the rattle of the hobble chains, the occasional tinkle of a bell when the clapper has come loose from its strap. It harmonises with the silence of the long paddock encountered by every traveller who ventures into central Australia without the distraction of a vehicle. Of great comfort was the *slosh, slosh, slosh* from the water jerrycans that I could hear if I walked close beside the string. We had almost half a ton of water on board as we left Mt Esther.

'A very neat turnout,' I admitted to myself, somewhat begrudgingly. A mob of working pack horses or camels was known as a plant or turnout in years gone by. Andrew's organisational skills were in high relief that first morning on the road. I hammered him with questions.

'Why don't all the camels have nose pegs?' From the time of the ancients, camels were led by a string attached from the nose peg of one animal to the butt of the tail of the camel in front. The lead camel was controlled by a string held by the cameleer and attached to its nose peg. The sharp peg, inserted in such a sensitive part of a camel's anatomy, made him think twice about misbehaving.

'The peg irritates them when a noseline is attached and makes them cranky. We'd have to peg all of them if we were riding them, but it's not necessary when we're walking. Ropes and halters do a better job,' he replied.

I had read of horrendous accidents that had befallen early explorers in deep scrub when the lines from the nose pegs snagged in the branches of trees, tearing the peg from the camel's nose or breaking the string, and leading to a shambles of stampeding camels and smashed gear. Andrew seemed unfazed by my endless questions.

I was counting strides and keeping a close eye on my watch. It was critical to gauge the camels' rate of travel before we hit the rough country. I counted about 1200 strides every eleven minutes – we were walking at about four kilometres an hour after allowing for stoppages to adjust gear. Suddenly – *crash*! Without any warning Morgan, the rear camel, fell face first into the dirt, landing hard on his knees with a shuddering thud. His saddle slammed forward and was saved from going over his head only by the crupper under his tail. He had collected a forked stick around one ankle and stumbled over it, but he was jerked to his feet again by the four camels in front of him who, oblivious of his predicament, kept striding out. He was the last carriage in the train. Morgan was walking again before we got to him. He looked around to check the lie of the land, but didn't utter a sound and just kept going.

'That's a relief,' I said. 'If that was a horse, he'd be lame now and would've bucked his saddle and gear all over the place.'

'They're pretty tough,' was Andrew's only comment.

We hooshed the camels down by the side of the track and had a quick lunch of kangaroo salami, dried tomatoes and cheese on dry Ryvita biscuits. This became a typical lunch. Over lunch that first day, I asked Andrew what a cob was.

He laughed. 'Why do you ask?'

I related the previous night's conversation with John. He laughed again and didn't answer immediately.

'That Wilko's a cheeky fellow, isn't he? "Cob"'s short for "cobber". It's a person, usually from the city, who doesn't know much about camels. The guests on my tours are cobs.' We both had a laugh and I promised to square up with John when next we met.

That first afternoon was a wake-up call as we strode along and the temperature climbed to 29°C. The expedition slogan was *Beyond the Sunset*, as we were walking mostly west or northwest the whole way. The implications of this hit me literally that first afternoon. The sun, as it dipped past its noontime zenith, was straight in our eyes, blasting up off the ground under my hat brim. My face began to fry. I was soon drenched in sweat as the temperature soared. The glare was savage. We had partly expected it. We were north of the Tropic of

Capricorn and subject to the tropical climate. Technically, the central desert never has a winter, only a wet and a dry season.

'It may be the dry season, but it's always summer in this part of the world,' I reflected as we walked along. We plodded on through the hot afternoon. At one point I startled a huge feral cat, which along with the fox is central Australia's most destructive predator. It was gone before I could get the rifle.

Late in the day we reached Murray Creek Dam, a large man-made waterhole surrounded by gum trees. Stuart had also camped at Murray Creek on his first day out from Central Mt Stuart. Like us, he found it was dry, but modern engineering had left us a man-made stock dam. We unpacked the camels in a brisk 24 minutes, and then it was a race to see who could get in the dam first. I wasn't tired so much as incredibly dirty. A body soaked in sweat and a sodden shirt had congealed with dirt from the woolly camels and the dust of the desert to make me crusty and in need of a wash.

'Better enjoy this,' Andrew said as I dived in. 'You won't get this every day.' He was right. Unbeknown to us, when we left Murray Creek Dam the next morning and headed west, we were leaving the last significant surface water for 700 kilometres. The next water I would swim in would be at Lake Gregory on the last day of our trip, five weeks hence. If I'd known this at the time, I may have turned around and gone straight back to Sydney.

Because of the late start, we walked only sixteen kilometres that first day at an average speed of four kilometres an hour. This was an easy pace and I relished the freedom of not lugging a backpack. My confidence began to lift. Dinner that night was Mexican chicken, corn chips and pasta. Cooked over an open fire, the dried ingredients were thrown in a pannikin with a couple of cups of water, brought to the boil, and stirred briskly. I thought it needed something extra, so I threw in some dried apricots. The pattern for evening meals for the rest of the journey was set.

The spirit of Chris Richards hung over us that night as we sat around the campfire. We were facing exactly the same challenges as Richards as we got to know each other. Richards' two female assistants lasted precisely one day, not even unrolling their swags before they fled. Though I found Andrew reserved and not much given to idle chatter, I couldn't help but make a joke of it. 'Well, that's it, Harper. You and your camels can get stuffed. I'm off. One day's more than enough for me. I'm going back to Alice Springs.' For a moment, he was shocked and thought I was serious. He recovered his composure.

'Knew you wouldn't last . . . thought you'd have quit earlier. Enjoy the walk to Alice. Tell Trevor to pick me up at Lake Gregory,' he said.

'Yeah, guess you're right. I'd better stick around. Can you imagine the look on the poor bastard's face when they told him they were leaving? If we get through tomorrow, at least we've made it further than they did,' I said.

Andrew looked at the fire without replying. He was a quiet type and was obviously still trying to figure me out. I was unsure just how far I could joke around, and decided to err on the side of caution.

Maybe he thinks we won't make it through tomorrow, I thought, as I said goodnight and headed for my swag.

N
W ✦ E
S

While I didn't share it with Andrew, I was having serious doubts about Stuart. By the time he'd reached the centre, his horses were tiring and his men were no better. Now that I had seen the country, I was convinced that he had been foolish to try to cross Australia with only thirteen horses and two companions. My experience showed that on any long pack-horse trip, at least a third of the horses will be lame at any one time. None of the pack or riding horses should be loaded or ridden on consecutive days, and therefore I just couldn't make the numbers add up. Gregory had taken 50 horses and seventeen other men on his northern expedition. He packed two years' provisions; Stuart took food for only three months when he left Chambers Creek in South Australia. By the time he got to Mt Stuart, two months of those provisions were gone. The coast near the mouth of the Victoria River was still 800 kilometres distant – a two-month round trip, at best. Then they had to get back to Chambers Creek, their starting point, which was another month's ride. A three-month journey thus confronted the group, who had only one month's provisions. If the horses managed the trip – and there were grave doubts about that – Stuart and his companions, Kekwick and Head, would certainly starve. Yet, he had pressed on . . .

These thoughts rumbled through my head in those first few days after leaving Mt Stuart as we tracked the footsteps of the little Scot.

'Where's your back-up crew?' Clint Campbell looked back towards Mt Stuart as if a large convoy was expected. Maybe he was thinking the same thoughts as I had about Stuart.

'This is it,' Andrew said.

'And you're going all the way to Western Australia?' He scratched his head in bewilderment. 'Well you'd better come in and have a cup of tea,' he offered.

'I've got some scones on, too,' Heidi, his wife, added.

We had reached Anninge Station about midday on the second day and had called to pay our courtesies to the homestead. Permission to cross the station had been received months ago – one of many things on my list. We were expected, but the warmth of the welcome was surprising. We were greeted with a pile of freshly baked scones, cream and strawberry jam. Andrew attacked it with gusto, and I thought I should extend the same courtesy and do my bit.

Like us, they were from down south – Clint from Young in southern New South Wales and Heidi from Canberra. Now they managed a station that was breathtaking in its isolation. They told us the history of the station, which is perched on the edge of the desert. The nearest station to the west is Tanami Downs on the Western Australian border, 600 kilometres away.

'Seen any mala while you've been here?' I asked Clint.

'No, not even any tracks. Don't think they're about,' he replied.

'Heard about the mala paddock, up at Lake Surprise on the Lander River?' I asked.

'Yeah, all gone. Couldn't keep the foxes out of it. They cleaned up the mala.'

I was shocked. 'What, so it's all been pulled down?' I didn't want to hear the answer.

'Yes, even the fences have been dismantled and taken away,' he replied. This was a devastating piece of news.

Too soon, an hour had elapsed and we said our goodbyes. The camels once more bent to their task and soon were heading inevitably west. Clint and Heidi stood at the sliprails and grew smaller until the homestead dropped below the horizon. Like people in a Russell Drysdale painting, they were absorbed by the landscape.

'I thought you said this desert travelling was tough? Only two days into the trip and we're getting filled with scones and strawberry jam. Mate, I'm so full I can hardly walk and my cholesterol meter's off the clock. I don't get scones at home; didn't expect them out here. Gee, they were good.'

'They sure were. Don't know how many more we'll get, though. Anninge may well be the only scone shop in the Tanami.'

'No, they'll have them in the coffee shop at Mt Leich-hardt, but I bet they're not as good as the Heidi scones,' I said, tongue-in-cheek.

'We'll see,' Andrew said equivocally. 'Is that coffee shop marked on the map?'

The afternoon sun did its usual frying job and all thoughts of luxurious lunches soon faded. Patient toil brought Mt Leichhardt to the horizon late in the afternoon. Stuart's landmark, the second-tallest mountain in central Australia after Mt Zeil, the dominant mountain on the plain and our first target, was dead ahead. We were on course. At 4.50 pm, as dusk drew near, we put the camels down and camped at the last of the bores before Anninge Station surrendered to the desert. It had been a long day.

'Bad news about the mala,' I said, as we unloaded the camels.

'Yes, we'll be lucky to see any. Still, we're on foot travelling slowly. You never know,' Andrew replied.

We managed to get water for the camels from the solar-powered bore. Although it was hot, they relished it. Unbeknown to them, or us, it would be their last drink for several weeks. My journal recorded my feelings at camp 3, on 17 July 2002: *Beautiful evening. Sun is setting as I write this – 1810 – Mt Leichhardt purple in the setting sun. Very quiet and still, camel bells tinkling in the distance. Walking time 6h 10m distance 24 km, ave speed 4 km/hr.*

All wasn't well, however. I pulled off my boots before turning in and found that the skin was wearing off the tops of my toes and a large piece of hide had disappeared from the inside joint of each big toe. My thick woollen socks and cotton sock liners were still sodden with sweat and I threw them over an acacia bush to dry, as I had each evening. I couldn't blame my boots. I wore a pair of Italian Scarpa hiking boots. Twelve years old and made of well worn-in leather, they fitted me like a pair of slippers. I had never had a problem with my feet before and so I took the easy route in problem solving – I ignored it, hoping it would go away.

I was handling the lifting of saddles and loading alright, but a growing pain in my lower back told me I was fighting a losing battle with the green boxes. On the first morning at Mt Esther, as we loaded the camels, Andrew had picked up one of the heavy metal boxes by the small handle attached to its lid. Carrying it in his right hand, he dropped it lightly on TC's near-side rack.

I bent to do the same, picking up the box in my right hand. It was partly raised when, with a sickening thud, I had to drop it. Again, I tried to lift it by getting my left hand underneath for extra support. The boxes contained the rifle and shotgun ammunition, the all-important rescue beacons, Andrew's expensive Nikon cameras, and all the reference and first-aid books.

'Bugger me, you must have the Mitchell Library in here,' I said, trying to make light of my difficulties.

'Hang on, I'll help you with it,' Trevor shouted, moving to assist.

'No, leave him. He's got to do it in the bush,' Andrew said, as he watched me stagger towards TC, bent almost double under the weight. I wrestled the box on to TC's rack. *Crash*. It was home. The box dropped on to the rack and I stood gasping, breathless from the exertion. Since then, I had tried everything, including lifting the box on to my right thigh for support, but then I couldn't walk to the camel. My back had been stiff and sore every morning and I blamed the dead weight of the 50-kilogram boxes. I didn't dare tell Andrew about my problems, though, and vowed to battle on.

On Thursday, 26 April 1860, Stuart had written while near our location:

No water. The country then became difficult to get through, in consequence of the number of dead mulga bushes . . . the grass ceased, and spinifex took its place, and continued to the banks of the next gum creek, which we crossed . . . the

bed sandy, and divided into a number of channels, . . . but
no water in them.

I read this to Andrew just before we left camp 3.

'The creek he mentions is Ingallan Creek, which we'll hit early afternoon,' I said. 'It'll be dry, though. Sounds like we're in for a difficult day. We're going to hit scrub.' He seemed unconcerned and we moved off.

Proving that the country hadn't changed since Stuart's time, it flattened out during the morning, with spinifex and anthills becoming more common. We were leaving the grasslands of Anninge behind. Even before we reached the creek, walking became almost impossible, our progress blocked by a tall, scrubby bush that I hadn't seen before.

'Mulga?' I asked Andrew at one stage, as we confronted a seemingly impenetrable barrier of the stuff. He nodded grimly before we resumed our march, smashing our way towards the creek. I had been introduced to the thick mulga scrub belts that dominate the central desert.

At 2.25 pm, I wrote in my notebook:

Reached the Ingallan creek, multi channel sandy bed
completely dry. Following S. [Stuart's] track exactly since
lunch. Crossed I. creek exactly where he did. Frightful
scrub dense spinifex could hardly walk through, no better
on W side of the creek. Bashed into it, very hard walking
into the sun, hands & face very burnt. Pitiless country.

Andrew was having a difficult time trying to drag the camels through the mulga on the western side of the creek. I had lost sight of Mt Leichhardt in the impenetrable thickets and was navigating entirely by compass. By mid-afternoon we could go no further and I altered course from west to west-northwest, hoping for a change in the country. Fortune favoured us and we soon broke through into country that had been burned bare the previous year. We had hardly spoken all day. In a pattern that would be repeated for the entire journey, I was 50 metres out in front trying to set a course and Andrew came behind, weaving in and out of the bush with the camels.

Late in the day we camped, worn out from our exertions. Tired and dirty, with clothes torn by the mulga, we had nevertheless walked another 24 kilometres off the clock, but had paid a high price in energy expended. Our battle with the mulga had begun, and although we didn't know it, that day was to become increasingly typical as the journey progressed. My feet were raw and swollen and became painful during the afternoon. I was too tired to worry about it and gratefully rolled into my swag. For the first time I realised that our journey was going to be a battle; a no–holds–barred contest – us versus the desert.

When urban Australians picture the interior of their country, they imagine a tall red–gum drooping in a sluggish river. Think Hans Heysen or Frederick McCubbin and you get the picture. Tourists see ours as a land of rainforests and beaches. The reality is starkly different. Australia is the land of the acacia, not the land of the gum tree. The humble wattle is king. This is especially so in central Australia where acacias cover a third of the landscape. Our particular *bête noire*, and the frontline combat soldier in the Tanami Desert's war on our expedition, was the mulga – *Acacia aneura*. Our battle with the mulga began on the banks of Ingallan Creek and would continue until we reached the Western Australian border.

I would develop a love–hate thing with this plant. Not quite a tree and too big for a shrub, it looks like the upswept, ruined umbrellas clutched by commuters on the Manly Ferry during a southerly gale. Its grey texture imparts a monotonous gloom to the desert landscape when viewed from a high ridge.

Almost impossible to walk through when it's dense, it rips at clothes, confounds camels and provides scant lunchtime shade. Nevertheless, in the weeks to come, it would sustain our camels when all other feed had vanished. Its dry, thorny stems, appearing impossibly devoid of nutrients, were a favourite meal for the animals. And when nothing else availed, it was to mulga trees, withered and blasted by the sun, that we tethered the camels for the first half of the trip, confident that they would still be there in the morning.

As we walked along, the ground rules for the expedition were being laid. The critical question would soon be answered – could Andrew and I, complete strangers, get along and function as a team? Andrew had pushed the door of his private world slightly ajar within the first couple of days. Like many conversations among men, it had begun with the subject of fathers.

'My father's Ian Harper. He was the Deniliquin doctor for 48 years. He's only just retired. His father was the doctor in Daylesford, Victoria, for 50 years.'

'That's a lot of doctors,' I said.

'Yes, I'm the first-born male Harper since 1790 who hasn't been either a doctor, a teacher or a clergyman. I'm the first to break the tradition,' he said.

I wanted to ask why, but held back. Instead, I asked, 'Did you live in Deniliquin when you were growing up?'

'No. I went to primary school there, then to Melbourne Grammar.' This confirmed what I had read in Andrew's résumé back in Sydney. I pondered over this as we walked along. Grammar, along with Scotch College, is a citadel of the Victorian private school system and has produced three prime ministers (including Malcolm Fraser), a governor general, numerous judges, business leaders, and the comedian Barry

Humphries. Prue had picked it on first meeting Andrew, saying that we came from very different sides of the tracks.

Country doctors, when I was growing up, were one notch above God on the social totem pole. Hard-working, community-minded, always highly educated, part healer, part confessor, part social worker, they fixed lives as well as bodies. My parents respected no one more than the town's general practitioner. My wife's family produced three generations of country GPs and although I had met Andrew only recently, I knew exactly the social environment that had moulded him. The Melbourne Grammar education was predictable. I had watched with great envy as some of my classmates, often the doctors' sons, headed off to St Ignatius' and St Joseph's colleges as we entered our teenage years. A Sydney education, however, was beyond my parents' means.

With Andrew's education and upbringing, he could have walked into any law or stockbroking firm on Collins Street, as many of his classmates doubtless did. The questions were obvious: with that sort of walk-up start, why didn't he go into business or the law? What did his family think of him breaking the medical tradition? How did a Melbourne Grammar boy end up hauling camels around some of the most dangerous country on earth? A small voice in my head counselled me not to pry. 'Mind your own business,' it warned.

Before our trip, I recalled Thor Heyerdahl's observations on men and expeditions. The veteran explorer who had sailed the *Kon-Tiki*, a balsawood raft crammed with men, across the Pacific believed that the only way to ensure harmony was to prevent the men talking about themselves and asking personal questions. Heyerdahl followed up the *Kon-Tiki* journey with a voyage across the Atlantic in the *Ra*, an Egyptian reed boat. He knew expeditions and he knew men. He allowed his crew to talk about the journey, the raft, the weather and the fish. Whenever anyone started a personal discussion that touched on their private life, it was squashed. I decided to do the same.

Andrew, I was learning, was a private person, reserved, bordering on shy, but so was I. If he wanted to tell me about his life, fine. If not, I wouldn't ask. I added politics and religion to the subjects to be avoided on the journey. It was something never stated between us, but the policy evolved and I hoped it would avoid crossed swords. We were strangers, forced to rely on each other in conditions of extreme duress, and we couldn't afford the luxury of having a dispute. Staying alive was our main concern.

CHAPTER 4

Seeking John Stuart: Mt Leichhardt and the desert

'It's got to be here *somewhere*,' I said in exasperation.

'Yes, there's a lot of animal tracks and a big pad up the western side of the creek,' Andrew said, studying the ground.

'Look at the bird tracks.' I pointed to the imprints in the dry mud. We decided to split up and continue the search.

We had arrived under the brow of Mt Leichhardt a little past noon on the fifth day of our journey. It had taken us five days to cover the 90 kilometres from Mt Stuart. Stuart and his men had made the same journey in two days. Travelling on foot, we couldn't match Stuart's speed; however, our low-maintenance camels would soon more than match his more mobile, but limited, horses. We hooshed the camels down near a dry creek that had been Stuart's camp and went in search of the spring that he had found there, known today as Leichhardt Spring. At 5 pm, I arrived back in camp after a fruitless search, just as Andrew also arrived.

'Did you see that big dry soak in the creek where the animals had been digging?' I asked.

'Yes, I saw your tracks go around it. That must've been it. We won't get much water out of there!'

I checked Stuart's journal: *After an hour's search I was success-ful, finding some rain water in a gum creek coming from the hills. The natives must have been there quite recently, as their fires were still warm*, he wrote after arriving at our location.

'Well, he certainly found it quicker then we did,' I said. Stuart, however, had moved through a crowded landscape and it is highly likely that he'd followed columns of Aboriginal campfire smoke to Mt Leichhardt and used this same smoke to locate the waterholes. We moved through a landscape devoid of people, the original inhabitants long gone, the waterholes no longer maintained. We were walking into a great loneliness.

A flight of birds caught our attention as they winged up the creek. I was certain there was water somewhere close by. 'I must be going crazy. I thought I heard a duck up there,' I said to Andrew, who looked surprised.

In his quiet, dry manner he immediately shot back, 'Yes, I heard him, too. He was coming out of the coffee shop.'

I was formally introduced to Andrew's wry sense of humour. His quick wit, often bordering on cynicism, would continually surprise me and often enliven a dull afternoon in the weeks ahead. A sense of humour is a great balm to the rigours of a desert.

We were camped in a grove of desert bloodwood trees, a common Tanami species and favourite camel food. Blood-wood apples, or 'desert coconuts', covered the trees. After we squared away the camp and attended to the camels, Andrew knocked down a couple of the apples with the shovel to have a closer look. They were about the size of a cricket ball and about as hard.

'Want some bush tucker?' Andrew came towards me with the apples and a brush saw that he had secreted away on one of the camels. Using the top of a water jerrycan as a work bench, he cut one of the apples in two to reveal what looked like the inside of a coconut. Unlike a coconut, however, it contained a large grub surrounded by hundreds of tiny, wriggling, purple larvae, which were attached to the white walls of apple meat. He plucked out the grub, popped it in his mouth and swallowed.

'I knew you'd take the best bits,' I said.

'You can have the larvae.' He handed me the apple and watched. I knew this was some sort of test, but if he expected me to flinch, he would be disappointed. I don't care if something's dead or still wriggling, cooked or raw – if I'm hungry enough, I'll eat it. I scraped out the inside of the apple with my knife and placed the squashy lump of larvae in my mouth, chewed and swallowed. Andrew was watching me closely for a reaction. I thought of Stuart's men eating the same food on their expedition. Speaking of the bloodwood gall nuts, one of them wrote: *We opened some of them and ate the larvae; which I fancied tasted like artichokes.* It wasn't bad, and if I concentrated very hard it did taste a little like an artichoke. However, I told Andrew that bloodwood apples were unlikely to show up on the menus of the better Sydney restaurants.

At his urging, I then tried the white, coconut-like material lining the apple. 'That's OK, tastes just like coconut,' I said. 'You've gotta work hard for a feed, though.'

Augustus Gregory wrote often of the folly of exploring expeditions attempting to live off the land in Australia, and it was easy to see why. I called our campsite under Mt Leichhardt the Bloodwood Apple Camp, in recognition of the *haute cuisine* enjoyed there.

We had always intended to climb Mt Leichhardt as Stuart had done, but the following morning Andrew vetoed the idea. We would be away all day and he didn't want to leave the camels tied up and unattended for that length of time. Mid-morning he left to climb a small ridge to the south to have a look at the country we were about to tackle, while I headed down the creek looking for a tree blazed by Stuart.

Returning before midday, I hauled out the sextant and other nineteenth-century navigational instruments to take a

noon sight of the sun and see what it was like for explorers in
the field using the old instruments to determine their location.
Nailing the location of Mt Leichhardt using these instruments
was a particular challenge. Stuart had used the noon sight for
latitude, but he had some problems of which I was free. *I find
today that my right eye, from long continuation of bad eyes, is now
become useless for taking observations; as proof of it I can see two
suns as well as one*, he wrote as he approached the centre. Errors
in this circumstance are inevitable and in the hands of a lesser
bushman would have been fatal.

As well as two healthy eyes, I had another advantage: a
modern quartz chronometer no bigger than a wristwatch,
which gave accurate Greenwich Mean Time. With it, I could
take longitude as well as latitude from the noon sight. Stuart
and Gregory would have shed blood for this tool. As I lifted
the Zeiss sextant and placed the telescope to my right eye,
the swarming flies around the campsite attacked me. They
crawled deep inside my ears; they crawled up inside my nose;
and they alighted in my left eye, which I had to keep open in
order to take the shot. They walked over my eyeball. As noon
approached and the sun neared its zenith, it resembled a
glowing green ball through the sextant shades. I felt for Stuart.
This was hard enough and I could see only one sun. I had to
sit absolutely still, not moving a muscle and not blinking. Both
hands were required for the sextant; I tried to ignore the flies.
I wound the index arm out slowly, slowly, desperately trying
to concentrate with the flies buzzing inside my ears. I kept
my mouth tightly shut. Finally, the sun culminated, hanging
motionless at local noon. I clicked the stop-watch to record
the precise time, then jumped to my feet and gouged
numerous flies from my cranial orifices. After several post-
meridian shots, the sextant went back in its box and the long
mathematical calculations necessary to derive latitude and
longitude were made in a small notebook. I sat with my back
to a straggly bloodwood. It was a scene that relived one of the

critical chores on early Australian exploring trips. However, while I sat there working the position, I came to a difficult decision – one that I would have to confront Andrew with.

I'd limped into the campsite the previous day, and after pulling off my boots, I realised this problem wasn't going away. My feet were rubbed raw. Dust and sand had mixed with sweat and had made the liners, when dry, as stiff as sandpaper – they were literally grinding my feet away. It was flex and bend time.

'We may need to make a couple of changes,' I said to Andrew, as we sat around the campfire that night. He looked at me, but said nothing. 'I'd like to use a small amount of water each night to wash the sweat out of my socks.'

'How much?'

'Not much – say, two cupfuls in a quart pot.'

'Well, we have to be really careful with the water. There's usually no water for washing on these trips, but if you think you need it. What else?'

'I think we should stop at about 11 to have a drink of water and some scroggin. Not sit down, just stop walking. A strict ten-minute break. I also think we should have a proper lunch – sit down, make a cup of tea and make it slightly later so that we walk longer in the morning.' We had pursued a punishing schedule, walking from 9 am to about 12.30, half an hour for lunch, usually eaten standing up. We then walked into the worst of the afternoon heat, often until 5 pm. The result, as we usually ate breakfast standing up, was that we were on our feet from about an hour before sunrise until an hour before sunset. This is a very different schedule from bushwalking, where a rest break about every two hours is mandatory. Not taking rest breaks had contributed to the problems with my feet. Neither of us had bothered to regularly make tea at lunchtime, which I also thought was unwise.

'I think we should walk until 1 o'clock each day and take a full hour's spell,' I suggested. 'The mulga and spinifex ahead is going to be really exhausting and I think we should pace ourselves, especially in the heat. This isn't a race. If we do what I'm suggesting, it'll break up the day into three blocks of roughly two hours' walking and keep us out of the sun during the worst heat of the day.' I watched Andrew with some trepidation, unsure of how he would react.

He thought for awhile. 'I think that makes a lot of sense,' he said, eventually. 'But we may not be able to make tea in the thick spinifex.'

'I brought a mountaineering MSR fuel stove. We can use that,' I said. It was no bigger than my clenched fist and was tucked in a bag with my gear.

'What else?'

'The green boxes.' Andrew laughed. He had already started subtly taking over the lifting of the camel-proof boxes. 'They're wrecking my back. If you can lift them on in the morning, I can handle all the other gear. But those boxes have beaten me.' This was a humiliating request. Despite all the training, my upper body strength, drained by injury and advancing years, was proving unequal to the task. Asking Andrew to cut me some slack was an admission of defeat. I hated asking for special treatment.

That night I cut all the loose skin off my feet with my clasp knife, washed them, rubbed in some zinc and castor oil cream, and strapped them with plaster. I put aside a pair of clean socks for the morning. Lying in my swag, looking at the stars, I reviewed all the training I'd done over the past year. Satisfied that I couldn't have pushed myself any harder, I had to admit that it wasn't enough. 'What a waste of time that was,' I lamented. I had, however, discovered that evening another of Andrew's qualities – his patience. He would have to flex and bend, and fill in the gaps I was leaving. He'd agreed to my requests without hesitation, although it meant he would have to work harder.

Disaster in the wilderness is never far away. When you're depending on animals for transport, it's indeed close. That Sunday at Mt Leichhardt started like any other day, an hour before sunrise. Andrew pulled the clapper straps on the camel bells and then untied the animals. They immediately ambled off to graze; hobble chains rattling and bells tinkling. The camels were never released without the hobbles in place. The hobble consists of two leather straps joined by a chain and swivel. The straps are buckled around each of the animals' front pasterns – in effect, the camel's front legs are chained together at the ankles, leaving him room to take short toddling steps and graze freely, but not to gallop away. It's a humane and time-honoured method in Australia for securing horses and camels.

I lit the fire. This would be a morning with a difference, however, as we were to speak to Ian McNamara's 'Australia All Over' radio program at 8 am on the satellite phone. The routine on which we had come to rely was slightly disturbed, although we didn't realise this at the time. Breakfast finished, we had the camp packed and all was in readiness to load as soon as the radio broadcast was finished. Taking longer than expected, we were nevertheless all done with the media at 8.30 and prepared to bring the camels in. No camels!

They had been grazing off to the northeast about half an hour before the call began; after that, we got preoccupied and took our eyes off them. We set off in pursuit. After two kilometres heading in the direction they were last seen, we lost their tracks among a profusion of wild camel tracks and I knew we were in trouble. The scrub began to close in, and when you can only see three metres in any direction, you won't see a brown camel camouflaged in the dusty bush. We stopped every couple of hundred metres and stood listening, concentrating, hoping for the slightest tinkle of a camel bell or rattle of a hobble chain on the breeze to reveal the fugitives' location. There was only a dreadful silence. We decided to split up and continue heading northeast.

If you want to experience desolation, try walking alone in a desert looking for straying pack animals. About a kilometre further on was a low ridge. Although I couldn't see Andrew, I knew instinctively that he would be heading towards it to get a better vantage point over the top of the acacia. My mind raced. If we couldn't find the camels, the nearest drinking water was at Anninge Station about 80 kilometres away. Travelling at night, we could walk it in two and a half days. We wouldn't be able to carry any food or gear. Could we carry enough water? As I reached the ridge, the scrub thinned and I saw that Andrew had already reached the top and was scanning the horizon with the miniature pair of binoculars he carried on his belt. Nothing seemed to be registering as he swung the glasses back and forth. I felt a hollow pit in my stomach as I saw our expedition ending in only its first week.

'What's the verdict?' I asked, expecting the worst, as he came down from the hill. The danger was that one of the older camels like Morgan or TC might break his hobbles and then start to drive the others back the way we had come. Worse still, if the feed was good the group might pursue it out into the desert. This would be a disaster.

'Back about a kilometre. I can see their heads sticking out above the scrub; we must've walked right past them. Got a bearing on them with the compass.' I breathed a great sigh of relief.

Back through the scrub we went, following the bearing Andrew had taken from the top of the hill. We found the delinquents grazing contentedly on the acacia. There is nothing so innocent as the look on the face of an animal that has successfully evaded its pursuers for a considerable time. They swung around at our approach and peered at us. Cooper gave me a smug look as if to say, 'Where've you blokes been? Thought you'd never get here. Were you looking for us?'

'Smart arse, Cooper,' I thought. 'We should load you up with all the full jerrycans.' They were only 100 metres beyond where we had lost their tracks. Even knowing where they were

I was staggered by how they blended into the landscape. Their camouflage was perfect. We headed back to camp, which was easy to find given the landmark of Mt Leichhardt. It crossed my mind that, while losing the camels was unthinkable, walking a long way from camp and its attendant water supply was also risky. Being unable to find the camp again would be fatal! Our experience certainly stood by us that day, but we never again allowed the camels to stray that far.

We had already walked more than six kilometres through the scrub without getting anywhere and had lost valuable time. While the experience had been frustrating as it meant a late start, it was a good lesson: the camels were almost two kilometres from the camp when we found them, and if a ridge hadn't been handy, we would've had real difficulty in spotting them. The old Arab proverb came to mind as we returned to camp: *Trust in God, but always tie up your horse.* I was about to share it with Andrew but I thought better of it.

After loading and as we prepared to leave, Andrew asked me for the course. Stuart wrote in his journal on Monday, 30 April 1860: *Started on a course, 315° across the plain towards Mt Barkly.* 'I think we should do the same, about 310° magnetic, hit the western end of it,' I said. We could just see the top of Mt Barkly to the north. 'After that, we cross the Lander River, where Stuart found an Aboriginal waterhole now called White Stone Well. I'd like to try to find it, too. There may be water there.'

'How far to his furthest point west from here?' Andrew asked.

'I reckon it'll take us about four days to get to the Studholme Hills and then another two days after that. Six all up, depending on the scrub.'

'How long did it take him?'

'Four days,' I replied.

'Let's get going, then. *Ibnah*, boys. Walk up.' *Ibnah* is the all-encompassing Afghan command to get up and start walking.

Stuart had marked a tree on the creek bank 'J.M.D.S' to record his campsite. Of this historic marker, probably burned in a scrub fire in the distant past, we found no trace.

Andrew was quiet as we moved off. I don't know if the morning's misadventure had rattled him as much as it'd rattled me, but I would learn in the weeks ahead that when things went wrong he didn't lose his temper and shout and swear or sulk and complain. I would get wound up like an eight-day clock and would sometimes brood and get discouraged. We not only came from different sides of the tracks, but our life experiences had given us very different temperaments. I suppose his long trip across Australia had taught him to cope with setbacks and then forget about them. He accepted difficulties, went very quiet, but then got on with it. At those times, I learned to leave him alone. His calm disposition made him a very agreeable travelling companion. However, he explained later that he had watched the direction the camels had taken that morning and was confident that we would have no difficulty finding them from the numerous vantage points around Mt Leichhardt.

As we moved north, away from Mt Leichhardt, it stood out from the plain a big, bare and weathered desert red. It looked ancient and immovable. It was a grand sight, one of the best of the journey.

I thought about John Stuart and Kekwick and Head, those three tiny figures on horseback travelling over the same country we were crossing and seeing the same sights we were seeing – only separated by 142 years. What sort of man was Stuart? A shipboard companion of his on the voyage to Australia later recalled: *He was a great reader, comparatively silent, very stubborn, yet withal an agreeable companion and rather a favourite among his fellow passengers.* This sounded a lot like Andrew, although I didn't tell him that. Maybe there were a few clues in this passage about the sort of man Stuart would become.

There is no doubt that Charles Sturt held the Scotsman in high regard. After Poole died on the Central Australian Expedition of 1844–45, Sturt appointed Stuart second in command. Sturt praised him as *a plucky little fellow* and noted *the valuable and cheerful assistance I received from Mr Stuart, whose zeal and spirits were equally conspicuous, and whose labour at the charts does him great credit.*

However, by the time he departed on the expedition that we were retracing, another sixteen years had elapsed and they had not been kind. Hard living had taken its toll. Stuart was damaged goods. Not long after his 44th birthday, he lamented that his body was failing him. *My eyes still very bad, and I suffer dreadfully from them . . . Today has been very hot, and the reflection from the white quartz and heated stones made it almost insufferable.* Stuart was suffering from the dreaded sandy blight, what we know today as trachoma, which is caused by a combination of dirt, exhaustion, glare and attack by flies. It is excruciatingly painful, especially when the sufferer is exposed to bright sunlight. Sandy blight eventually leads to blindness, which was Stuart's fate on several occasions during his expeditions. He would have benefited enormously from the UV-resistant sunglasses worn by Andrew and me.

'You know, Stuart was suffering from trachoma as well as scurvy when he rode up here. Poor bugger was nearly blind – could hardly use his sextant,' I said to Andrew around the campfire later that night. 'I don't know how the early explorers got along without sunglasses in this heat and glare. The top-drawer explorers like Gregory hated taking people over the age of 25 on their expeditions. That was seen as the cut-off. He wouldn't have taken someone of Stuart's age along. Maybe that was one of Stuart's problems – he didn't know when to quit.'

'Yes, but if he'd quit, he never would've crossed Australia,' Andrew replied.

Stuart's other problem must also have dogged him. His weakness for the drink had made him notorious in Adelaide for making a fool of himself and getting thrown out of society dinners. Probably he preferred the rough comforts of the bush with all its attendant simplicity to the complicated life of the town. None of the early explorers seemed to have had time for women in their lives, either. Gus and Henry Gregory never married; Stuart was a bachelor. Neither Andrew nor I was hanging out for a whisky as we tracked north from Mt Leichhardt, but I spared a thought for Stuart, who probably had been. There were no hotels in the Tanami where he could slake his thirst.

We reached the partially burned ruins of Mt Barkly Station at lunchtime on the second day out from Mt Leichhardt. The walking had been easier, mostly through open grassland. An old windmill still turned, pumping water from deep in the artesian basin into a trough, rich in mineral accretion. People and cattle were long gone, as the owners had lost their fight with the desert, but thousands of zebra finches had invaded the damp microclimate around the tank and were thriving. They rose like a blizzard as we walked to the tank.

'They're a seed-eating bird and require a lot of water. Bit of a sign that water is handy out here,' Andrew said. At ten centimetres, the zebra finch is the smallest Australian finch. This tiny grey bird with its distinctive red–orange bill would reappear in other parts of the Tanami, and the apparently waterless locations where we spied them would confound the theory that they need abundant water to survive. They whirred about, protesting our presence while we had lunch.

'There must be at least 100,000 in this flock,' I said. Andrew nodded. He tried to get the camels to drink, but the clanking windmill and burned-out buildings disturbed them.

'Pretty impressive,' I said to Andrew, pointing to Mt Barkly, which dominated the eastern horizon.

'*My word!* Not as tall as Mt Leichhardt, though. Did Stuart climb that?'

'Yep, there on the western face. He wrote in his journal that he *did not like the appearance of the country before us*. He still kept going, though,' I said. So did we. We punched into the afternoon, heading for a low line of gums on the western horizon marking the Lander River, our next objective. Hopefully, we would find the waterhole that saved Stuart. Secretly I hoped for a big waterhole, a swim, and a release from the caked-on dirt and sweat.

Late in the afternoon more abundant animal tracks told us that we were nearing the river and a water source. With two hours of daylight remaining, we hit the east channel of the Lander. Its bed was broad, dry and sandy, as expected. We split up, Andrew heading north, me heading south. I checked Stuart's bearings from Mt Barkly — we should've been standing on his well. Hot, tired and thirsty, I trudged along the dry riverbed, cursing these central Australian 'rivers' — rivers in name only; rivers of sand that flowed once a year in a good season and thereafter were a murderous stretch of aridity, maddening the weary traveller.

'What twisted bastard called that a river?' I said, when we met back at camp with dusk closing in. 'Hasn't been too much water skiing there,' I grumbled.

'There's water here somewhere, though. Look at the animal tracks,' Andrew said. For the first time on the trip, he looked genuinely puzzled. A herd of wild horses, station stock from the days when Mt Barkly was a working property, had galloped away as we arrived.

We unloaded the camels. By now it was routine, and anything over 40 minutes to complete the task was unacceptable to both of us. The camels were led in, still roped together and hooshed down, always facing west into the dying sun. They preferred it that way. I put hobbles on TC and Cooper, the front two camels, and Andrew did the back three – Sang, Char and Morgan. We then swapped and unroped each camel. I undid Char and Morgan's crupper, girth and breastplate and folded the tack neatly on top of their saddles. Andrew untacked the front three in the same time I did the back two, a revealing measure of relative efficiency. With the gear undone, we converged on Morgan and began unloading the gear from the racks. It was important to unweight the saddles evenly so that if Andrew pulled two jerrycans from the near side, I had to pull two from the off side, otherwise the saddle would slip, and the animal would stand up and possibly panic and bolt. At best, there would be gear scattered everywhere. We worked methodically on each camel, moving down the line as each one was relieved of its weight. We worked the same side of the string for the entire time we were in the bush.

With all the gear off, we went back to Morgan again. We unloaded Morgan – the rear camel – first, as the animals sometimes stood up when the weight came off. Working from the back discourages all the camels from standing in sympathy as they can't see what's happening behind them. With Andrew gripping the front of the saddle and me the back, the heavy encumbrance was lifted off – up and over the hump – and placed on Andrew's side of the string. By the end of the first week, I could do this in my sleep and I rejoiced in the fact that it was a lot easier getting those saddles off in the evening than it was getting them on in the morning.

My big problem was keeping up with Andrew. His practised fingers fairly flew over the myriad knots keeping the jerrycans and boxes tight in the racks. He did it by instinct, me by concentration. If my concentration ever faulted, which it often did, Andrew would stand on his side waiting to lift off while I was still about three knots behind him. Nevertheless, he was always patient and never demanded that I hurry up. I eventually got faster, and it seemed adequate, as he never complained.

With their saddles off and hobbles on, the camels received a friendly pat from Andrew, who also checked their backs for tender spots in the saddle area. Then they were stood up and shooed out of the camp and allowed to graze for the hour before sunset. This is where I came into my own – captain of the shovel and the campfire. Inevitably, a space would have to be cleared for the fire, a space big enough so that we didn't set fire to the surrounding spinifex. To do so would have started a conflagration totally beyond our control. I cleared an area while Andrew brought over the 'lunchboxes'. Firewood was collected and sorted into 'tonight' and 'tomorrow' piles and in heaps according to size – from kindling to logs, although big timber was scarce in the Tanami. We raced against the encroaching darkness, doing as much as possible while we could still see. Andrew put an apple, a muesli bar and a Popper fruit drink for each of us in the box. That was tomorrow's lunch. Anything else that was required was also topped up. He put out a can of tinned fruit for breakfast. He was always thinking ahead, to the next meal, the next day, the next camp. I filled two billies and got the fire going.

The camp was established the same way every day: facing west, as this was how the gear was unloaded, in the shade if possible. The wood was stacked in the smoke, as we never sat there, and the two food boxes were placed upwind of the fire. Next to the food boxes was a water jerrycan for drinking and for filling the water bottles for tomorrow's march. Only this nominated jerrycan could be opened. When all was in order, the swags were brought to the fire and placed near, but not on top of, the food boxes. Nothing was left in 'no-man's-land' between the fire and the food boxes. The order and organisation was immensely practical, for when night fell we always knew where everything was. All this was done and we had yet to sit down! We still had to take the shovel and clear a space for our tarps and swags.

It was camp design and camp practice according to the Harper template: order, discipline, safety and routine, routine,

routine. There was a rule for doing everything, even down to where to light a lunchtime fire – never in the shade, as shade is scarce and that's where people want to sit. It was tried and proven, it worked and it was based on common sense. Many people would find it monotonous. It was, but it kept us alive, so I didn't complain. I began calling Andrew 'Coach' because that's what he reminded me of – an old football coach dispensing wisdom. Still, doing something exactly the way another person wants it done – all the time – is difficult, no matter how much it's rationalised. There is no room for ego on an exploring trip, and asking Andrew for help with the boxes and relentlessly doing things his way, dented mine. I had to swallow my pride, and pride – like fishbones – doesn't slide down my gullet easily!

When we finally got to sit down in the afternoons, I ripped off my boots and socks to let my feet breathe and we mixed up one of Prue's magic drinks. Vitafresh is a New Zealand-made powdered fruit juice high in glucose and citric acid. I don't know where Prue found it, but Andrew and I shared a litre of it every afternoon and it quenched our thirst in a way that water never could. We followed this up with a litre of water each and then several cups of tea, while we were furiously writing in our journals and updating the maps in the fading light and munching on the one apple we allowed ourselves each day.

Andrew seemed to find some of the things I did very strange. Like me, he was a disciplined journal keeper. Unlike me, he managed to record the day's events in half a page, taking no more than five minutes immediately after he sat down. I would sometimes start before I cooked the evening meal and would still be going late in the night after Andrew was in his swag. Sometimes, I would write up to ten pages, recording time spent walking, distances, temperature, humidity, the state of the camels, and observations on Andrew, the desert and how I was travelling. Everything that I had written in my small notebook during the day went into my journal at night. I painstakingly logged our route on the maps, recording the traverses, course changes, camp-sites and places of interest.

'What on earth do you write in that journal?' Andrew said one night as I scribbled away.

'Everything that happens. I like to think we're keeping a journal that one day people might compare to the early explorers' journals.' He thought about this while looking at the fire.

'There's another reason. I don't have anything from my parents or grandparents, something that I can point to and say, "That's been in my family for a long time." I want these journals and maps and my compass and sextants to go to my kids. Hopefully, they'll pass them on to their kids, and so on.' I picked up the heavy brass prismatic compass made by Francis Barker in London. It was a work of art, but nevertheless was very practical and had accompanied me on all my expeditions.

'They may not. They mightn't be interested,' Andrew said.

'Possibly, but just imagine in 100 years' time my great-grandson might be trawling through a dusty attic and find this compass and the journals and be fired up to come out here and retrace our steps or find the plaques we've left behind. I can only imagine what it would be like to know that this compass had been on one of my great-grandfather's expeditions,' I said, sliding the instrument into its leather case.

'Have you got anything handed down from your family?' I asked.

'Yes, my father's got some heirlooms that came out on the ship with the family in 1856,' Andrew replied.

I would like to have discovered what these items were, but Andrew didn't volunteer so I didn't push it. 'You're lucky,' I said.

'So, what did Stuart's journal say about this place?' Andrew asked later that evening at the Lander.

I pulled out Stuart's journal. 'He got here on Tuesday, 1 May 1860, and said that ten kilometres northwest of Mt Barkly he *came upon a large gum creek divided into numerous channels; searched it carefully without finding any surface water; but I discovered a native well about four feet deep, in the east channel, close to a small hill of rocks. Cleared it out and watered the horses with a quart pot which took us long after dark* . . . Each horse drank 45 litres – not much for a working horse – about two of our jerrycans.' A working horse in a hot climate requires at least that amount of water daily to maintain condition. It wasn't enough for the punishing conditions Stuart was about to put his horses through. Stuart wrote that they discovered numerous recent human footprints in the sand, further evidence of the crowded landscape through which he moved.

'I've checked this about a dozen times. I don't know what I'm missing. Where's the small hill of rocks he's writing about? Stuart didn't call it White Stone Well. It must have been christened that later. I wonder what the white stone –'

Bang!

We looked at each other.

Bang! Bang!

We jumped to our feet. Rifle fire, large calibre, close-up, southeast.

'Who the hell could *that* be?' I said.

Bang! Bang! The echo trailed down the creek.

'Willowra mob out hunting, I expect,' Andrew replied calmly. Willowra was a remote Aboriginal community about 40 kilometres to the north. He quickly loaded the shotgun and loosed off a shell to alert the hunters to our presence. The last thing we needed was someone shooting in the direction of our camp or taking a pot shot at the camels. There were no further shots, but shortly we heard the faint tremor on the breeze of a vehicle engine coming towards us. A moment later, a battered four-wheel drive emerged from the scrub heading our way. Andrew went to say hello. I went to hunt the camels back.

He was back within five minutes as our visitors disappeared over the river. 'Willowra mob out after a steer. Water's just across the river, directly opposite the camp.'

'You're kidding!' I had missed it by about 200 metres. 'You know, nothing much has changed out here. A couple of white fellas out exploring bump into the locals out hunting, and the locals have to show the white fellas where the water is. History keeps repeating itself.'

'I suppose it does, when you put it like that,' Andrew said, smiling.

I pointed out to Andrew that night that we had completed our first week on the road, 126 kilometres in seven days, and about 624 kilometres to go. 'Too soon to break out the champagne,' I said. 'It's a long way even to the half-way mark.' The enormity of our task was frightening. That evening was overcast; one of the few nights on the entire trip that we wouldn't see the stars. The sunset – first red, then pink, then purple – defied description.

'So, Stuart discovered this river and named it the Lander?' Andrew asked as he wrote in his journal that night and we sat with cups of tea watching the fire die.

'Yes, he discovered it; but no, he didn't name it the Lander. He called it the Fisher, after Sir James Hurtle Fisher, but he was robbed.' The Lander rises in the Giles Range and flows north away from the highlands of central Australia, emptying out on to the floodout of the Tanami plain. It seldom contains water. 'Bill Gosse, the surveyor, came along thirteen years after Stuart, rediscovered the river and named it the Lander. That name stuck.'

'Stuart got a bad deal all around, didn't he?' Andrew said, gazing into the fire. I had already shown him the mistakes made on the modern topographic maps of the area. Stuart gave the name Mt Denison to the towering landmark that dominates the Tanami plain and under which we had camped two days earlier. The Mt Denison shown on modern maps is a trivial peak neither climbed nor named by Stuart. It's nowhere near his route. There were many other significant mistakes.

'This Mt Peake map of the Northern Territory is a shambles,' I said. 'They should tear it up and start again.' Mt Esther, named by Stuart and the site of our first camp, isn't even identified on the modern maps.

That night I dreamed that I was loading the camels and all the boxes were of green metal, two solid rows of them. I tried to lift one but it wouldn't budge, and as I struggled, Andrew was cracking up with laughter. I opened the box to find that he had bolted it to the ground. I frantically ran along to each box, opening them to find they were all securely bolted down. Andrew was a keen student of dreams and had even brought along a small reference book. In the morning, I asked him for an interpretation.

He made a great show of studying the book's index. 'Sorry, there's no chapter in here dealing with green boxes.'

CHAPTER 5

Crossing the frontier: White Stone Well to Stuart's furthest point west

We walked into the riverbed not long after sunrise, the camels churning through the deep sand, revelling in conditions for which they had evolved. Coming out of the eastern channel of the river, I saw sticking up out of the dense gum thickets lining the banks a tall outcrop of white quartz. 'That's why it's called White Stone Well,' I said to Andrew. 'That's the small hill of rocks Stuart wrote about.' I couldn't believe I had missed it the previous day.

I climbed the small outcrop to photograph the camels crossing the Lander and saw the small puddle in the western river channel at about the same time Andrew called out, 'Here it is!' By the time I reached them, man and animals were standing around a puddle of muddy water in the middle of the sandy riverbed. A metre square, it was no more than 50 milli-metres deep. The sand around it was churned by the constant traffic of animals, and kangaroo tracks were everywhere. It was supporting a huge amount of life. This was Stuart's well. Stuart reported in his journal that the well, carefully tended by Aborigines, was over a metre deep when he visited. I was a bit overawed by the history of the place. Stuart had camped here on his first night out from Mt Leichhardt. Here the little Scotsman had watered his horses with a quart pot. It was this tiny splash of water that had saved his life and those of his horses and men when they retreated from their furthest point west in danger of perishing from thirst.

'Well, there's one reason we missed it. It's in the *western* river channel, not the *eastern* channel, as Stuart recorded,' I said.

'Yes, he might've made a mistake, but it's more likely the riverbed's changed since then.' Andrew was trying to urge the camels to drink, by throwing water on to their snouts. TC sniffed at it, but couldn't be enticed. Char, the young camel, held back, watching to see what his older colleagues did. 'C'mon, boys. Don't be so fussy, have a drink. You've got a long, dry stretch in front of you. Still not ready for a drink? Mustn't be thirsty.'

Although they hadn't enjoyed a drink since we left the solar bore six days before, they were indifferent. 'I bet they'd drink if they knew what was in front of them,' I thought. 'Imagine trying to water these camels with our quart pots. I wouldn't live that long,' I said as I watched Andrew tempting the camels.

'Yes, you'd be here for a while, and it would be hard to clean out the well and deepen it, with this sand here,' he said.

We crossed the river, the camels burning up the sandy western bank. Crossing the Lander was a psychological milestone – no more cattle stations, no more bore tracks or abandoned settlements, and no more cranking old windmills. We were crossing the frontier. Here was desolation; here was the majesty of the Tanami. Stretching out in front of us was a flat plain covered in dense spinifex and scrub.

'Well, mate, this is the real deal. Here we go. Next stop the Studholme Hills, and I think we've got some ugly country to cover,' I said.

We plunged into the spinifex. As the sun rose, I knew we would cop it. The overnight minimum had been 10°C – high considering that the nighttime minimum had been hovering around 0°C for the first week. I noticed that the colder the night, the cooler the following day. We were in for a hot one. The country varied between dense spinifex and charred wilderness, the sun roasting off the red clay as it climbed higher. The only sound as I walked along about 50 metres in front of the camels was my boots crunching on the burned spinifex stubble. Otherwise, it was deathly quiet.

As we moved away from the Lander the line of white ghost gums marking its channel to the north provided a stark contrast to the grey–green of the dry, dusty mulga scrub. Gradually, the Lander faded from sight.

'I don't understand,' I said later, looking back towards the river, now a faint line of trees on the horizon. We'd come together for one of our regular water stops. A chance for snatched conversation. Andrew put down his canteen and looked at me. 'If I wanted to get north from here, I would've followed the Lander. Sure, it's dry, but he found one waterhole and there must be others. It seems like a lifeline going north through the bush but he ignored it and pressed on into this country.'

'He was obviously determined to go northwest and reach the Victoria River or Lake Gregory, as you said,' Andrew replied. The headwaters of the Victoria River, on the other side of the desert, were only 450 kilometres from where we stood, and Lake Gregory not much further.

'I suppose so, but I really have doubts about this bloke's judgment sometimes. Not his guts, just his judgment. I would've at least followed the river down for a while.' Stuart wasn't to know, but if he had followed the river, whose course swings around to the northwest, he just might have made it.

Andrew was still making up his mind about Stuart and wasn't yet ready to join any Sydney investment banker's censure of the acclaimed pioneer. 'Yes, I think I would've at least had a look at the river,' was all he would offer. 'Maybe he did and decided against it,' he added.

As I'd predicted, the day was a scorcher, especially the afternoon. My journal of 23 July recorded:

1330 dep. Heading 325°m [magnetic] temp 32.5°c
probably the hottest day so far. At 1345 saw a bull camel,
big old one who ran off. Brutal burnt country, completely
savage & unforgiving. Got so hot today that drinking
water was hot, sunscreen melted and came out of the tube
like milk. Jerrycans are leaking as water heats up.

Hot air, expanding and forcing water out of the jerrycan lids was a continuing problem. Jerrycan lids were screwed down and checked each day before loading.

Stumbling along in the afternoon murder between 1400
and 1600 backs of hands & face burning in the sun. Sun
heating tops of boots. Have to drink about every hour.
Water warm. Something between a plod, a shuffle & a
trudge late in the afternoon definitely not a walk. Hard to
walk a compass bearing as all scrub up ahead looks the
same and I quickly lose the bearing point.

My water bladder was stored on the front of TC's saddle, together with Andrew's canteen. Periodically, we would pull up and both have a mouthful of water. The sun heated the water so much that day, we were forced to move the containers to the back of the saddle into the shade of a green box. It would have been undrinkable otherwise.

As we settled into the reality of a desert expedition, heat was only one of our concerns. During the planning phase, we had discussed many times the numerous things in the desert that could kill a camel. Peter Egerton Warburton, who followed

Stuart into the Tanami in a vain attempt to reach Lake Gregory, had lamented when losing a camel: *Obliged to halt; our master bull camel has eaten poison, and is very ill; . . . Our lives almost depend on this sick camel. We have nothing to give the poor beast but a bottle of mustard, and that does not seem to do it much good.* The following day, he recorded: *The old camel is unable to stand, so we were obliged to leave it.* Two days later, the explorer lost two more camels to poisoning and had to abandon them. A fourth was so sick it was killed and its meat jerked. Warburton's Afghans blamed the recent deaths on certain stars being in the ascent and a poisonous 'night wind'. We had other ideas.

Poison bushes plagued the horses and camels of all the outback explorers. We were no different. It was the unimaginatively named camel poison bush that killed Warburton's animals and we were wary of it.

West of the Lander, we noticed dense groves of a poplar-like tree whose green colouring made it stand out from the grey mulga. The camels attacked it with relish, snatching mouthfuls as they walked along, not breaking their stride. Sometimes TC would almost pull Andrew over, trying to get at the plant as he strode along.

At our first camp past the river, the camels were grazing the poplars hard, ignoring all else. I watched Morgan grab a branch of the tree near the trunk, close his mouth gently over the branch, then swipe it clean of fruit and leaves with a sideways toss of his head. A few quick chews, swallow and then on to the next one. Morgan and TC could strip a large poplar in a matter of minutes, reducing it to a spectral skeleton of trunk and bare limbs.

Andrew was watching the camels intently, as they tore into the trees immediately after being unloaded. Suddenly, he grabbed the stockwhip from TC's saddle and began driving the camels away from the poplar grove. Resounding cracks echoed through the silent bush. The hobbled camels trotted away and cast him

a sad look like chastised children caught with a hand in a for-
bidden biscuit tin. I saw Andrew examining one of the trees.

'What's up?' I asked, joining him. He was looking at a
handful of bell-shaped fruit from a tree.

'I don't like this tree; it looks a bit like *Gyrostemon ramulosus*, which grows in the Simpson – camel poison bush. Good
gutful of it will kill one of these camels, especially if there's no
other tucker to graze on,' he said.

I didn't know what to say. Only experience counted in
a place like this.

'It's not *ramulosus*,' he continued, 'but it's got that "keep
away" look to it. See the blood-red colour of the stalks and the
bell-shaped fruit?' He looked around. The plant was much
taller than the surrounding scrub. 'It also gets out of the ground
faster than the other plants after a fire. Sure sign of a *Gyrostemon*,
but it looks different from the ones in the Simpson,' he said
with a frown. This was only the second time I had seen him
perplexed. His efforts to keep the camels away from the trees
were futile. No sooner had we sat down than they descended
once more on the poplar grove and methodically stripped
each tree.

'Mate, I wouldn't worry too much. The wild camels have
been having a pretty good feed.' I had noticed when we set
up camp that many of the trees had already been stripped.
Camel tracks were everywhere around the grove. 'If it was
poisonous, the wild camels wouldn't eat it, and if it won't kill
wild camels it won't kill our boys,' I said with more authority
than I possessed.

'No, that's not altogether a good sign, as wild camels
will eat poison bush without any side effects even though it
will make my camels sick or even kill them. I don't know
why.' Andrew explained that he was relying on the age and
desert experience of the older camels. 'Most of our older chaps
have a pretty good idea of what not to eat, and the younger
camels usually won't eat anything until Morgan or TC has

tried it. Still, as we don't know *exactly* what it is, it'd be wise to keep the humps away from it if we can.'

He tied the three 'night camels' to shrubs some distance from the poplar grove, but after dark we heard the untethered animals dining with great relish. Andrew tried without success on several occasions to drive them away. I went to sleep fearful that tomorrow at least some of the camels would be on their side, seriously ill. To my great relief they were all hale and hearty in the morning. Showing their busy work, not a leaf remained on any of the poplars around the camp.

I named that first camp west of the Lander the Mulga Ant Camp, in recognition of the giant arthropods stomping around the campsite and their distinctive mound nests lurking in the scrub. Mulga ants have the most distinctive nest of any Australian ant – a circular mound of soil with a palisade of twigs surrounds a funnel-shaped hole, into which the curious city traveller like me may peer. The mound acts as a berm or levee-bank to stop the occasional flooding that occurs after desert rainstorms, when water sheets across the whole land-scape. They are a masterpiece of engineering and I had noticed them on most days of the journey so far. With its savage fangs, *Polyrhachis macropa* is probably the most prolific animal in the region west of the Lander and is one of the great desert survivors, but not someone to share your sleeping bag with.

On reflection, I should have named the camp after myself and called it the Really Useless Camp! It had been a long, hot day and I was tired. As darkness fell, I took the billy off the fire after it had boiled, put some tea in it and left it to draw. I then turned my attention to cooking dinner. Going to the food boxes to fetch the salt, I connected the billy with my boot, and the billy, hot water and tea went flying. I immediately looked at Andrew. He said nothing and just looked at the fire. I was mortified. I had left the billy in no-man's-land, breaking one of the camp rules. I had then distinguished myself further by booting it into the darkness! It had a big dent in it. If there is a bigger crime than kicking over a freshly brewed billy of tea in a bush camp, I don't know what it is. There was nothing for it but to get more water, fill it with tea and start again.

'Sorry about that,' was all I could think to say.

Moonrise at the Mulga Ant Camp. The moon was almost full and huge as it rose in the east. It was a beautiful scene. Moonlight bathed the landscape in a golden light, turning the camp, the saddles and the drought-blasted scrub from commonplace objects dreary to the eye into things of great beauty. The camels dozed in the moonlight, some with their heads and necks stretched on the ground, others sitting quietly, heads up, not moving. During the night, I awoke to see the moon's glowing face. In the old days, the explorers had sometimes put a cloth over their faces to keep out the light.

The following day we walked up a long incline not marked on the charts. At the top was a small ridge covered in quartz. While Andrew brought the camels up, I raced ahead and made the short climb. The view was of desert desolation; to the south, Mt Barkley, Mt Leichhardt and Mt Denison were mere blue smudges on an otherwise uninterrupted horizon. Away to the north, the Studholme Hills, our next target, swam in the heat haze. I looked out over an endless sea of dark-grey, scorched acacia scrub. I named it Prudence Ridge, so as to leave my wife's name somewhere on the map.

'He should've quit here,' I said as Andrew joined me on the ridge. 'There's no water in front of us and he could still see back to Mt Barkley, so he's got his landmarks. It was poor bushmanship to continue past here.'

Andrew scanned the horizon, unconvinced. 'Not nec-essarily. He may've had enough water on his horses. Maybe he was just managing the situation, taking a calculated risk.'

'No, I think he was a mad bastard who didn't know when to quit. He wasn't reading the country. He was just driven by hope; pushing on and just hoping for the best. Plenty of guts, but bloody reckless.'

Andrew clearly didn't agree, but it wasn't worth starting an argument over.

Looking at the empty vastness, I felt fear of the bush for the first time in my life. I was shocked to feel the twisting sensation in my guts. Dorothea Mackellar wrote of the beauty and the terror of Australia. I had seen plenty of its beauty; I was now getting a close look at its terror. My fear stayed my own. Unlike food and water, fear on exploring trips shouldn't be shared; it's best hoarded.

We walked off the ridge and had lunch in the long grass. The camels dozed in the heat. After lunch we pushed on for the Studholme Hills. Four large fires – our worst nightmare – burned all day along the horizon as we marched northwest towards the hills.

He was shadowing us for about two hours. I couldn't see him, but I knew he was back there in the scrub. The low *burble, burble, burble* gave him away; a bachelor bull camel in heat, trailing the scent of our camels. Every time we stopped, Morgan would swing around and look back the way we had come. It falls to the bull camel in the mob to protect his charges from lions, bunyips and anything else that may threaten the group, and Morgan took his responsibilities seriously, despite his losses in reproductive anatomy. His lordship wanted the challenge – all his instincts told him to go and fight. For us, that would be a disaster. An injury to Morgan would probably mean the end of the trip.

He came out of the scrub about 50 metres to our right, a tall, imperious young bull in the peak of condition. A ball of muscle, he looked like one of our camels jacked on steroids. He planted his front legs and bellowed his challenge. At the same time, his tail, wet with urine, slapped repeatedly on his back, while the bladder in his jowls blew out and a spray of slobber vented into the breeze. Impatiently, he waved his head from side to side.

'Come out and fight!' he challenged our camels. 'Come out and fight!' He was magnificent, and we stopped and stared.

'He's a beauty, isn't he? Crikey, we could load *him* up with some weight. Look at the muscles,' Andrew said admiringly.

Our camels, long domesticated and gelded, looked at the stranger with an air of faint amusement. Only Morgan, gelded late but ignoring his loss, struggled to break his halter and lead rope and get at him. He would accept the challenge on behalf of the other camels.

'Look at Morgan. He stills thinks he's a bull!' Andrew said, watching Morgan's struggles.

'Maybe you should break the news to him. Want me to drive this bugger off?' I asked.

'No, let's keep going for a while and see if he loses interest,' Andrew replied.

We held our course and so did the bull, walking parallel with us, about 50 metres away. Periodically, he would stop and throw out his ritualised invitation to fight, but he was getting confused as no one was answering his challenge. I could almost see him thinking: 'They don't smell like bulls and they won't come out and fight. They must be cows. I'll go and have a closer look. I've got nothing to be afraid of.'

He gradually walked closer while still keeping some distance.

Andrew decided the issue. 'I want to camp here, but this fellow's being a nuisance. I don't want him hanging around the camels after dark. Take the shotgun and see if you can scare him off. Just shoot over the top of him and try to run at him so that he gets the message.'

TC was hooshed down and I untied the shotgun. It was a single-barrel, Boehler Blitz, an Austrian antique made sometime before World War II. Andrew grabbed the belt holding the shotgun shells from a green box. I buckled on the ammunition belt, cracked the gun open and slipped a twelve-gauge shell into the breech. Andrew walked off with the camels and I tackled our guest.

As he watched me approaching him, he didn't know that the gun cracked open and resting across my shoulder could seriously injure him. It wouldn't kill him, except at very close range, but it could inflict no end of pain. That I wouldn't do, so I shadowed him for a while, walking between him and the camels. I pushed him out about 50 metres by singing out and shouting. It was inspiring to see how he covered the ground. Nevertheless, he was tiring of this game and picked up speed, breaking into a trot in the hope of getting around in front of me towards Andrew. I snapped the gun shut while shouting at him and making as much noise as possible. I then fired from the hip, aiming well over his head. He didn't even blink, didn't even break his stride.

Having picked the campsite for the night, Andrew was leading the camels around in a circle and hooshing them down. All except Morgan. We were in a clearing just under the brow of the Studholme Hills and he was getting a clear view of the action. He wanted into the brawl and let out a furious bellow. Andrew got him down and foreleg-tied him, with the lead-rope dangling from his halter.

'Try again,' he shouted out.

I cracked open the shotgun, extracted the spent shell and slipped in another.

'Come on, you big bastard. Piss off,' I said, running towards him, but he just circled out of the way and headed for the seated camels. I snapped the gun shut and aimed just behind his hump. The shotgun pellets shredded the leaves of a tree behind him and he swung and looked at me. I think a few pellets hit him in the backside. Undeterred, he began to circle the campsite, keeping to a distance of about 50 metres. I walked back to Andrew, who had begun to unload the camels, which he had tied down in case of trouble.

'It doesn't seem like he wants to go away,' he said.

'I think you'd better let me knock him over. He's not going to give up and it's nearly dark. We won't be able to get a clear shot in soon,' I said, handing him the shotgun and ammunition belt. The distress this caused him was evident on his face. I guessed he hated this part of the job. He pulled the .308 Remington rifle out of its scabbard and handed me a plastic, six-shot cartridge clip.

'Thanks. Go for the brisket shot?' I asked.

'No, too much bone in front. Go for the head shot. That'll bring him down and you'll need another to finish him off.'

'Will do,' I said, shouldering the rifle and walking towards the stranger who was pacing back and forth at the side of the clearing only about twenty metres away. *Rumble, rumble, rumble; slobber, slobber, slobber; slap, slap, slap*; he was becoming more and more agitated.

He didn't immediately back up as I walked towards him and I got a very close look at a healthy, wild, central Australian bull camel. Tanked full of testosterone and eager for a fight, he was huge. If he attacked and I was unarmed, I wouldn't stand a chance. He slowly fell back as I advanced towards him, shifting uneasily. This time he sensed the danger, even though he had probably never seen a human being before, possibly because I was totally silent as I walked towards him.

He slowly retreated. He had one last chance. I loaded a single .308 cartridge into the breech, then knelt and laid the rifle across the top of a small termite mound, cushioning the stock with my left arm. I snapped the bolt shut and took aim through the telescopic sight. It was horrible. The camel's head filled the telescope and he was looking straight down the tube at me, straight into my eye. He looked like one of our camels. I set the crosshairs on the bridge of his nose. A shot there would be a clean kill. Between the eyes.

'He won't feel a thing,' I told myself, not feeling assured.

There was another murmur in the back of my head, a pleading voice that surprised me: 'Please walk away, mate. Just bugger off back into the desert. Don't make me do this.' The camel took a step forward. I took first pressure on the trigger.

I was finding this very difficult. I had shot only once before through a telescopic sight. As a child on our farm at Wellington, I had happily laid waste rabbits and foxes by the hundreds – feral pests shot with iron sights in comfortable long-range anonymity. This was different – a large animal, and through the 'scope I could see the individual hairs on his head.

'Please, walk away. Leave us alone. We don't have to do this . . .'

Camels look at humans with none of the wariness often shown by horses. Down the telescope came the face of a curious animal, peering at me with large brown eyes set wide apart on his head. I was becoming more attached to these animals than I had realised. No wonder Andrew found it so hard to shoot them.

I started to steady my breathing. The camel turned his head towards the camp and took another couple of steps and then stopped, staring at the animals and sniffing the breeze. I laid the crosshairs just below his left ear. My father's advice came back to me. He had stood behind me the first day I picked up a rifle and gave an eager twelve-year-old some expert coaching: 'Get comfortable first. Feel the breeze on your cheek and the backs of your hands. *Squeeze* the trigger, don't pull. Let the barrel come up as you breathe in, let it fall as you breathe out. Don't take forever over the shot, or your eyes will lose focus . . .'

The animal took another step forward. My finger began to curl around the trigger as the pressure increased.

'One last chance, mate. Please, don't make me do this . . .'
He took another step.

'Squeeze, don't pull. Feel the breeze . . .'

The crosshairs sat below his ear. I could see his eyelashes.

'Let the barrel come down . . .'

The rifle slammed back into my shoulder and the sound of gunfire echoed around the Studholme Hills. The brass cartridge case caught the dying rays of the sun as it spun end over end, and a million ants were mobilised to drink of the blood that pooled under the spinifex. The circle of life and death in the desert, old as time, went on.

While the Tanami Desert is a place of unrelenting harshness by day, it's a thing of wonder by night. I awoke the next morning just as the moon was setting. It was full and luminous. I watched the horizon turn from black to purple to royal blue. As I rolled out of my swag, Orion was rising in the still-dark eastern sky. I had to stop and watch. The things we miss by living inside! I had been watching a waxing moon every night since we left Mt Stuart. It was growing in luminosity and I eagerly awaited its evening visit. Moonset was no less spectacular. I felt close to nature and its wonders each night as I looked up from my swag.

At 9 am we led the camels up on to the first ridge of the Studholme Hills. Named by Michael Terry in 1928 for Miss F. N. Studholme, of Hindhead, England, in 'appreciation of her encouragement', they were an important landmark for us and confirmed that we were on Stuart's track. Stuart had passed in this direction a century and a half ago, and Terry had camped right where we had on his east-to-west truck trip across the desert.

As Andrew weaved through the scrub, hauling the camels and taking the easiest course over the ridge, I scanned the route ahead from the highest point. It was a look at infinity. The Studholme Hills are a collection of small domes, insignificant in the vastness that surrounds them. They do, however, provide a perch from which to view the country we were about to travel through. No mountain, not even a bump, disturbed the horizon. From east to west was an unbroken sea of scrub. There wasn't the slightest indication of water such as a line of green trees snaking through the scrub marking a watercourse. Not even a lonely ghost gum to break up the monotony of the vista. Until now, there had been landmarks to guide us – Mt Leichhardt, Mt Barkly or the Studholme Hills. Always something in front to aim at. Now there was the horizon perched at infinity rolling back even as we walked towards it.

Stuart had stood where we were standing and he had seen what we were seeing, and yet he kept going. Andrew saw the view when he came up with the camels. I didn't say anything. I didn't need to. From the top of the Studholme Hills I estimated it was 44 kilometres to Stuart's furthest point west, about two days' march.

The enormity of what we were doing hit me on top of the Studholme Hills – this was no small thing we were attempting. Get lost out here and we could wander around in circles forever and no one would find us. Get bitten by a snake, burned in a fire, injured by one of the camels – rescue couldn't come in time. Despite our high-tech satellite phone and our rescue beacons, a bad head injury or an accident with the large-calibre firearms we carried could cost us our lives. A vehicle couldn't get to us; there's no place to land a fixed-wing aircraft, it would have to be a helicopter. Where a helicopter with that flight range could come from was anyone's guess.

My journal recorded the tough country as we left the Studholme Hills behind and indicates my frame of mind and attitude to deserts:

*1300, lunch under a scrubby gum in the middle of dense
spinifex plain. Plenty of ant hills. Horrible morning. Thick
scrub, dense spinifex, hard to walk through. No more
landmarks, Mount Barkly gone. Country really crook
north of Studholme Hills. 32.1°C at lunchtime – hot.
This is horrible country and the Tanami only seems to get
worse the deeper we get into it.*

Mid-afternoon I was a long way ahead of Andrew and the
camels, so I stopped to let them catch up. I opened my notebook and wrote: *Thirsty, hot, dirty. Filthy-dirty hands, arms, clothes,
face, hair, scalp – covered in sunscreen and dirt.* I wrote standing in
the scant shade provided by a drought-blasted native orange
tree. *Boots white, all polish gone.* The spinifex had stripped all the
colour from my boots and they were back to bare leather. That
notebook never left my top pocket; as I walked along, I jotted
down our course, speed, time of march and anything else that
took my fancy. By this stage of the trip it was filthy, with
droplets of sweat, dirt, grass seeds and squashed insects
smudging its pages. At night I transferred these notebook
scribblings to my journal. I did this religiously, as soon as I had
finished eating.

I must have been a picture. My clothes were black from
campfire smoke, sweat and dirt. My eyelids were gummy from
sweat and congealed dirt. The backs of my hands were black
from sunburn, and the hairs were gone – burned off from dives
at a billy sitting on countless campfires. I had worn the same
trousers for a fortnight, and all manner of vegetation, spinifex
resin, camel hair and dirt had made them putrid. Highwater
marks of dried salt on my shirt marked the tidal flow of each
day's sweat.

As I walked north of the Studholme Hills, some of the
doubts that had assailed me before I left Sydney returned and
I began to wonder – seriously wonder – what we were doing.
'Is this a socially useful undertaking?' I asked myself, standing

under a tree, looking out at the far horizon and the dot that was Andrew and the camels slowly moving towards me. 'If this was useful, we'd be getting paid to do it,' I thought. 'Out here, we won't find any new grazing lands, any unknown inland waterways, no new mineral deposits, nothing new to science and nothing useful to society. Society has no need or use for what we're doing out here, so why are we doing it?' I couldn't really come up with an answer. Men in the 21st century work, look after their families and pay off their mortgages. They don't go exploring. It's no longer a socially useful profession. I was born 150 years too late.

That night the stress and strains of the journey almost boiled to the surface. The scrub had been so dense that we couldn't find a camp until 4.50 pm, not long before dark. I cleared a space for the fire and was preparing the evening meal, my nightly challenge to make an interesting feed – a tin of corn and a single onion added to a serve of dried, braised beef and beans with a side serve of mashed potato.

I fanned the fire with my hat to stir the coals into flame. Unfortunately, a light shower of ash blew up towards Andrew, who was sitting near the fire and, unbeknown to me, cleaning his F5 Nikon camera. 'Lucky I had my camera closed when you did that,' he said.

'Get stuffed. You shouldn't have been cleaning it near the fire, you stupid bastard,' was my ready reply. But before I could utter my thoughts, a voice – clear as a bell – jumped into my head: 'You say that and you won't have an expedition tomorrow morning. *You* decide.'

I fumed and fumed. Andrew had had a go at me the previous evening about stacking the fire too high and getting twigs in the billy of tea.

'If you worked for me and made a fire like that, I'd sack you,' he'd said, with some venom. All the frustrations, the dirt, the sweat and the exhaustion boiled up inside me. My humiliation at having knocked over the billy still tore at me.

I'd also taken water from the wrong jerrycan some nights previously. I didn't realise my mistake until I saw Andrew the following morning re-weighting the jerrycans by tipping water out of one and into another. He didn't say anything. He didn't have to. I got the message and chastised myself and – being my own taskmaster – I was merciless.

Despite being demoralised and feeling pretty low, I didn't reply to Andrew's complaint about the flying ash. I didn't say sorry – I just said nothing. This was the downside of doing things by the Harper camp template – I had to learn to do everything Andrew's way. It's not easy for a man to admit that another knows more, or knows a better way of doing things, especially in the pressure-cooker environment of a remote expedition. I learned the Harper method by making mistakes, and most of my mistakes, even the minor ones, really stood out. Unfortunately, I had to bend to Andrew's way of doing things for the simple reason that I could never suggest a better alternative. I copped it and vowed to myself never to make the same mistake twice. It was bend or break time!

That night I lay in my swag, sticky with sweat, analysing my predicament. Andrew never seems to make mistakes, and I make them all the time, I thought. One of the difficulties was that my travelling companion never got tired, never got rattled, never got despondent – at least, he never seemed to. And it was clearly *his* show – he owned the camels, he had the desert experience and so we would do it his way. It didn't seem like a team effort. He had to bend to my shortcomings, particularly my inability to lift the green boxes, but I had to bend to his methods. Again, I swallowed my pride, finding it an unpalatable dish.

I watched Scorpius come up to its zenith and then pass into the west. A debate raged in my brain. 'I can't do this, it's too hard,' one side of my brain said. 'Have some resolution. It's bloody hard, but that's what makes it interesting and that's why no one's done it before. Have some courage,' the other side countered. The debate went on all night.

Midnight came and went, and sleep wouldn't come. Through the early hours of the morning, I was still awake. In no time, Orion came up to signal the impending dawn. I was as weary as I've ever been when I rolled out of my swag before sunrise. I had washed my hands and face in the remains of last night's billy of tea before turning in. The rest of me had missed out. My hair was stiff with sweat, and the rest of me was rank. I stank as only someone can stink who is working long hours day after day, in a hot desert, without the benefit of an evening wash. I was weary. Weary and muscle-sore, and not looking forward to getting up and moving more than a ton of gear on to the backs of the camels.

Andrew was stirring at the other end of the camp, so I had to get moving. A small voice in my head encouraged me to lie in for a bit longer. But another, sterner, voice commanded, 'I'm going to count to three, and by three you'll be up and putting your boots on.' I don't know whose voice this was, but I heard it every morning as Orion faded, and it always won out.

The *tinkle, tinkle, tinkle* of several bells out in the dark shortly after signalled that Andrew was pulling the clapper straps on the camel bells and turning loose the animals, which had been tethered overnight to trees near the camp. We met several minutes later at the remains of last night's fire.

'Morning,' he said, in his usual cheerful voice. 'Sleep well?'

I removed the mound of sand which I had heaped on the ashes the previous night and we fell into our practised routine. 'Bloody dreadful. I just can't get used to sleeping dirty,' I said, yawning. 'Gee, we're soft in the city. We're so used to being clean.'

I placed a small tuft of spinifex underneath some thin twigs and chose some thicker bloodwood branches from the pile we'd made the previous evening. A boot on top of the lot crushed it into a small pile and made for a twig-free cup of tea. Andrew believed that there was only one proper way to light a fire and boil tea.

'It takes a bit of getting used to, but after you've been out here for six months without a wash you won't notice the sweat and dirt at all,' Andrew said.

'Thanks. I'm really encouraged by that,' I laughed, and stuck a lit match into the spinifex, which burst into flame, igniting the dead, dry bloodwood kindling. The billy of water, with two sticks underneath to allow the heat to circulate, was enveloped in flame. A thin swirl of smoke rose on the desert air. The light illuminated the food boxes, jerrycans, shovel and woodpile all arranged methodically around the campfire the previous evening.

'I wonder how the early explorers and stockmen got on,' I said. 'Going for months at a time without a wash and just rolling themselves in a blanket at the end of the day, not even taking their clothes off. I think a lot of them even slept with their boots on so that they could get going if the horses or cattle bolted during the night.'

'They would've been cold last night in just a blanket. Tough men, but that's what they did for a living. They would've been used to it.' Andrew said.

As we often did at that time of the day, we stood for a while in silence, looking at the flames and waiting for the water to boil, each lost in his private thoughts. That short period was the only time Andrew would stand still and not be attending to the numerous needs of the camp or the camels.

'Camels camp alright?' I asked, breaking the silence.

'They were eating well on the bloodwoods, but the bells were making so much noise I got up during the night and turned them off,' he replied, moving to the food boxes to make a bowl of muesli, his morning treat. Turning off the bells meant pushing the clapper of the bell through a hole in the tongue of the neck-strap to prevent it from swinging as the animal moved and thus rendering it silent. No mean feat in the dark.

'A bit colder last night. What did it get down to?' Andrew asked.

'Minimum of 1°C, humidity 24 per cent,' I said, reaching down and pulling the boiling billy off the fire with the pliers of the Leatherman tool I carried permanently on my belt. I checked the overnight temperature each morning, as soon as I rolled out of my swag, and recorded it religiously in my journal.

I put the second billy on and soon had water for a pannikin of porridge. This was topped up with sultanas or dates and smothered in golden syrup. We also split between us a small tin of fruit – one of the great luxuries of the journey. Nevertheless, it wasn't a leisurely breakfast. As usual, it was eaten standing up and while packing various bits of gear back in boxes where they belonged. Breakfast finished, I smothered the fire once more and washed my pannikin in the remains of the tea. No fancy pot scrapers or detergent – it was hot tea and vigorous fingers. A quick flick at the end got rid of the excess water. As the sky turned pink in the east, heralding piccaninny daylight – the small dawn – Andrew led the five camels into the camp and hooshed them down next to the saddles, which had been lined up with military precision the previous evening. As the sun rose, loading began and another day was under way.

The saddles, heavy at the best of times, felt like refrigerators after my sleepless night. My legs were a dead weight.

'How're you feeling?' Andrew said cheerily as he walked along the string checking gear after we finished loading.

'Flat as a shit-carter's hat,' I said, trying to sound equally cheerful.

'What course? Same as yesterday?' he asked, laughing at my remark. The fully loaded camels were lined up behind him and looked expectantly out over the top of the scrub in the direction of the day's travel. The sun was well up now, the cool dawn air was gone, jackets were already stowed on the lead camel, and I knew that within an hour the sweat would be running down my back.

'Yeah, same as usual: 315° magnetic. I reckon it's about twenty kilometres to Stuart's last camp before he turned back. Should get there around 4 o'clock, depending on the scrub,' I said, setting the course on my compass before replacing it in the small leather case on my belt.

I looked at Andrew to see if he agreed. While I set the course, he had the final say and was free to disagree, although he hadn't so far. He set the bezel on his compass, before looking one last time at the camels behind him.

'*Ibnah*, boys. *Ibnah*, TC. *Ibnah*, Cooper. On, boys. Walk up, Sang. Up, Char. Walk on, Morgan,' Andrew said, tugging TC's lead rope. The animals responded immediately, moving off obediently in single file behind Andrew as they had done on so many days of their working lives. They were soon into their rhythmic gait. We left camp 10, which I called the Spinifex Camp, just after 9 am.

The coming day would be one of the longest of my life – long and very hot. However, it wasn't without its bright moments. Walking in front, not long after we began the day's march, I startled two brilliant white corellas who flew off to the north. Along with a pair of tawny frogmouth owls, they were the only bird life we had seen since leaving the Lander.

I took my usual position about 100 metres ahead of Andrew and the camels, giving them a course to follow. I consulted the compass constantly as we entered solid thickets of mulga then burst on to vast plains where even these shrubs couldn't survive. Here a dense covering of spinifex blanketed the landscape.

At 12.55, we halted the camels near a native orange whose scant foliage was the only shade on the plain. The morning coolness was but a memory as the temperature hit 30°C. The big swings in temperature were killing me. Years of working in air-conditioned offices had left a legacy that was hard to shake and I didn't acclimatise easily.

'Kangaroo salami's all gone, so you'll have to open the

jerky,' Andrew said, as he pulled the lunch items out of the grey boxes. I busied myself with setting up the small fuel stove for boiling water. There was hardly room to sit down and the spinifex pressed in on every side. To light a fire would be certain death. We sliced the jerky out of its cryo-vacuum pack and tipped the contents into a cotton sack. The rich aroma of the dried beef seemed out of place in the desert. It smelled like the butcher's shop in Chatswood where the beef was dried and packed. Lunch was dried tomatoes and cheese served on dry wheat biscuits with a handful of jerky. A few dried prunes and a strong cup of tea was dessert. It tasted great.

While we munched away, I checked the map.

'How're we going? Andrew asked.

'We're tracking his route exactly,' I replied. 'I make his camp a bit over six kilometres bearing about 320° magnetic. He was mad to bring horses out here. He was lucky he didn't get himself killed.'

'We'll know when we get to his camp tonight what made him turn back,' Andrew said.

'Mate, I think he was a punter. All that made him turn back was he ran out of water. He should've quit days before this. Mad bastard! I'll read you his journal when we get there tonight,' I said.

We were soon out into the full blast of the afternoon heat. A broad band of mulga blocked our path shortly after lunch and we began crashing and pushing through it. It sapped energy and I quickly worked up a parching thirst. Ahead, just above the top of the scrub, was the line of ridge we were aiming for – the point where Stuart decided he couldn't go on. We arrived at 3.30 as the sun was doing its worst. Even the camels were feeling the heat and tried to stand in the shade of the sun-blasted scrub, while Andrew and I deliberated. I'm sure that if they could have talked, they would have said, 'Will you two make up your mind where you're going to camp so that we can get this stuff off our backs!'

Retreating about half a kilometre from the top of the ridge, we camped at 4.05. I photographed the camels arriving at the historic spot, and after unloading the gear, we nailed an aluminium plaque to the lonely ghost gum that marked the site, recording the visit to this spot by our Central Australian Expedition, the camp number and the date. Andrew used a metal letter punch and hammer, which materialised out of the green boxes at significant occasions such as this. The stuff he had secreted away in those green boxes was remarkable. 'No wonder they're so bloody heavy,' I thought, watching him work.

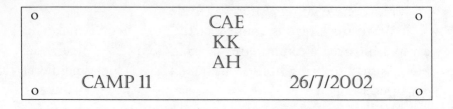

```
o                      CAE                      o
                       KK
                       AH
o          CAMP 11              26/7/2002        o
```

I recorded our position, using a GPS, as latitude 20° 53' 56.3" south and longitude 131° 53' 19.8" east. We had walked 213 kilometres in the twelve days since leaving Mt Stuart. Stuart and his crew had taken eight days on horseback. While they travelled faster than us, we were in good order compared to them. We were tired, but healthy and free of the sandy blight and scurvy that had plagued the Scotsman.

Late in the afternoon, I did a rough check of the water. We were using about ten litres per day – exactly on budget. Food consumption, after a rummage through the boxes, was also going exactly to plan. We were in good shape. Our animals, too, were doing better than Stuart's. His horses had travelled faster than our patient beasts but were on their last legs when they reached the ridge. Nevertheless, our animals had to be watched constantly. The previous day, I was decanting water out of a jerrycan on Sang, the third camel in the string, into my water bladder. Char, the timid camel, seated immediately behind Sang, paid rapt attention as I carefully poured the water and tried to avoid spilling any. Suddenly, Char stretched his long neck forward and gently nuzzled the back of my hand, sniffing the precious liquid. He looked up at me and licked the back of my hand. At the sound of the water running into my canteen, TC and Cooper, the two lead camels, also looked around, indicating that our beasts were becoming increasingly thirsty. Even I could smell the aroma of the water, distinct in the dry desert air. Andrew assured me that there was no cause for concern – not yet!

We had reached our first major objective. Reaching this important target on Friday, 26 July 2002 was cause for a bush celebration.

Andrew relaxed his tight grip on the jerrycans and we drew off a quart pot each – about three cups of water – for a bath. Using a sports towel, I washed off the accumulated sweat and grime and had a shave. It made a marvellous difference to my mood. I felt I could take on the world. I put on a clean shirt; my previous one – a blue R.M. Williams shirt – had turned black. We broke out the medicinal port, carried for snakebite and other such emergencies, and toasted the health of Stuart, Kekwick and Head. It was just a splash in the bottom of a quart pot, but I'm sure that if Stuart's spirit had been there on that lonely ridge, he would have joined us for a drink.

As I had pounded through the scrub that afternoon, coming up to the ridge where Stuart had made his crucial decision, the words of a poem that my mother used to recite years ago came to me. In the afternoon's desert silence, with nothing to distract and the long horizon the only point of reference, childhood memories came flooding back to an astonishing degree. I wrote the lines in my notebook as I walked along, then read it aloud by the fire and dedicated it to the little Scotsman and all those other Australian explorers who had tried to make sense of a strange new land.

The narrow ways of English folk are not for such as we
They bear the long accustomed yoke of staid conservancy
But all our roads are new and strange and through our
blood there runs
The vagabonding love of change that drove us westward of
the range and westward of the suns.

I remembered my mother reciting the poem, which was written by A.B. 'Banjo' Paterson, one of her favourite poets, but I couldn't remember its name. On returning to Sydney, I found that it was called 'The Old Australian Ways'. It was probably appropriate for our situation, as it could apply to Andrew and me, as well as to Stuart and his mates.

'Friday evenings are a bit tough out here, aren't they?' I said, as we sat over our ports.

'Is it Friday?' he asked. 'I didn't realise. No, every day's the same to me.'

'I was just thinking of the rush and bustle of a Friday evening in Sydney. People pouring out of those tall buildings, the pubs filling up, my mates having a few beers on the back of the Manly ferry on the way home. On a Friday night in Sydney, everyone would be going home, looking forward to the weekend. Looking forward to spending time with their wives, looking forward to Saturday sport with the kids.'

'Well, this is *my* office,' Andrew said, sweeping his arm around to take in the clearing, the saddles and the camels grazing out in the gloom.

'The office with no walls,' I said.

'So, every day's the same out here. Sunday's no different from Friday. But every day's also different. There's always something new to see – that's why I like it so much.'

'Well, that's one of the frustrating things. Some of this country's bloody monotonous; it goes from dense scrub to thin scrub to thick spinifex, then back to dense scrub. There's no reward in this country.'

'What do you mean?'

'Well, we've worked really hard since we left Mt Stuart. We've pushed through scrub, through spinifex; we're dirty and tired and cut to pieces – and the country's given us nothing. No waterholes, no nice billabongs – some days we've hardly had a shade tree to sit under to eat our lunch.'

'That's why it's called a desert,' he said.

'Yes, I know, but in every other part of Australia I've been in, there's always been a pleasant surprise – a waterhole you didn't expect, a cave that no one had mentioned, or maybe some rock art. I feel this is more like a contest and the desert is saying: "You can come out here and challenge me, but I make the rules and I won't let up, and if you make the slightest mistake – I'll kill you." I find it relentless and merciless. It never gives up.' Privately, I felt that the Tanami had had its foot on my throat since we left Mt Stuart and was going to leave it there until further notice.

Andrew stared into the fire, thinking about what I had said. 'Well, that's what deserts are. They're not like other parts of Australia. You just have to accept them for what they are. You're right in one respect, though. I could never bring tourists out here on a commercial trip and ask them to bash through this – they just wouldn't do it. A lot of them *couldn't* do it. The country doesn't change quickly enough to keep them interested, either.'

There was no doubt that the desert was giving me a beating. Not just physically – I had prepared for that – but mentally, too. It was the mental part that I was finding exhausting. I recalled Stuart's words printed in the Adelaide *Register* newspaper after his exploring days were done: *When the summit of the dark blue hill ahead is at last reached there comes into view its counterpart, far away in the distance. The magnitude of each*

succeeding plain is appalling. The solitude becomes almost unbearable. I read those words months ago in my study in Sydney. I was now finding out exactly what he meant. I had always felt that exploration was a physical test, a test of courage and endurance and athleticism. A realisation was growing that it was also a test of mental fortitude. How I would cope with this side of the challenge, I had no idea.

Day jobs: Kieran Kelly, Investment Banker, Circular Quay, Sydney.

Andrew Harper, Outback Camel Co., a desert somewhere.

The journey begins, Mt Esther Camp, 16 July 2002. TC, our lead camel, waits patiently.

Dawn, camp 3. I record the overnight temperature and proposed course in my notebook. Mt Leichhardt, our first target, is in the background.

Camp 4, west of Anninge Station. Unloading finished, I revive with a cup of tea and watch the sunset.

Tireless in his attention to the animals and gear, Andrew adjusts a saddle cuttah at camp 4.

Mt Leichhardt, a significant navigational landmark in the desert for Stuart's expedition and our own. TC is unimpressed.

Bush tucker at Bloodwood Apple Camp near Mt Leichhardt. The grub and larvae tasted a bit like artichokes.

RIGHT: The billy and my quart pot, essential equipment, tied to Sang's packsaddle.

Loading water jerrycans on Morgan before leaving Mt Leichhardt.

Desert sunrise, White Stone Well Camp beside the Lander River.

TC surveys the world at a lunch stop west of the Lander. Andrew's swag is on top of the saddle; the white rifle scabbard is under the jerrycans.

BELOW: Morgan, our imperious boss camel, who mistakenly believed he was still an entire male. Between camps 8 and 9 west of the Lander.

Lunch in the spinifex. We cleared a place to sit down. The cotton sack of beef jerky is at my feet.

Andrew and the camels arrive at Stuart's furthest point west, 26 July 2002.
The spinifex looks like wheat but conceals a spiky misery beneath.

Beyond Stuart's furthest point west we encountered almost impenetrable
scrub. Andrew leads the camels through mulga and chest-high spinifex.

I check our compass course on Mac's Bump. The clear area on the bump provided a brief respite from the spinifex jungle.

Freezing dawn at Long Grass II Camp. Saddles and gear are laid out with military precision, according to the Harper template.

Andrew repairs a packsaddle amongst the dense spinifex. No Trees Camp, 29 July 2002.

The largest termite mounds in Australia, in the bed of the Tanami's ancient river channel, dwarfed us and the camels.

Char, our smallest camel, ponders the sunset at Anthill Camp.

LEFT: 'She's dry.' The well at Thomson's Rockhole. I was disappointed in my hope to have a swim.

Alec Thomson, the first white visitor to the rockhole, left his mark in 1926, but he was a very late arrival to the site.

Jack Keyser contemplates the dry rockhole on Michael Terry's 1928 expedition.

History repeated. The rockhole has changed little since Terry's visit.

Spinifex north of Godforsaken Camp. The atrocious conditions had prompted a course change.

Loading camels at Granites Mine Camp on 4 August. The ridges that give the Granites its name can be seen in the background.

A caravan of the ages. Andrew, TC, Cooper, Sang, Char and Morgan crossing a ridge west of Dead Bullock Soak.

The source of my nightmares: Andrew loading a camel-proof green box.

'The turnout's buggered.' Lunch on a Western Australian saltpan. No shade, no firewood and no cup of tea, but plenty of salt.

TC discusses life with a trainee cameleer as we approach Mt Wilson. He souvenired my hat shortly thereafter.

Our goal accomplished. At Mt Wilson we linked the expeditions of the earlier explorers, Augustus Gregory and John McDouall Stuart.

I keep a close watch on a large scrub fire bearing down on us between Mt Wilson and Lake Gregory. Sang seems unconcerned.

A bath at last. Despite the hobbles the camels enjoy a wallow at Lake Gregory.

Journey's end. We place a plaque on the ghost gum at Lake Gregory, recording our arrival from Central Mount Stuart on the last day of the expedition.

CHAPTER 6

Australia's Stonehenge: The search for Thomson's Rockhole

The end of day arrives quietly in the desert. The setting sun spreads a veil of stillness and peace that I have never experienced in the city. Every afternoon, as the rim of the sun touched the far horizon, men and camels stopped what they were doing and turned to watch the last rays of another dying day. Seven heads all turned to the west. The light softened from its harsh midday fierceness. The very air became golden, and the edges of the scrubby bloodwoods, the thorny acacia and spiny spinifex were bathed in purple, pink and red. For a moment, the scrub was transformed. The temperature dropped and sweat cooled. The strain of the afternoon's trudge was briefly forgotten in the silent contemplation of one of inland Australia's great sights – the giant red ball falling to the unbroken horizon. That afternoon on Stuart's ridge was no different.

If the spirits of Stuart, Kekwick and Head looked down on the eastern Tanami that July evening in 2002, they would have seen a tiny campfire deep in the wilderness, just below a ridge, with two men sitting on swags on either side of the fire as they did every night. The younger man's head leaned on his hand as he stared absentmindedly into the fire, which he poked occasionally with a stick. He listened as the older man read from a journal written by the first explorer to camp on that ridge 142 years earlier.

'What time did he arrive here?' the one poking the fire asked.

'At 1550, about the same time as us,' the other man replied, referring to the journal. 'And listen to this. They were all stuffed – horses, men, the lot – when they got here: *Some of my horses being nearly done up from want of water, and having nothing to eat but spinifex.*'

'Does he say why he turned back here?' Andrew asked.

'Not exactly, but he sounds pretty depressed: *We are expecting every moment to come upon a gum creek, but hope is disappointed. I have not so much as seen a water-course since I left the Fisher [Lander River], and how far this country may continue it is impossible to tell. I intended to have turned back sooner, but I was expecting every moment to meet with a creek . . . I wish I had turned back earlier for I am almost afraid that I have allowed myself to come too far. I am doubtful if all my horses will be able to get back to water.*

'So, I think that shows that Stuart turned back here because he was out of water and he realised it was hopeless,' I said. 'I don't think he had any water at all on his horses. I don't think the animals had had a drink since they left the Lander. He just took a punt and came out here hoping he'd find some. But there's nothing special about this place. If he'd been a better bushman, he would've turned back earlier, probably at the Studholme Hills, and not risked his men's lives.'

Andrew was unmoved, so I kept talking. 'See, he's admitting his mistake: *I intended to have turned back sooner . . . I wish I had turned back earlier.* He says it twice. He realises his mistake and the terrible situation he's put everyone in.'

In the deepening gloom, Andrew turned and looked back down the plain. He was mulling over what Stuart had written, trying to balance it against his experience of the country we had just walked through. It was a grim scene. 'Well, for one thing, they'd lost their landmarks,' he said. We had been able to see Mt Barkly and Mt Leichhardt for quite a way up the plain, but they were now gone. We could have been in the middle of the ocean for all the navigational guidance the topography gave us. 'So, they got back to Central Mt Stuart from here?' he asked.

'Yes, but only just. It took them two days to get back to White Stone Well at the Lander River, and the horses and men were on their last legs, dying of thirst, just about buggered.'

Sitting on that ridge, Stuart had made his historic decision. *To-morrow morning I must unwillingly retreat to water for my horses.*

'What does he say of the country up ahead? Does he have an opinion?' Andrew asked.

'Yes, he says: *There is no chance of getting to the north-west in this direction, unless the plain soon terminates. From what I could see there is little hope of its doing so for a long distance.*'

'Well, that's cheerful,' Andrew said. 'But I agree with him; this country in front of us isn't going to break for a long time. Does he say if Aborigines came out here then?' He continued poking the fire.

'Yes, he does, as a matter of fact: *At times this country is visited by blacks, but it must be seldom, as since we left the Fisher we have only seen the track of one . . .*'

'Nothing's changed. They certainly don't come out here west of the river at all now,' Andrew observed.

Later that night, with dinner complete and our lunchboxes packed away ready for tomorrow, we stood for a moment enjoying the last flicker of the fire before it was drowned in its nightly deluge of sand.

'You know, most Australians would consider where we are now impossibly remote,' I said. 'They wouldn't even *think* of coming out here. But really, Alice is only 400 kilometres away and we have a satellite phone and EPIRBs [Emergency position indicating radio beacon]. Imagine how isolated Stuart must have felt sitting here! The nearest town in his time was Adelaide, and it's 1800 kilometres away. It would have taken a rescue party about three months to get here and then they would have had to find him. He had no communication, either – no radios back then – so he couldn't have called for help anyway.'

'No, it's impossible out here,' Andrew replied. 'You get lost, no one would ever find you. There are just too many places to look. But I agree with you, it sure *seems* remote.'

We talked of Peter Falconio that night, the British tourist who had recently been murdered on the Stuart Highway. We both agreed that if his body had been dumped out here some-where, it would never be found; the mulga ants would see to that.

'Poor old Stuart, sitting here rotten with scurvy, half-blind and desperate for a whisky. He must've been miserable,' I said.

That night as I lay in my swag looking up at the stars – I thought of the three men – John Stuart, his offsider Bill Kekwick, a superb bushman, and Ben Head, the big eighteen-year-old stockman on his first journey into the interior. I felt their presence there on the ridge as I had every day since we left Mt Stuart, not in a vanished sense but as if they were there as part of our group. I imagined that tomorrow we would all shake hands, and they would turn back and we'd keep going. I could feel the fear and doubt they must have felt about getting back to water. I looked towards the north where the line of scrub on the ridge obliterated the stars.

During the next two days, we would find an answer to the question that had intrigued me for so long: what would've happened to Stuart and his men if they'd kept going? I felt tremendous excitement at the prospect. I'm no expert, but even my city brain tells me that if Stuart had crossed that ridge he was a dead man, was one of the many thoughts that rattled around in my mind before I went to sleep. I felt like we were perched on the edge of the world and feared, like the old mariners did, that we were about to topple off into a void. I had packed Stuart's journal and maps away for the last time before I went to bed. I had relied on these documents, nearly 140 years old, to guide us over the opening days of the expedition. I had followed Stuart's route and compass bearings religiously – from hill, to river, to ridge, not deviating at all. Now we were truly on our own. I had to set our course knowing nothing of the terrain and with few landmarks as a guide. I could only guess what lay ahead. I could only imagine what would have been Stuart's fate. The remoteness of our surroundings heightened my anxiety, but I was thrilled by the challenge. I wanted a challenge and I wanted adventure, and I was about to get both.

I was sobered by Stuart's assessment. He wrote while sitting on the ridge that the Tanami country *is very alluring and apt to lead the traveller into serious mistakes.* I hoped we weren't making a mistake. We would soon know. In the twilight world between sleeping and wakefulness, I saw Scorpius sweep overhead. A wet towel and a glass of port were a balm for the weary traveller and I was soon deep in sleep.

Stuart's retreat from the ridge on which we camped is one of those harrowing tales of exploration. He was in a desperate situation. Our camels hadn't tasted water for nine days when we arrived at Stuart's ridge, yet they weren't greatly distressed. Stuart's horses hadn't drunk since they left White Stone Well two days earlier and they were perishing. A working horse sweats prodigiously; a working camel sweats hardly at all. When I took the saddlecloths off Morgan, Char and the others in the evenings, I was always amazed that they were almost dry. A pack horse's saddlecloth in a similar situation would be sopping wet – you could wring the sweat out of it. The water pours out of a horse and each needs between 45 and 70 litres a day when working just to survive. If he doesn't get it, he will lose condition and die. Gregory and Stuart were both superb horse handlers and expert judges of what their animals could bear. Stuart had given each of his horses 45 litres at White Stone Well and that's all they'd had for the two-day, 114-kilometre ride from the Lander. Although his horses made it, they were suffering – and now they had to do the return journey with no water – a four-day round trip! A tired, thirsty horse couldn't carry a man or a pack for four days without water. Stuart knew this. Well might he lament that he had allowed himself to come too far.

His bull-headed persistence in pushing into the arid desert west of the Lander had been a punt. His gamble hadn't come off and he now faced losing his own life and those of Kekwick, Head and the horses. His statement that he was *doubtful if all my horses will be able to get back to water* is an admission of the limitations of horses for desert travel. If he didn't find water before nightfall, *I should lose the whole of the horses and our own lives into the bargain*, he wrote.

Stuart, Kekwick and Head left at 7.10 am, the morning after arriving at that terrible ridge. They were riding for their lives and covered 50 kilometres on their failing horses. What words passed between them we will never know. The country was the bone-dry, scrub-infested desert that both they and we had traversed. Death stalked them, but it was to be denied. Fortune favoured them. Proving that not only the Irish have luck, in the middle of that dry, inhospitable plain, Stuart's wager paid off and they stumbled on to a small *native well, with a little grass round it; the bottom was moist*. This unassuming little soak would save their lives.

Having lost their shovel, they were reduced to cleaning out the well with a quart pot and a tin dish. To their dismay, the water dribbled in only slowly – about four litres an hour – and the smell drove the horses mad, so it was a constant battle to dig and at the same time stop the horses stampeding into the well. *One of us is required to be constantly with them to keep them back, and that he can hardly do; some of them will get away from him do all he can,* Stuart wrote in frustration. The folly of bringing only three men on a pack-horse trip was never more starkly demonstrated. They were up all night baling the well and keeping the horses out of it.

By 11 am the next day, without the benefit of any sleep and working with quart pots through the night, they had managed to get some water – about 23 litres – into each horse, about half what they needed. Again, they flew south, arriving back at the White Stone Well at sundown. Then they did it all over again. The well had collapsed and they were digging in the dark and fighting the desperate horses until 3 am. They survived, but it was a predicament that more measured explorers such as Gregory avoided. Stuart and his men had had only two hours' sleep in two days of riding, walking and digging.

The desperate straits that Stuart found himself in as a result of losing his shovel led Andrew to play occasional practical jokes on our modern expedition. One of my jobs was to ensure that our shovel was tied securely on Morgan each morning and again after lunch. The handle slid in between the ribs of Morgan's saddle, and I secured the blade with a piece of rope and three half-hitches through a ring in the shovel's metalwork. This was a sacred trust. We used the shovel to build campfires, clear spinifex for sitting down and sleeping, for making a bush toilet, for getting girths under camels, and for putting out or banking the fire. It was one of our most vital tools.

Andrew would sometimes walk behind Morgan during the morning halt or a water stop and shout: 'Hey, Kelly. The shovel's gone.' This would nearly stop my heart and make me

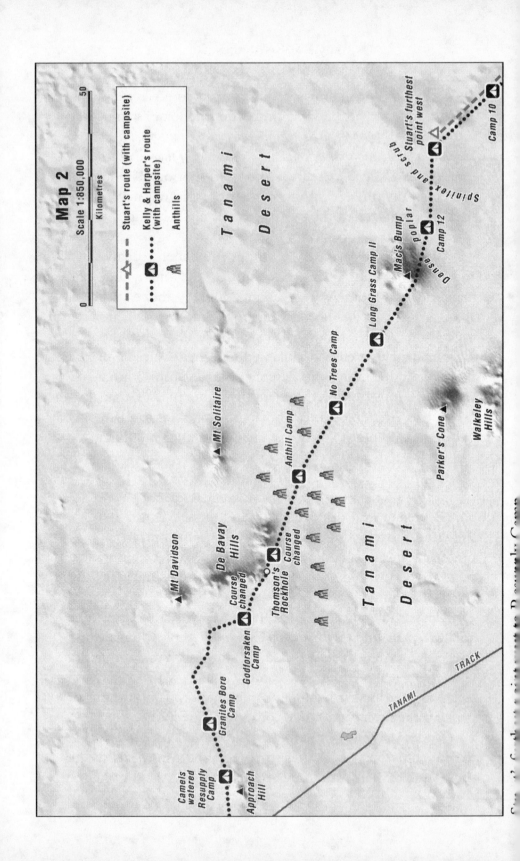

Map 2

Scale 1:850,000

Kilometres

0   50

- ⊲ — — — Stuart's route (with campsite)
- ◀ ········· Kelly & Harper's route (with campsite)
- 🐜 Anthills

Tanami Desert

Mt Solitaire ▲

Mt Davidson ▲

De Bavay Hills

Course changed

Thomson's Rockhole

Course changed

Anthill Camp

No Trees Camp

Long Grass Camp II

Mac's Bump

Dense poplar

Spinifex and scrub

Stuart's furthest point west

Camp 12

Camp 10

Parker's Cone ▲

Walkeley Hills

Tanami Desert

Godforsaken Camp

Granites Bore Camp

Camels watered
Resupply Camp

Approach Hill ▲

TANAMI

TRACK

break into an even more profuse sweat. I would run to the back of the string, to be greeted by, 'Sorry, it's still there.'

'Mate, *don't* do that,' I would say.

'You'll have to walk back and get it if it comes loose,' he would say, laughing.

'If it comes loose, I'll walk into the bush and you'll never see me again.'

That shovel caused me stress every day until we got to Lake Gregory.

N
W ◇ E
S

The morning after our arrival at Stuart's furthest point west we were awake, as usual, before sunrise. After breakfast the food boxes were packed and lined up alongside the saddles with the jerrycans. We buried the fire in sand, filled our water bottles and led in the camels and hooshed them down. By now our routine was well rehearsed, and within 40 minutes we had the animals saddled and the gear loaded. On went the water canteens and food boxes, the swags and tarps, safety equipment and clothing, cameras and navigational equipment, the rifle and shotgun – everything that was required to keep two men alive in a desert for 35 days.

While we worked, Andrew peppered me with questions about Stuart. He was obviously still trying to make up his mind.

'How many men and horses did he bring out here? Did he leave anyone at Mt Stuart?' he asked.

'Two other men, thirteen horses. No one was left at Mt Stuart,' I replied.

'You might be right. I certainly wouldn't bring horses out here. Even today, I wouldn't bring horses out here,' he said. I never did discover what Andrew thought about Stuart. He listened to me over the campfire while I read the journals and expounded my theories, but his conclusions remained his own.

The camels were roped together and standing in a line patiently waiting for Andrew's command. I had to ask, 'Well, mate, Stuart got to here and packed it in, and he was a pretty good explorer. There's probably no water for the next 200 kilometres, and you can see what's in front of us. What do you think?'

'I think Stuart didn't have these guys,' he laughed, patting big TC. After looking around the historic campsite one last time, we plunged once more into the scrub. My guiding landmarks – Mt Barkly and Mt Leichhardt – had vanished and we were alone in a desert wilderness relying on compasses and experience.

Our next landmark, Thomson's Rockhole, was five days' march away, our guide a rough map drawn 72 years earlier by the pioneering Tanami gold prospector, Michael Terry. The rockhole is a semi-mythical jumble of granite boulders perched in the middle of the desert and shading a permanent well of fresh water.

I was in a much better frame of mind as we left Stuart's redoubt. After 45 minutes, we broke out of the mulga covering the ridge and came on to a broad, almost treeless plain. A lonely white gum, barely visible on the horizon, became my navigational marker. When we finally reached it, we were disappointed to find not a magnificent eucalypt, but a scrubby, narrow gum, thin of limb and spare of leaf.

'Wouldn't it be great to find a dirty great big kurrajong tree, something to give us some shade?' I said. This would be a continuing phenomenon: a huge tree dominating the bare plain which, when finally walked to, proved to be nothing more than a shrubby native orange or scorched bloodwood. Such are the frustrations and illusions that plague the eye and vex the mind of the desert traveller. Late in the afternoon, the spinifex was as dense as anything we had encountered. Impossible to walk through, I had to lift my legs high like a clockwork soldier. It produced a biting thirst. I began to dream of coming across a stall selling cold lemonade and cordial.

Hour after hour, we pounded through the dense spinifex. Our speed dropped alarmingly. We had averaged four and a half kilometres an hour at the start of the trip. Around Stuart's furthest point west, our speed fell to 3.75 kilometres an hour. By Sunday, 28 July, it had fallen to 2.76 kilometres per hour. Over a six-and-a-half-hour walking day, this was the difference between covering 26 kilometres and eighteen kilometres. While this might not seem much of a difference, it was of great concern to me as all my water and food budgets were based on our covering twenty kilometres a day. Despite our best efforts, 28 July produced only 17.7 kilometres as we walked through the scrub towards the Long Grass Camp II. Thankfully, this was to be the slowest day of the trip.

Each luncheon spot and evening campsite had to be cleared with the shovel to enable us to sit down, unload boxes and find somewhere to sleep. The camp names northwest of Stuart's ridge tell the story – Long Grass Camp (27 July), Long Grass Camp II (28 July), No Trees Camp (29 July).

Walking through the spinifex was like walking on a million different-sized spiky basketballs. 'You can't put your feet down properly,' I complained to Andrew.

'Yes, the camels hate it. It sticks into their legs and they can't see where to put their feet.'

Andrew also must have been suffering. His legs and arms were black. Shorts and a sleeveless shirt weren't the best uniform for this type of adventure. When I tackled him about it, he said he found long trousers and long-sleeved shirts, which I wore, too restrictive and hot in this sort of climate.

'You must have tough skin,' I thought. A rash of spinifex punctures covered my legs where the needle-sharp spines had sliced through my trousers. We both had knee-length gaiters for such an eventuality, but it was so hot I left them packed in the gear. Spiked shins I could endure. The extra heat of wearing gaiters I could not.

But it wasn't all bad news. The 11 am scroggin halt had become a ritual since leaving Mt Leichhardt and Andrew needed no encouragement to pull the camels up for our ten-minute morning tea. We were eating well. One night I would cook a dried lamb fettuccine with carrots, dried peas and powdered mashed potato; another night dried tuna mornay with pasta. Lunch was generally dry biscuits, cheese, dried tomatoes and beef jerky. Some days we swapped the Ryvita dry biscuits for the dried rye or pumpernickel bread Prue had contributed. Dessert was wheat biscuits with strawberry jam, peanut butter or Vegemite. It was filling and proved adequate to get us through the day. The kangaroo salami that I'd spied in Alice Springs and added as an afterthought was gone but had been a great success – nutritious and impervious to the heat. It was superseded by the jerky, which also proved a great success.

No matter how tired we were or how dense the spinifex, we always cleared some ground at lunchtime to sit on, even if we had only a square metre for the food boxes and ourselves. I always unpacked the small fuel stove and made tea. The tea gave me strength to face the afternoon. Although it was a nuisance, I always unlaced my boots, pulling each one off, allowing my feet to dry and massaging them to get the blood flowing. I did the same thing each afternoon as soon as we set up camp. Despite having hobbled into Mt Leichhardt, the new routine meant that I had no further trouble. I had spent the first week putting strapping on my feet, and in the second week taking it off; by the third week, the burning and chaffing had disappeared along with the bruises and was replaced by hard calluses. The soreness in my back vanished as soon as Andrew took over the handling of the green boxes.

We had encountered numerous obstacles, but we overcame

them with teamwork. At No Trees Camp on the morning of 30 July, a southeasterly gale was blowing as we rolled out of our swags and I was reluctant to light the fire. We needed a hot meal, however, and setting off on the morning's march without having had a billy of tea was unthinkable. Andrew solved the problem by digging a deep pit in which I built the fire. Only the tips of the flames were visible above the rim of the pit, despite the roaring wind.

Nevertheless, the trip was tiring and difficult. The temperature would often swing between 0° at sunrise to 32°C in the middle of the day. To a person from Sydney's temperate climate, used to air-conditioned buildings where the temperature never varies, this was a real hardship. It required a lot of getting used to, a lot of acclimatisation. 'That's one of the hardest things out here,' I said to Andrew one night around the campfire. 'I've slept on the ground every day for a fortnight and haven't seen the inside of a house. It's tough. I'm amazed at how soft I've become.'

'It's the same with most city people I take on trips,' he replied. The idea of living outside all the time is foreign to most people. Years ago, it was the norm to live outside. Gregory and Stuart would've felt strange to be inside. They were out here for years at a time, never sleeping under a roof, always sleeping under the stars. Imagine how strange it must've been for them to sleep in a bed?'

'It doesn't bother you?'

'No, this is my home as well as my office. This is where I live. When I go home to Deni [Deniliquin], I often roll a swag on the lawn – I get claustrophobic sleeping inside. So, no, it doesn't make me tired and the big swings in temperature don't bother me. This is my day job, remember? My office travels with me in those green boxes on the back of the camels,' he said.

'Mate, I *know* that – I've tried to lift 'em.'

He thought for a while. 'It would really bother me sitting

in an air-conditioned office all day, like you do. I couldn't do it.'

Our navigation north of Stuart's ridge had to be exact. I used the Francis Barker prismatic compass. Often I could only see ten metres in front of us, so I had to consult it constantly. There had been no visible landmarks since the Studholme Hills. Walking up an incline two days past Stuart's furthest point west, I spied above the scrub a bare dome devoid of vegetation. It was a great relief to feel my boots' *crunch, crunch, crunch* on the weathered granite gravel covering the top of the bump. The views to the south were magnificent, probably 40 kilometres. But Mt Leichhardt and Mt Barkly were long gone now, below the horizon, emphasising how far we had come. To my great relief, Parker's Cone was visible above the scrub about ten kilometres away to the southwest, confirming that we were on course.

Andrew wound his way up the dome with the camels. He looked around, apparently enjoying the broad vista as much as I was.

'Great to get out of the spinifex jungle,' I said, as he got busy with the cameras.

'Does this place have a name on the map?' Andrew asked.

'No, but I think it deserves one. Let's call it Mt McNamara.' Ian McNamara, the host of the ABC's popular 'Australia All Over' radio program, had shown an enormous interest in our journey.

'I don't think it's a mountain. It's more like a knob,' Andrew said.

'Well, we can't call it McNamara's Knob,' I said. 'That sounds obscene.'

He burst out laughing. 'What about McNamara's Lump?'

'No, that sounds like a disease.'

'McNamara's Dome, then?'

'No, that sounds like he's bald,' I said.

'Mac's Bump? What about Mac's Bump?'

I thought about it and agreed. I added 'Mac's Bump' to the chart and a piece of the Northern Territory now celebrates the Sydney radio broadcaster.

It was only a brief rest and the scrub swallowed us once more as we walked down the back of the dome, heading northwest.

Mac's Bump was ringed with a dense poplar forest; the tree that resembled the dreaded camel poison bush. Many of the trees had not only been stripped of fruit and leaves, but also had been violently knocked over, their trunks broken off about 60 centimetres above the ground. Dead trees lay everywhere. We already knew the reason. After crossing the Lander, we had noticed that our camels stripped all the vegetation from the trees reaching as high as their long necks would allow. Nevertheless, the top metre or so of each tree usually escaped their straining necks and ravenous appetites. They had a simple expedient. One of the older, taller camels, Morgan or TC usually, would lean against the tree-trunk, whipping it back and forth, faster and faster, until with a violent crack, the trunk split and the ravenous mob would descend on the remaining morsels of leaves and fruit at the top of the now prostrate tree. They were so organised that the smaller camels like Char would often stand under a tree and look around for Morgan or TC, who would amble over and obligingly knock it down. Methodical and diligent, Morgan would sometimes knock over two or three trees, allowing all the camels to graze unhindered. I had watched this ritual many times since we crossed the Lander. How our domesticated animals learned so quickly to copy their bush cousins remains a mystery.

'Mate, wild camels must be having a devastating impact on the environment out here,' I said. At every grove we came to, it was obvious that wild camels had been there first. Tracks were everywhere.

'Yes, it takes a lot to fill them up,' Andrew replied, looking at the ravaged poplar forest. It looked like the flattened forests of the Tunguska region in Siberia following the 1908 meteor strike.

It is estimated that there are between 600,000 and 750,000 wild camels in Australia, and their numbers are exploding. In some places in the desert, they outnumber red kangaroos by 100 to one. Australia's feral camel herd is one of the biggest and healthiest in the world, but even my untrained eye could see the damage they were doing. Their great range – we found their tracks right across the desert, even in places too parched for kangaroos – means they are invading very fragile country and must be competing with native animals for food and water. I admired our hard-working pack animals, but something will have to be done about their wild relations before irreparable harm is done to the desert.

'Going to have to be a big shooting program out here, or round them all up and sell them,' I ventured gingerly to Andrew, as we walked north from the bump. Surprisingly, he agreed.

Two days later, on the morning of 30 July, after consulting the maps, I told Andrew that soon, probably that day, we should see the De Bavay Hills for the first time. I'd decided to have a bet – match my bushmanship against his. It was probably not a good bet to take, but it would add some interest to the day.

A cold, strong wind was blowing from the southeast as we stood with the camels getting ready to begin the day's march. 'I'll bet you a schooner of beer that I see the De Bavays first, and I bet I can guess the time,' I said.

He thought about it for a while. 'OK, you're on. I'll back myself to see them first at, say, hmmm, 1440. Just after lunch.'

'Ah, that's a good bet, but too optimistic. I'll say 1600. Later in the day,' I said.

Three hours later, I saw another small outcrop of granite directly in our path. I raced to the top, expecting to claim the bet from this unexpected vantage point. I pulled out the Francis Barker compass, fixed the bezel for a rough bearing of the elusive hills and looked down the prism through the sighting line at the distant horizon. I waited for the swinging compass card to settle. There was nothing there. There were no hills. No blue bumps on the horizon. Just shimmering heat haze. I checked the map. Checked the bearing on the bezel. Sighted again. Nothing. Looked once more at the map. My heart sank. Although it was earlier than we had expected, I thought my vantage point would throw up the mysterious hills. Fear and dread clutched at my stomach. I was looking at more of the same country – a flat, endless plain where the De Bavay Hills were supposed to be. Maybe they had been marked in completely the wrong position on the modern map? Terry's latitude and longitude were out; maybe the modern maps were too? Who knows? There was no one to ask. I had to rely on my own gut feel. I was sure of our navigation because we had been plotting it so carefully, so I knew where we were. I just didn't know where the hills were. I walked down off the back of the dome feeling very discouraged and resumed the march.

'What the hell is that?' I said. We peered ahead.

'Bit difficult to say, but it looks just like an English haystack, or a little thatched hut,' I said, answering my own question while peering into the heat haze. 'Either that or the back of a camel sitting down.' We were too far away to tell. We changed course and started to walk towards it.

'You know what that is?' Andrew said while we were still some distance away. 'That's a termite mound.'

'It can't be. It would have to be five to six metres high. It would be taller than the camels.'

'Yes, I know. It's amazing, but that's what I think it is,' he said.

Sure enough, the object sticking out of the scrub proved to be a prodigious termite mound. The kiosk-shaped structure, made entirely of mud and home to billions of termites, towered over the camels, who regarded it with great suspicion. Initially, they couldn't be coaxed to approach it. I walked up and looked. It was remarkable. It must have been ten or twelve metres around the base and it was at least three times my height.

'Imagine how long it would have taken termites to build this,' I said to Andrew. 'Have you ever seen anything like it in other deserts?'

'No,' he admitted. 'I've seen a lot of termite mounds, but this is huge.' The camels waited patiently while we photographed it, bug-eyed with amazement. It was a foretaste of things to come.

After lunch, the scrub gradually thinned until suddenly and without warning it vanished. We found ourselves on the edge of a vast plain. There wasn't a tree in sight, but thousands of termite mounds, all five to six metres in height, were scattered over the plain – termite mounds all the way to the horizon. These silent sentinels looked just like haystacks in an English field of wheat. The wheat, of course, was spinifex, blowing gently in the breeze. It gave the impression of a vast, cultivated, agricultural plain. Of course, we knew better. It was a bitter, arid desert. It was one of the strangest things I have seen during my time visiting the bush.

The plain was an ancient swamp, the remains of a very old river that once flowed through central Australia. The river, now deep underground is the water source for the mound builders. The termites often burrow up to 100 metres underground, allowing the subterranean moisture to evaporate upwards. It condenses in the myriad passageways of the above-ground shelters as evening temperatures plummet. Existing on spinifex and dead timber, these tiny creatures, totally in tune with their environment, are the desert's most abundant grazing animals. While the river is subterranean, its ancient channel, about 40 kilometres wide, remains on the surface. Paradoxically, the river channel floods in the downpours that occasionally deluge the Tanami. If we'd been standing in the same spot just a year earlier, we would've been up to our knees in a broad lagoon.

I saw it immediately as we began walking northwest across the plain. My heart leapt – a low blue line on the horizon. That's got to be it! I thought. It was off to the left of our line of march and I checked the compass bearing. It must have been there for a while without me realising. It was no more than a faint line appearing, disappearing and reappearing in the shimmering heat haze along the horizon.

'That's got to be it!' I said to Andrew, as he brought the camels up and saw me checking the compass. This jolted him from deep in his afternoon reverie. 'Anyway, I hope it is,' I added. He immediately pulled out his small binoculars.

'Looks like hills, and the bearing's about right. Looks like you owe me a beer,' he said, looking at his watch. It was 2.40 pm. He had correctly guessed the time. I reminded him that I had seen them first. He didn't comment. An hour later, he pointed to another conical hill to the right of our line. It was only a blue lump, but it indicated a large peak, although a long way off.

'Has to be Mt Solitaire. You beauty!' I said. Mt Solitaire sat on the plain northeast of the supposed location of the De Bavay Hills. We were closing in on our mysterious target.

Our camp that night was on the treeless plain. We had walked late into the afternoon, in a vain search for forage trees, and that night the camels were tethered to small shrubs. This was the downside of leaving the mulga – there's nothing for the camels to eat. They wandered around mournfully sniffing the termite mounds. When they realised there was no hope of eating them, they retreated into the shade of the giant mud structures and stood silently. They sniffed at the spinifex, but no matter how hungry they were, they couldn't eat it. There wasn't a patch of bare ground, so I set to work with the shovel. I soon had the tufts of spinifex flying through the air.

Andrew walked past, intending to take some photographs of the camels and the termite mounds in the dying light.

I worked furiously with the shovel and soon had a space about six metres square cleared for the fire, the food boxes and the wood heap. Getting out of the scrub and on to that eerie plain had energised me. I thought of my shovel work as doing the gardening, the Tanami gardening – digging up the weeds. While I hated doing it at home, I was happy to do it in the bush. I felt a growing sense of confidence that I knew exactly what to do every afternoon to get the camp established and that Andrew trusted me with this routine. That afternoon was one of the most memorable I've had in the bush. As the sun touched the horizon, camels and men stopped what we were doing. I leaned on the shovel in awe. The camels looked at us, then at the sun, and became very still. Not a sound broke the silence. The giant termite mounds glowed a copper colour. When silhouetted by the sun, they looked like an army standing mute on the plain. They could have been a group of high-rise buildings in a city like Sydney. The waving seed heads of the spinifex were stilled as the breeze died, and the camels were immovable in their contemplation of the desert sunset. It was a picture as old as time. The camels glowed orange and red. We waited and watched. No one moved. Darkness crept up. Venus glowed bright, impossibly bright, in the clear desert air.

To the east, Mt Solitaire stood out distinctly. The De Bavay Hills over in the west, after teasing us with a view in the afternoon, were lost in the mirage and heat haze of the sunset.

I hope they're still there tomorrow, I thought.

My journal records camp 15 of 30 July 2002 as the Anthill Camp.

The book was over 70 years old. I had unwrapped it gingerly, after the courier delivered it to my home in Seaforth. The words on the spine, *Hidden Wealth and Hiding People*, were faded, as was the author's name, Michael Terry. Bought over the Internet after a considerable search, it told the story of the first vehicle expedition into the Tanami Desert in 1928. It was a predecessor of today's four-wheel-drive tag-along tour, only it was done in open-canopied, six-wheeled, primitive Morris trucks. One of my many weaknesses is a passion for old books on Australian exploration. When I can find them, and if I can afford them, I snap them up. I always run the risk of earning my wife's considerable displeasure and of having her carry out her threat to move out of the house if more bookshelves are installed. I got away with it this time.

Hidden Wealth and Hiding People describes how Terry took two trucks and a group of prospecting companions and went looking for gold in central Australia. Beginning in Port Hedland, he ended up in Alice Springs four months later. With this journey, the first across the Tanami Desert in a motor vehicle, he wrote himself into Australian history.

At the back of the book, folded neatly and unopened for many years, was a map. Terry's map showed his route sitting squarely across the journey that Andrew and I proposed to travel. In the middle was a rockhole, and beside it the words 'Thomson's Rockhole'.

Bingo! Water in the middle of the desert, I had thought.

My problem was a simple one. The De Bavay Hills and Thomson's Rockhole are only marked on modern maps in an approximate position. In fact, the hills aren't marked at all; just the words appear on the map. The size, shape and contours of the hills are left to the explorer's imagination. At least Terry had sketched an outline of the hills on his map – they appeared as a rough L. When I plotted Terry's coordinates on to a modern topographical map, however, it was clear that he was badly adrift. His map showed the rockhole and the hills as being fourteen kilometres south of their location on a modern map. His longitude was about right, but his latitude was flawed. I went to his journal. Pushing his trucks east over the desert from the Granites, one of the major watering holes in the Tanami, he had driven towards a run of low hills extending south along the horizon. He believed that Thomson's Rockhole lay at the southern end of those hills.

Ascending the north–south ridge as a vantage point, he observed *a run of hills coming in from the east til opposite the last of those coming down from the north, stood clear and strong before us where they changed direction to skirt around the flat a mile across, separating each run of hills. And that flat was where the granite boulders hiding the Rockhole should lie.*

Keyser was the first to spot some lighter colour about the middle of the flat. It might be dried grass, it might be granite – we could go and look-see. And sure enough a heap of granite tors, interesting in their freakish distortions, stood among poor, withered Sturt bean trees. This fragment is what I would use to find the rockhole. The difference between the coordinates on Terry's map and the modern map was too great for me to rely on either, especially as the modern map only recorded an approximate position. The clue was in the words. Terry had identified a range of hills; one running east–west, another north–south, like a human arm bent into an L shape. In the elbow of these two ranges stood our water source. I was aiming for the southern part of the forearm, below the elbow.

The Tanami had thrown everything at us over the five days it took to walk from Stuart's ridge to the De Bavays: dense acacia scrub, sharp spinifex, burning-hot days, freezing nights, heat, thirst, aridity, and the largest termite mounds I had ever seen. The evening camps were often under any stunted bloodwood trees we could find to tie the camels to. The country showed us no water, not even a watercourse, and slowly the animal tracks disappeared. However, the camels plodded patiently onward and so did we.

Wednesday, 31 July, was a cold morning as we prepared for our push to the hills from the Anthill Camp. My journal recorded:

Heated half a billy of water last night and had a wash all over. Washed my hair for the first time since the start of the trip. Felt really clean until I had to put on the same shirt that I have been wearing for about the last eight days – it is stiff with sweat & dirt. Wore tracksuit pants for sleeping but that left the top half of my body cold – dozed all night. Min o'night temp. –0.1°C. When I awoke at 0515 still pitch dark – went to pull on shirt but it was still wet with sweat & really cold. Looked at temp when I got up 0°C. 0545 AH and me shivering and doing a joint effort at the fire. Sun still not up. I had put on a jumper until the fire was up – warmed up my shirt & tried to dry it, by the fire. I cooked us both a big pot of porridge with honey & prunes. After that we knocked off a tin of peach & mango slices while we had a cup of tea and watched a beautiful sunrise silhouette the giant anthills. Really magnificent – horizon just one long straight line.

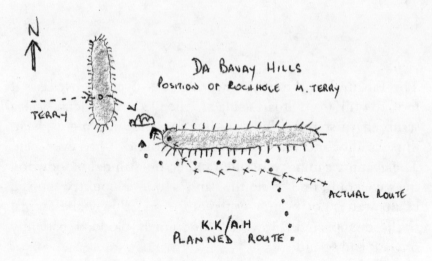

DA BAVAY HILLS
POSITION OF ROCKHOLE M. TERRY

TERRY

ACTUAL ROUTE

K.K/A.H
PLANNED ROUTE

Position of Thomson's Rockhole from M. Terry's journal,
K. Kelly's journal, 31 July 2002

'Something's wrong,' I said to Andrew around midday. The march had been through varying country, open one minute, dense scrub the next. For a while the compass was in its case, as we could see the hills. Then it was in hand as we walked a 284° magnetic bearing, as I could barely see a metre in front. The long ridge, sighted the previous day as a blur stretching across the horizon, was quite distinct now. The problem was we were walking roughly parallel with it.

I drew a sketch on the ground with a stick when Andrew came up with the camels. 'If this *is* the De Bavay Hills,' I said, pointing the stick at the ridge – it looked nothing like the hills I had expected – 'then we should have hit the bottom half of the L in a perpendicular fashion. It should block our path, but we're walking parallel with it. I hope we haven't missed the western end of the hills and are now walking up the north–south part. That would mean we're already past the rockhole.' We had no way of knowing, as the topography of the hills wasn't shown on the modern maps. Its L shape was shown on Terry's map, but Terry's location was already well to the south of us. I was exasperated and a bit confused trying to reconcile a 70-year-old map that I *knew* was wrong, with a modern map that *probably* was wrong.

'I hope this is the De Bavays,' I said, waving my stick at the ridge.

'Got to be,' Andrew said, with more conviction than I felt.

We pressed on. At lunchtime, with more stick diagrams and earnest discussion over a cup of tea, we solved the mystery. A cup of tea and a talk will usually solve any conundrum, especially those concerned with navigation. We had come into the hills travelling in a northwesterly direction, gradually turning left to follow the run of the ridge. In so doing, we had ended up walking parallel to them. Back in my study in Seaforth, I had planned an approach in a straight line from the south, with a turn to the west when we hit the east–west ridge. This wasn't Seaforth, and there are no straight lines in the desert. Flex, bend and adapt.

We plodded west–northwest following the ridge. If Terry's journal was correct, this ridge should gradually peter out and we would walk around the end of it and start heading north. After lunch, we crossed a burned ridge bare of vegetation and I was stunned by the view. I was looking at the ocean! Mt Solitaire, now a giant landmark in the northeast, was floating in a blue inland sea, a sea as blue as the Pacific Ocean at Manly. The mountain looked like an island far out to sea.

'Mate, I would've been no good out here as a pioneer. I would've taken one look at that, ripped off all my kit, and gone tearing across the flat shouting, "The inland sea! The inland sea!" and dived head-first into the spinifex,' I said.

'Yes, it's really deceptive, isn't it?' Andrew replied.

I stood still, astonished. My first sight of the great inland mirage is something I will never forget. It had bays and inlets, little coves among the hills that looked like beaches. And everywhere, the deep blue rolling up from the horizon almost to my feet, giving the impression of a broad ocean.

'We should start the Tanami Yacht Squadron,' Andrew said.

As we had hoped, the ridge petered out and we were standing at its extreme western end. Another range of hills began on the other side of the flat, running north–south. The rockhole should be right in front of us, although I could see nothing but a broad plain.

'Can you put Cooper down and let me get the binoculars? I'm going to climb the ridge and see if I can spot it from above.' Without comment, Andrew began tugging on Cooper's lead rope to induce him to kneel.

'*Hoosh*, Cooper. *Hoosh*,' he said. The camel dropped obediently to his knees and I retrieved a powerful pair of 12 x 50 Pentax field-glasses which I carried in a Pelican waterproof/dustproof/shockproof case on top of Cooper.

After taking several big mouthfuls of water, I set off up the ridge but I hadn't reached its crest when a shout from below told me that the thrill of seeing the rockhole first wasn't to be mine.

'There it is! Straight ahead about 288°,' Andrew shouted. I looked down and saw him peering intently through his miniature binoculars. I have seldom felt such a jolt of excitement. And relief! I quickly checked the bearing with my compass and raised the field-glasses, scanning the surrounding plain in the direction he'd indicated. Yes, Andrew had beaten me to it. Swimming in the heat haze, less than three kilometres away, was a jumble of granite boulders.

'That's got to be it,' I shouted down to where he waited with the camels. 'Looks like the photographs in his book.' The rockhole was right where Terry's map said it would be in relation to the surrounding hills. His navigational fix was wrong, but his written instructions were exact. The rockhole stood on a plain, in an elbow in the hills. Bare of scrub, it looked like an Australian Stonehenge. This shrine, however, stood in a desert of red and orange under a dazzling blue sky, rather than on an English plain. Battered by the sun, it seldom felt the touch of rain. Its grey English cousin, shrouded in mist and drizzle and with grass lapping up to its breastwork, couldn't have been more different. I stood and stared.

'This is better than Stonehenge. Those are *my* colours, *my* country,' I thought. I was looking at something of enormous significance to Australian heritage. Something symbolic of the country that had borne me, shaped me and nurtured me. Foreign Stonehenge, in a grey, faraway land, couldn't compete for inspiration.

'There's Mt Davidson,' Andrew shouted. Sure enough, away to the northeast, jutting out of the blue mirage, was the peak that, along with Mt Solitaire, provides the best landmark west of the Lander. I had been keeping a watchful eye that day but had missed it in the excitement. We were on course and for that I was truly grateful.

We headed off across the plain. I was eagerly anticipating a deep rock pool. So were the camels. I'm sure they could smell water; their stride lengthened and they had a very purposeful look. Their gaze didn't deviate from the clump of boulders we were approaching.

'You know, I brought my Speedos,' I said to Andrew

'You're kidding! You brought your swimmers?' he replied.

'Bloody oath, I did! Two of my goals on this trip – do a lap up Thomson's Rockhole and have a swim at Lake Gregory. I'm not coming all this way and not have a swim,' I told him emphatically.

'Wonder if there'll be any lifeguards on duty,' Andrew said.

'I don't care, as long as it's full of water.'

'Well, Kelly, you'll make history. The first person to carry a pair of Speedos across the Tanami Desert.'

We all stepped out. I was walking faster and faster, and Andrew was moving as quickly as the camels would allow. 'I'm going ahead to photograph the camels coming into the rockhole,' I said.

'Don't dive in the shallow end!' he shouted as I strode ahead.

I arrived about ten minutes ahead of Andrew and the camels. There was time to climb up to the highest point of the tumbled granite boulders and survey the scene.

It wasn't as Michael Terry had described it: *At the southern extremity of the rocks there is a high gaping crack in the side of a smooth granite whaleback, alone, rising straight out of the earth. Wedged in this crack is a very large pear-shaped boulder, which gives shade to the soakage beneath it. A regular trampled way leads from the ground to a little wet hole ten feet below, where normally the blacks get supply.*

Jack Keyser, a young member of Terry's expedition, was photographed sitting above this crack in the whaleback, his feet dangling near the pear-shaped rock. I could find neither. The horrible thought occurred to me as Andrew pulled up with the camels that this wasn't Thomson's Rockhole, but just a pile of boulders in the desert. I didn't relish the thought of breaking the news to Andrew that my navigational skills may have brought us to the wrong place.

CHAPTER 7

Dreamtime: Thomson's Rockhole
to the Granites

Australian waterholes are of two types. A soak is a pool of water sometimes fed by an underground spring, sometimes just a shallow claypan that fills after rain and disappears. Sometimes they are just a small puddle in the bed of an otherwise dry creek bed. White Stone Well is a typical outback soak. The other form of water catchment is the rockhole, of which there are various types. The gnamma hole is an indentation in granite rock, which forms a pool of transient water, varying in size from a coffee cup to a washbasin to a swimming pool. The explorer Ernest Giles, whose life was saved on numerous occasions by these holes, called them *cups in the rock*. They usually fill only after rain and are prone to evaporation from wind and sun, so the Aborigines often covered the smaller ones with stone slabs, spinifex or saplings. They were jealously guarded from explorers. A single camel could easily drink a precious gnamma hole dry. Granite traps are another type of rockhole where water is collected as run-off by the granite and trapped in a cool, shady place. If fed by artesian water, these rockholes can often provide that most blessed sanctuary in the desert – permanent water. Thomson's Rockhole is a granite trap.

'Look at this. It's amazing!' Andrew pointed to a cone-shaped piece of rock soaring into the sky. He had joined me on top of a mammoth granite boulder after tying the camels in a grove of bean trees near the rocks. Covering the granite cone were numerous cupolas, as if a grapefruit had been pressed repeatedly into the hard rock when it was still molten, dimpling its surface.

'Can you imagine how long it must have taken to carve those holes into the rock?' I wondered aloud. 'Probably hundreds of years, with someone chipping away with stone tools. I wonder what their significance is?'

Andrew was equally at a loss. 'Look at the carvings over here – they look like water symbols,' he said, pointing to a gallery carved into the rock. Everywhere we looked there were signs of human craft, of human art. The antiquity of the place, and the great energy expended there, was striking. Unfortunately, after examining most of the site, there was no sign of Terry's cleft in the rock or of the well guarded by the pear-shaped rock.

I pulled out the Jack Keyser photograph and studied it closely. 'Where could it possibly be?' I thought.

'I hope I haven't brought us to the wrong place, but I can't find this anywhere,' I said to Andrew, showing him the Keyser photograph.

'No. This has to be it. There were no other piles of rocks on the plain, or none that I saw,' he replied. 'Anyway, let's find a campsite, get the humps unloaded and come back and have a better look.'

We collected the camels and started in the direction of a grove of native pines about 300 metres to the southeast of the rocks. We had decided that, given the totemic symbols on the rocks, it may be a site of spiritual significance to the Aborigines and so should be treated with respect.

Half-way across the flat to the campsite, I realised that in all the excitement I had left my camera at the rockhole. I turned around and walked back to the rocks. As I bent to retrieve the camera from its position on a rock shelf, I glanced to my left and nearly fell over in surprise. There it was! I was looking straight down the cleft in the granite, directly at the pear-shaped rock in Terry's photograph.

'Andrew! Andrew! I've found it!' I shouted across the flat. I ran to the top of a large boulder about six metres above the plain. 'I found it! I found it!' I waved my hat at his figure retreating across the plain, but he was already too far away. I raced up to the cleft and peered in, keen to see its cool waters. It was dry!

'Bugger. Never mind, I've found it,' I thought, as it sunk in that we were once again to be disappointed. I stood looking down into the well for several seconds and then took off across the flat, running as fast as a pair of hiking boots and tired legs would allow. I was breathless when I caught up, just as Andrew entered the grove of pines with the camels. 'I found it. We walked right past it,' I said. 'It's at the back of the rock complex.'

'Water?' he asked.

'Dry.'

'Never mind. Let's get the camels unloaded and make camp,' he said.

No matter what we found or what occurred, it wouldn't disturb Andrew's routine. The camels came first. They were hooshed, hobbled and unloaded. The camp was organised, food for the evening meal arranged as well as for tomorrow's lunchbox. Water bottles were topped up, and firewood was collected and sorted. A place was made for the fire. I mixed up a litre of the magic Vitafresh fruit drink, shaking it vigorously in a one-litre Nalgene water bottle. After a refreshing gorge, mind and body were restored and I was ready for anything. Andrew took one last look around the camp, and at the camels grazing nearby. Happy that everything was in order he grabbed his camera and I grabbed the shovel. We set off once more to the rocks.

The rockhole was as Michael Terry had described it. A yawning cleft in the granite acted as a scoop for wet season downpours, funnelling run-off into a sheer-sided granite well about three metres deep. Deep in the dry season, the water was now underground. Hoping to reach it, small animals had dug a tunnel into the floor of the well. I climbed into the well carrying the shovel and peered into the tunnel. It was dark and cool. It smelled of subterranean water. I managed to extract a mound of damp sand from the tunnel and sniffed it. Water alright.

'Don't have to worry about diving in the shallow end,' Andrew said, looking from the top of the well as I worked with the shovel.

'Well, there's definitely water here, but I'm not about to start swimming laps,' I replied.

A breach in the rock formed a pathway that must have been used by Aborigines to access the water. Through the breach came the tracks of small animals heading for the tunnel. 'If we had a couple of days to spare, we could clean this out. I'm sure we'd get a good flow,' I said, leaning on the shovel. 'Nothing's changed since Terry's time.'

'Dry for him too, was it?'

'Sure was, both times he was here.' Terry had written in 1928: *A regular trampled way leads from the ground to a little wet hole ten feet below, where normally the blacks get supply. But alas, there was none for us. We dug for some time, clearing away bones, fur and debris of animals, till at length black wet earth stuck to the shovel, but she wouldn't make — the soak was dry.*

The unmistakable clank of hobble chain and Condamine bell told us that our colleagues had joined us. As I walked out of the well, I saw the five camels standing at the edge of the rocks, peering at us intently. As usual, TC, Cooper and Morgan were at the front, eying the rocks to see if they could clamber up.

'The boys can smell the water,' Andrew said. 'They must have just about galloped across the flat to get here that fast.' The camels shuffled back and forth, sniffing the air, not game to walk up on to the large round boulders that towered over them.

'Poor buggers. There's no way they could ever get access to the water down that well, even if it was full,' I said.

I climbed out and Andrew walked down to have a look. He lay prone on the floor of the well and extended his arm and then his head into the tunnel at the bottom. Every warning bell went off in my head. 'You're a dead man,' I thought. My mouth opened to scream out, but I was struck dumb with horror. I had visions of a death adder or mulga snake, spitting fire after my earlier intrusion with the shovel into its lair.

Snakes will often seek shade in the hot part of the day, and it was cool inside the small tunnel. The presence of water made it doubly attractive, doubly dangerous. I expected to see Andrew come recoiling out of the hole with one of these lethal reptiles attached to his arm. He had committed his first mistake of the journey – a mistake that could kill him. An ironclad rule in the bush is that you never, under any circumstances, reach into a place you cannot see – not into a hole, not up a log and not under a rock. That's why I'd used the shovel. I'm sure this rule was in the Harper template, but he must have forgotten it. I had a vision of taking his body into the Granites wrapped in a blanket and strapped over Morgan's back. Having to tell Ian Harper that his only son was coming home in a body bag wouldn't be fun.

I let out a sigh of relief as he said sheepishly, 'I shouldn't have done that. There's probably a tiger snake down there.'

'No, mate,' I thought. 'Not a tiger snake – wrong part of the world – but that wasn't a smart thing to do. Could've been something even worse than a tiger snake.'

After we had exhausted all our efforts to obtain any water from the tunnel, we turned our attention to the rest of the site.

'Hello, look at this. This must have been the boardroom,' I said. Near the well, nature had hewn an outdoor amphitheatre from the granite. A ledge ran along one side forming a backrest; the floor was flat stone. It was a natural place to sit, stretch our legs and relax, so we did, leaning back against the ledge. I loosened my boots, let out a sigh and took it all in. Opposite us, arranged in a semicircle, were blocks of stone so placed as to provide convenient seats. It was theatre in the round, with the centre-piece a small depression where the campfire once blazed.

'Mate, imagine the old boys sitting here, yarning, arguing, making laws, settling disputes and disciplining the young blokes. Big corroboree going on out there on the flat, pile of water next door, kangaroos in the hills. What a magic place!' I said to Andrew.

'Yes, it's a natural place to sit for a while. Look at how the rock has been worn smooth over the years,' he replied. We sat with our backs to the rock wall, just as others must have done in antiquity. The passage of feet, backsides and hands had, over the millennia, burnished the stone to a smooth sheen – it was the texture of marble.

We sat for some time saying nothing, relishing the pleasure of sitting on something resembling a chair rather than on a swag, which had been the seat of necessity in recent weeks. I revelled in the atmosphere of the place.

'What do you think they talked about?' Andrew asked, breaking the silence.

'Same as us, I guess. Probably went crook about their wives – they often had a few of 'em – and their kids. I suppose they talked a lot about hunting and food, and about water. I bet there were a lot of people coming and going here. I'll read you what Terry said,' I offered, and opened his book.

> . . . a sharp exclamation from Keyser, perched high on a granite boulder surveying the world in general, brought everyone to attention. We listened.

'Cou, cou, cou.'

Singing out to attract attention, two finely-built bucks, naked, in the pink of condition, issued from the scrub. Of course unarmed, they approached the camp boldly, and as we were on the march no objection was taken to this friendly visit. Being true myalls, and therefore unable to speak a word of English, they imitated every word and sentence as nearly as they could. They imitated actions also, all the while almost exploding with great peals of laughter, slapping their thighs meanwhile. Talk about amusing mimicry. Why, they would have turned a burial party into an uproarious glee meeting.

We asked: 'Which way nappa? Watchila Kuppi?'

Both meant the same — where is water?

But this might have been the greatest joke ever, for they simply repeated each phrase and burst out into deafening guffaws of merriment, which made the place ring. At length, by pantomime, we got them to understand, whereupon each pointed about north-northwest and traced the passage of the sun, equal to about two hours. They meant they knew of water in the direction of pointing. In fact, convinced we must need it, they began to walk that way and motioned us repeatedly to follow. Our visitors were quite downfallen when no further interest was shown.

Pointing to Keyser, we said 'Jack.' The blacks seemed to grasp it was his name and, repeating 'Jaggie,' went up to him to bestow pats of good fellowship. Unwittingly someone slapped his thigh, and immediately each black did the same, laughed boisterously. We slapped again. They slapped again, laughed at the huge joke, and in no time by their infectious glee had the whole camp laughing too. Like a lot of silly kids. Encouraged, they approached Keyser's truck timidly, touched it, touched it again, then laughed; repeated the performance till they simply had to be given a tin of tea to shut them up. Bits of damper they did not

*seem to appreciate, but quickly drained the tea and held
out the tin for more.*

*Having grabbed a chunk of meat and damper, the billy
was passed round. Each man filled his quart pot and got
busy with the meal. In a minute or two North looked up.
'That's pretty slick – Jacky's gone!' It was true. Though one
minute close up, the next they were gone, silently, mysteri-
ously, as in arrival. The bucks had just melted away . . .*

This is the first recorded meeting of whites and blacks at
Thomson's Rockhole and took place only 24 years before
I was born. Terry's book included a wonderful photograph of
the two locals laughing heartily, observed closely by one of the
explorers puffing happily on his pipe. *The laughing bucks of
Thomson's rockhole*, reads the caption.

Andrew photographed me sitting with my legs dangling
in the rockhole, just as Jack Keyser was photographed 74 years
before. By studying the photo we could tell the exact spot
where Terry had stood to take it and the time of day. We
examined numerous grooves used for sharpening spears and
grinding stones that were used for food preparation. The intri-
cate carved patterns in the hard rock were everywhere.

As the sun moved lower, I made a startling discovery.
'Here, look at this,' I said. Just to the left of where I was sitting
someone had scratched the letters: AIT 26. Faint and weathered from the years, it appeared to have been chipped into the
rock with the pointy end of a geologist's hammer. 'Wonder
who he was? Maybe the T stands for Thomson,' I pondered
aloud. 'The 26 would stand for 1926, two years before Terry's
visit.'

'Who was the rockhole named after?' Andrew asked.

'Terry was the first one to call it Thomson's Rockhole, but
I don't know who Thomson was or if he ever came here,'
I replied.

'You'd have to think he did, for Terry to name the place

after him,' Andrew said. The strange inscription remained a mystery until I returned to Sydney.

We sat and watched as the sun dipped towards the horizon and cloaked the granite tors in fantastic shadows. We wondered aloud about AIT's identity and what was the Aboriginal name for the rockhole.

Soon after returning home from the trip I trawled through Michael Terry's books and finally came up with the solution to the puzzling inscription. Terry had driven across the Tanami in 1928. In *Hidden Wealth and Hiding People*, he wrote that a prospector called Alec Thomson rode into their camp and told them of a rockhole that he had discovered out in the desert to the east. *Two years previously, prospecting south of Mount Davidson, Thomson had used a granite rock hole forty miles east of No. 1 Granite*, Terry wrote. Terry named it Thomson's Rockhole, *as he was the first white to use it*. This confirmed that in 1926, two years before Terry's visit, Thomson had visited the rockhole and left his mark with the tip of a geologist's hammer. Thomson and Terry were, however, late arrivals at a spot that had been visited by humans for millennia.

Our camp that night was probably our best one so far. A bare area of low grass under the pines meant minimal shovel work and was a welcome respite from the spinifex. Over dinner, our elation at finding this ancient and remote outpost banished memories of the many hardships we'd endured in getting there.

'You know, people may've been coming here for 60,000 years, as long as humans have occupied Australia,' I said to Andrew over the flickering firelight. It was the last day of July 2002, a Wednesday and our sixteenth campsite.

'It's a shame that no one comes here now. There would've been people coming and going all the time here once. What's worse, if more was known about this place, we probably wouldn't be allowed to come here.'

'Why, because it's a sacred site?' I asked.

'Yes, exactly.'

'But we don't know it's a sacred site,' I queried.

'Well, how do you define a sacred site? It was obviously an important watering place for tribes hunting out in the desert. Lots of people watered and congregated here over a very long period of time.'

'Yes, but that doesn't mean it's a sacred site,' I reminded him. 'We don't know if ceremonies were performed here, or if the place had special significance other than for the water. People in our society congregate at the beach or in office buildings or at the pub, but that doesn't make them sacred places. Our sacred places are churches. Aboriginal culture may have been no different. Not everywhere they congregated may have been sacred to them.'

'It'd be good to know – to have someone out here explain it all,' Andrew said.

'Too right. Maybe *everywhere* was sacred.'

Another log went on the fire and the billy was topped up again from the jerrycan *du jour*. This was a marathon gab session for us. I watched the billy boil and put a small handful of tea in from the cotton sack, then lifted off the blackened can with my knife.

'Anyway, it's a sacred site to me,' I said. 'Part of *my* Dreamtime. So I don't think I'd be stopped from coming here.'

Andrew looked a bit surprised. 'So, you've got a Dreamtime too, have you?'

'Sure do! I see these places like Mt Leichhardt or the Lander or this rockhole,' I said, pointing to the giant boulders silhouetted against the stars, 'and I don't see a mountain or a river or granite boulders. I see the stories that happened there.

I don't see Mt Stuart and think, That's a mountain. I think, Stuart climbed that and he read these words – stuff like that. I look at the landscape and see it differently from other blokes. I see the history of the country, not the geography. That's why I like reading explorers' journals where they were written. I feel I can see the storyline, feel the history and know the people who went before. I call it "white fella Dreamtime". Bit of ancestor worship, I suppose.'

'I agree with you, but I think you'd have a lot of trouble convincing some people in this country that there can be "white fella Dreamtime",' Andrew said, looking at me sceptically over the campfire.

'Mate, I rode a horse through Wickham Gorge and fulfilled a dream I'd had since I was a kid. But I wasn't thinking, This is a gorge with a river in it. Nope, I was thinking, Gus Gregory rode through here and saw what I'm seeing. I could follow his route exactly from his maps, like a storyline or a songline. I've dreamed about coming to places like Thomson's Rockhole for years. And whether you like it or not, this place's now part of *your* family's history, too – part of *your* dreaming.'

We both fell silent for a moment. I wondered if I was breaking the Heyerdahl principle. I didn't think we were getting close to having an argument, so I ploughed on.

'Look at us. We came up out of the desert to this rockhole with our tongues hanging out of our heads. We're only the most recent visitors in a tradition going back thousands of years. Doesn't matter if we're black fellas or white fellas, we're just thirsty fellas. I bet if we had rolled up here 100 years ago, like Terry did, the locals wouldn't have said, "You can't drink here." I bet they would've welcomed us.'

'I understand what you're saying,' Andrew said. 'But I think there are a lot of people who would disagree with you.'

'Well, possibly. But in a longwinded way I'm saying that these places are special to me, too,' I replied. 'Australia's the most spiritual place on earth, I reckon. I've seen St Peter's

Basilica and the Sistine Chapel in Rome, and visited the Duomo Cathedral in Florence. I've lined up with other tourists to gawk at Michelangelo's *Pietà*, but nothing moves me like these places in Australia. They make the hairs on the back of my neck stand on end.' Andrew took this in without replying.

We sat looking at the fire for a while. 'That'll do me for the day. See you in the morning,' Andrew said, draining the last of his tea.

'Yeah, see you, mate. Made it all worthwhile, even if there's no water.'

'Sure did.' His voice came from out of the dark.

I banked the fire, walked to my camping spot and unrolled my swag. As I did so, I was drawn to the ghostly shape of the granite tors brooding on the plain. I walked out of the pines, captivated by the scene. A flat area the size of several football fields lay between the pines and the rockhole. Grasses waving in the light breeze turned silver in the moonlight.

'This place is really ancient,' I thought. People were coming here before Stonehenge was built and before Cheops built the Great Pyramid in Egypt.'

The loneliness of the place struck me. Terry wrote of coolamons, woomeras and digging sticks scattered around the site, now all gone. No laughing bucks came up to greet Andrew and me. Only a great silence welcomed us. The clap of the singing sticks and the wail of the didgeridoo, which must have rolled across this flat like audio thunder since time immemorial, were gone. A place of vibrant human activity for 60,000 years had been snuffed out in a little over a century.

Gee, there must've been some high old times here when the tribes came in out of the desert, I thought, looking at the moonlit corroboree ground. I pictured a hundred fires scattered around the flat, with sparks jumping into the night sky and the shadows of dancers flitting across the trees. The noise, oh the noise – the thump of the dancers' feet pounding the ground, the clapping of hands in time to the singing sticks, the laughter, the shouts in anger or delight, the cries of picca-ninnies, the barking of dogs, the chants of singers. This place knew the whine of the bull-roarers. I imagined the cloud of dust swirling into the night air and the gleaming sweat of the naked bodies decorated in ochre. Many people had enjoyed themselves here, and all of this was only possible because of the water beneath those boulders.

Strangely, I felt a sense of loss, of something gone that will never return. The words of another of my mother's favourite poems came back to me. I immediately went back to my swag, turned on my head torch and wrote them down. I could only remember three verses:

> *For his eyes have been full with a smouldering thought*
> *But he dreams of the hunts of yore*
> *And of foes that he sought, and of fights that he fought*
> *With those who will battle no more*
> *Who will go to the battle no more.*
>
> *And he sees through the rents of the scattering fogs*
> *The corroboree warlike and grim*
> *And the lubra who sat by the fire on the logs*
> *To watch like a mourner for him*
> *Like a mother and mourner for him.*
>
> *Will he go in his sleep from these desolate lands*
> *Like a chief to the rest of his race*
> *With the honey-voiced woman who beckons and stands*
> *And gleams like a dream in his face*
> *Like a marvellous dream in his face?*

I learned on my return to Sydney that the lines were from a poem called 'The Last of His Tribe', by Henry Kendall. I dedicated it that night to the laughing bucks of Thomson's Rockhole. I rolled into my swag and was asleep in seconds.

After a dreamless sleep and a good breakfast, we went to the rockhole to farewell the spirits that dwelled there. With great reluctance, I took one last look around before we returned to the pines, loaded the camels and prepared to leave. I'd plotted the exact position of the rockhole on the charts the previous evening and confirmed that it was fourteen kilometres from Terry's fix.

We had walked for seventeen days to reach Thomson's Rockhole and had covered 310 kilometres. The desert we had crossed had at least answered the question: what would have happened to Stuart if he hadn't turned back in 1860? He would have died somewhere between his furthest point west and the De Bavay Hills. No matter which direction he'd taken, he wouldn't have found water.

We were closing in on the half-way point of our journey. We were succeeding where Stuart had failed, because we had camels and he'd had horses. Every day our five camels were led in and loaded with about 300 kilograms each of food, equipment and water. Uncomplaining, they trudged on day after day and mile after mile, their only water obtained from the food they ate. My experience is with horses, so the camels were a revelation. Obedient, easy to load and lead, they required no grooming or shoeing, and the sore backs, girth galls, stone bruises and other plagues of Stuart's pack horses were completely foreign to camels. In the roughest scrub, dense with spinifex and devoid of grass, a camel can be tied to a stunted bloodwood tree or acacia bush and is happy in the morning, having browsed the plant he was tied to. From these dry and thorny shrubs and trees came the life-giving water that the animals needed to survive and which the desert couldn't provide.

Nevertheless, even camels have their limits and our failure

to obtain water for them at the rockhole meant a change in plans. Our camels hadn't had a drink for fourteen days, the last at the solar bore on Anninge Station. They were travelling well, but couldn't go on forever without water. They were blood, bone and muscle, not machines!

Andrew and I had discussed this eventuality many times in recent days. In Seaforth, when planning the expedition, I plotted a course due west from the rockhole, crossing the Tanami track at Fiddlers Lake, a large saltpan. This would skirt the Granites goldmine with its people, trucks and noise. This wasn't to be.

'We could probably get them to the Western Australian border by giving them some of our water, but we'd have to go on really strict rations,' Andrew had said the previous evening. 'We couldn't allow ourselves more than four litres a day each.'

This was a big ask, as it would mean no water for small luxuries like cleaning our teeth, hands or face, and cooking would have to be carefully controlled as dried food uses a lot of water. So far, we hadn't gone to bed thirsty or hungry on any night. 'It would leave no room for error. We'd have to hit one of those bores on the border and they'd have to be working,' he said.

I had studied the nest of bores on Tanami Downs Station, far to the west. The map was so inaccurate, there was no guarantee that they would still be working. We wouldn't know until we got there.

'Well, we can swing around to the northwest and track straight into the first of the Granites' bores,' I suggested. This was located east of the mine, about 35 kilometres away. I showed Andrew the map. 'The problem with that course is we'll have to go straight through the mine property to get to the border. Makes for a longer journey, too. Not an ideal outcome.'

'I know, but I can't see any alternative,' Andrew said.

I was bitterly disappointed. I had hoped to see the salt lake system south of the Granites and the sandhill country there. The proposed route would add needless extra kilometres of no historical interest. As a stockbroker, I had been on many mine-site visits all over Australia and knew that an open-cut gold-mine means huge pits, mullock heaps, large haulage trucks, ore-crushing ball mills and the hand of man on the landscape. We would soon be leaving the wilderness.

Disappointment on exploring expeditions, like pride and fear, is best handled by chewing it vigorously and then swallowing. I never let on as to how disappointed I felt. Andrew owned the camels and had the final say in anything concerning them. If he said we needed to go into the Granites for water, then that's what we'd do. I supported this decision without hesitation. I had no understanding of the limits of a camel's physiology, so I backed his judgment unequivocally. This was one of the positives of my lack of knowledge about camels – there was no room for argument. All I knew was that if we had left Mt Stuart with horses, they'd all be dead by now. Maybe we would be, too.

We set off at 10.30 am over bare stony ground, the late start due to our final visit to the rockhole. It slowly fell away behind us and was soon lost below the horizon. The Granites goldmine, our destination, was the only known source of water in the region. I estimated four to five days to reach it. The brief respite we had enjoyed on the bare ridges around Thomson's Rockhole and our jubilation at reaching the historic site were soon lost. We had walked up the northern edge of the ancient swamp and the scrub returned, dusty and grim and intent on retribution. The country closed in, with the spinifex the worst I've seen.

Mid-afternoon, the mulga piled up and a chest-high ledge of spinifex, hundreds of metres wide, confronted me. 'Well, I can't go through it and I can't go around. I'll have to go over it,' I said to myself. I lifted one leg, stepped up and began to walk across the top of the tangled mass. I went ten metres, sharp spines going straight through my trousers, and didn't touch the ground. The spinifex formed a thick, thorny, horrible, blanket. I reached the other side and it was no better. The mulga closed in. It was still too hot for gaiters. Andrew must've been suffering. He was still wearing shorts, and his legs were again black from spinifex resin. The tight stands of mulga meant he had to weave around with the camels and couldn't walk a straight course. Sometimes I could see only the top of his hat and TC's head above the scrub when I turned to check on their progress. It must've been exhausting work, towing those camels, but he never complained.

Our progress slowed to a crawl. By late afternoon I was so tired I was stumbling as my boots became tangled in the bush. Several times, I almost went down.

Thursday, 1 August: our first camp north of Thomson's Rockhole I called the Godforsaken Camp. We gave up looking for a clearing and hooshed the camels down where they had stopped walking. They flopped into the dense spinifex, oblivious of its spines.

'Shit, this is going to be hard work!' I said to Andrew.

I unbuckled TC's hobbles from his halter and reached into the spinifex that surrounded his forelegs. It immediately lacerated my hands. A seated camel with legs folded under him is a difficult beast to hobble, especially with only one good hand. When the animal is knee-deep in spinifex, it draws prodigious profanities from the camel handler. No hoary old Afghan, long of beard and short of temper, could have matched me that afternoon in the profanity department. I secured one side of the hobble around the near-side foreleg, then moved around to the other side to discover that the camel was sitting with his legs slightly too far apart and the chain wouldn't reach.

'You did that on purpose, you old bastard, didn't you?' I said, giving TC a pat on the head. He looked straight ahead with studied indifference, chewing away. 'Cunning old bugger.'

I sat down in the spinifex, getting a bumful for my troubles, grasped the loose end of the hobble chain and with one boot against TC's shoulder pulled with all my strength. It's not easy to move the foreleg of a 600-kilogram camel, especially when he's sitting on it, but it worked and I secured the chain to the off-side foreleg with the leather strap. During all this pushing, pulling and heaving, TC just ignored me.

I wouldn't have been game to do that a couple of weeks ago, I thought.

I moved to Cooper, the second camel in line, sat down and repeated the procedue. 'This job *is* a pain in the arse, Coop, *literally*,' I said aloud.

Cooper, his soft underbelly spiked by the bristling spinifex on which he sat, had problems of his own and wasn't interested in my complaints.

I was sweating, breathless and had spinifex punctures over the backs of my hands and in my bum as a souvenir. I found that swearing endlessly to myself helped. Andrew, as was his habit, worked quickly and silently at the other end of the string, applying hobbles.

I had previously asked him why the camels couldn't be hobbled standing up, the way horses are, as it would be so much easier.

'True, but it's harder for the animal to kneel with its front feet tied together,' he replied. 'A horse doesn't have to kneel down. It would also be easier for them to strike you. They can't lash out if they're sitting on their feet.'

'I thought you said they never lash out,' I said.

'Well, I'll never say "never", and it doesn't hurt to be careful.'

When all their loads were removed, the camels remained seated. Normally they would leap to their feet and go off into the scrub to graze, or simply stand in the shade. That night, at the Godforsaken Camp, they just sat in the spinifex, immovable. One or two moaned quietly. I noticed that the bellowing and roaring of the early days had been replaced with an air of resignation at loading and unloading times.

'Why aren't they getting up?' I asked.

'They're starting to get a bit thirsty,' Andrew said. 'When they have plenty of water, they'll eat anything, the drier and thornier and rougher the better. As they get thirsty, they become more selective, adjusting their feeding habits to the tougher conditions.'

After a space was cleared for the fire and the swags, I went to the day's jerrycan and poured out some water. As the gurgling sound reached them, the two lead camels, TC and Cooper, stood up and walked towards me with a determined air, stepping carefully around the food boxes and saddles. They tried to follow the brimming billy, but when Andrew hunted them away, they went and licked the lids of the jerrycans. Unsatisfied, they stood around the camp, watching Andrew and me make tea. Impenetrable spinifex and acacia scrub pressed in on all sides. They looked sad.

'That was one tough day,' I said to Andrew as we sat gulping our tea. 'I was stumbling through that stuff. This country hasn't been burned in years. If we start a fire we're stuffed!'

'Yes, the camels hate it. They have to look where to put their feet because they can't see the ground. I have to tow them. That's why it's so slow. We'll never get there if this keeps up,' he said. It was one of the first times I had seen him genuinely exasperated.

'And you'll get a very long arm from towing!'

Even boiling the billy was a chore. We were both terrified of starting a fire, and the scarce wood was so anaemic it took an eternity to make the tea. We needed a small mountain of wood just to boil a quart pot. Andrew watched the camels constantly. I could tell their distress caused him anxiety, but he didn't comment on it, so I didn't ask.

With a steaming pannikin on offer, our spirits revived. We watched the sunset and pored over the map. To our north it showed an old track from the deserted Mt Davidson out-station. It ran into the Granites and offered the prospect of some relief from the dense scrub. To reach it required another

course change from northwest to north and additional kilometres for the seven weary members of our expedition. It
was frustrating. When I had plotted the course in Sydney,
I believed we would be going west at this stage; instead, we were
about to go north. I was determined, though, to be flexible and
to change course as the circumstances required. Anyway, we had
no choice.

That night we drew off precious drinking water for a wash
and shave – not much, about a quart pot, but it was a great
relief. I was sitting having a wash when Cooper, hobbled
though he was, shuffled up behind me and put his snout in my
pot, leaving no room as both my hands were also in the small
steel vessel. I pushed his nose out of the way, but he left his
head resting on my shoulder while he sniffed despondently at
the soapy water. That big animal and I were united in our need
for the small amount of liquid in that pot. I was amazed at how
docile he was. He weighed over 600 kilograms and yet rested
his head gently on my shoulder without the slightest malice.
He had walked so softly that I hadn't heard him approach.

'You've got a friend there,' Andrew said. 'He'll be getting
in your swag next.'

'Mate, I read in the papers before I came up here how
horrible these blokes are. The Chris Richards story in the
Herald said they bite and kick and are unfriendly. I'd be launch-
ing a defamation action, if I was you.' I knew this would get a
rise out of Andrew. He constantly complained about how
poorly camels were perceived by the public and was always
coming to their defence.

'Their reputation's undeserved. And they don't spit. Well,
not much anyway – only at you. I really don't know where it
comes from. I think they've been framed,' Andrew said.

'They need a good public relations manager,' I agreed,
chasing Cooper out of the camp. However, two of our troopers,
TC and Morgan, had crossed Australia with Andrew along the
Tropic of Capricorn in 1999, and all were experienced desert

campaigners. In Andrew, they had a patient handler who never struck them, swore at them or lost his temper. All domesticated animals reflect the personality of their owner, and Andrew's camels were no different.

Like all our camps, that night at the Godforsaken Camp was quiet. No birds farewell the sunset in the desert or greet the day. No songbirds sing in the eastern Tanami. Nevertheless, fortune favoured us. Just before we arrived at our campsite we had discovered, buried in the scrub, the remnants of an old seismic line, a cleared track through the vegetation. It wasn't marked on the maps. We estimated it was probably 30 years old and overgrown. Nevertheless, the mulga hadn't regrown as densely as it was in the virgin scrub. Passage, at least for the camels, would be easier from here.

That night, the camp was the scene of a near disaster. I was in a deep sleep, but through the fog of my dreaming I heard one of the untethered camels grazing close up. Its clanking hobble chains briefly woke me. I saw his shadow about five metres away silhouetted against the stars. Unperturbed, I immediately fell asleep again. In the early hours, I sat up with a start – the camel had eaten my journal! The journal was in a leather case made by the highly respected Katherine saddler, Geoff Newton. The case had been on every expedition I had under-taken and was already regarded as a family heirloom. It was always placed near my head as I slept. My heart sank. All the work of keeping the diary up to date was wasted. I reached out in the dark to the place where the journal customarily resided. It was there untouched and unharmed. I had been dreaming.

'Good night's sleep?' Andrew asked, as he joined me at the fire in the morning.

'No! Bloody camel ate my journal,' I replied.

'What? Are you serious? That's terrible!' He looked genuinely concerned, knowing how much work I had put into it, and I let it hang for a minute.

'Nah. Not really. It was only a nightmare.'

He burst out laughing. He seemed to find many of my struggles in the bush highly amusing and this was no exception. He often referred to it during the remainder of the journey, promising retribution if any of his camels were injured from eating my journal.

Getting the saddles and girths secure that morning was as big a chore as the hobbles had been. The camel sits on its pedestal, the bony protuberance jutting down between its front legs. Behind the pedestal goes the girth, effectively around the camel's gut. However, because the animal is sitting, there is no room between gut and ground to poke the rope girth through, from one side to the other. Ordinarily, girthing a seated camel is a difficult job, akin to pushing a piece of string under a car tyre; when the camel sits on a solid nest of spinifex plants, the job is nearly impossible and very painful. And I thought that *clients* could be difficult! I tried everything: digging with my hands, using the shovel, pleading with the camel to breathe in, and swearing very loudly. At the Godforsaken Camp, I needed a combination of the above. I didn't need to ask why the girths couldn't be attached and tightened after the camel stood up – common sense dictated that as the animal lurched to its feet, saddles and gear would tumble off, the camel would bolt across the flat, mayhem would follow and the whole thing would have to be done again. So, everything was done with the animal sitting down, no matter how awkward it was.

We set off heading north. As the string moved off from the campsite, I had one last look around. I did this 'emu-bob' every day after Andrew and the animals left, to check that nothing was left behind. I scrutinised each camel as it went by. Here was the genius of the Harper method. Even a 'cob' like me could check all the obvious places and see if anything was missing. I looked around in the spinifex, which came up to my waist.

Finding a billy or the shovel or a camera, or any other vital piece of expedition gear, would be impossible. Andrew relied on everything having its place. Checking the ground was really overkill – the real check was made on the backs of the animals.

My hands were a mass of cuts from the spinifex and tannin-brown from washing in waste tea. The palms were black from sooty billies and handling burned campfire kindling. But these trials were soon forgotten in facing the challenges of the bush and negotiating the track we had discovered the previous evening. Sometimes we saw the track, sometimes we lost it, weaving around the regrowth and dodging the worst of the spinifex. The track's course was constant – due north – the way we'd decided to go. Finally, a ridge ahead foreshadowed the main Mt Davidson track. 'It'll be along the top of that ridge,' I said to Andrew. Shortly after, we crested the stony ridge to find an old dirt road heading west. The termite mounds springing up along it were evidence that it carried very little traffic.

The camels looked around in shock at the open country surrounding them and we took in the view. After being hemmed in for so long, the prospect of a marked track was a great relief.

'Scroggin time,' I said, checking my watch. The expedition had been going long enough now to have developed its own traditions, the 11 am halt being one of them since Mt Leichhardt. I reached up and opened the off-side green box on TC's saddle. The scroggin packet was placed strategically on the bottom tier of the box so that I could get at it without having to put the camel down. Andrew grabbed his water canteen from the back of TC's saddle, also accessible without putting the animal down.

I upended the packet, ladling the scroggin into Andrew's cupped hands. The nuts and sultanas, dates and dried apricots came tumbling out, along with the birdseed. But it was the chocolate-coated almonds Andrew was waiting for. A lump of congealed chocolate, nuts and sultanas plopped into his hands.

'Mate, you always get the best part. *You* get the chocolate-coated almonds and *I* get the birdseed,' I said. We were allowed one cupped handful each – no more, no less – and it was a lucky dip as to what you got. I tried to make each one-kilogram packet last a week.

My scroggin recipe is ancient, its origins lost in time. I start with a basic mix, like Naytura Trail Mix, consisting of almonds, muscatel raisins, cashew nuts, pumpkin kernels, sunflower seeds, brazil nuts, dried nectarines and pears. Ian McNamara had supplied about six packets of this mix to the expedition, each weighing about 250 grams. 'Call it the Australian Broadcasting Corporation's contribution to the trip,' he'd said. This was the basic birdseed. To this I add sliced dates, dried apricots, sultanas and dried figs until each packet is bulked up to about a kilogram. It is then weighed, dumped into a plastic, zip-lock bag, and sealed with ducting tape and thick rubber bands to ensure freshness. The secret ingredient is the chocolate-coated almonds. This was the luxury touch and the jackpot in each day's 11 am scroggin lucky dip. I had brought six, one-kilogram packets of home-made scroggin on the journey.

My philosophy with the mixture was to provide an alternative food source that we could carry in an emergency. It could be eaten without water, unlike the dried evening meals and salted beef jerky. It didn't have to be cooked and didn't go off in the heat. Along with the powdered fruit juice, the scroggin's sultanas, dried apricots and dates provided the vitamin C we weren't getting from the rest of our diet. This prevented an attack of Barcoo rot, a close cousin of scurvy. The scroggin was also a luxury and reward, something to look forward to every morning as the sun climbed higher and the temperature increased. High in calories, it also gave our tired legs an energy burst. The scroggin halt split the morning in half, two hours after the start and two hours before lunch.

We stood next to the camels munching away in silence, each lost in thought. I tried to make the handful go as far as possible by eating slowly.

'Civilisation!' Andrew said, looking down the dusty track. 'Good to get out of that scrub.'

'My word!' he replied.

'Speed should pick up a bit now. Scroggin's good,' I said.

'Too right! Those chocolate almonds are good.'

'Dunno. I didn't get any,' I said, giving him a stir. I never admitted to getting any chocolate-coated almonds during the whole trip. In reality, I always tried to ensure that Andrew got more of them than me; and in the mornings, if I opened the tinned fruit, I never took a full half-share. This ploy also came from Thor Heyerdahl. Arguments over food are one of the most common causes of an expedition collapsing and the only way to avoid it is for the person who is dishing out the food to take the smallest share. I followed the same policy at night making sure that Andrew's pot was always fuller than mine. Chocolate-coated almonds included, we didn't exchange one cross word about food during the whole trip.

'So, how far to the bore?' Andrew asked, watching me studying the map.

'Bit hard to say; I'd have to guess where we've cut this track but I think it's about eighteen kilometres. So we'll get there this afternoon, but late – say, 5 o'clock. Speed will pick up now that we're out of the scrub. We should do about four and a half kilometres an hour from here, which is about double what we've been doing. Have to get going, though,' I said, handing him the map. I gulped down several mouthfuls of water and we headed off. Finally, we were walking west, towards the sunset and the Western Australian border.

I felt elated that morning, walking along the track. We had found Thomson's Rockhole. We had encountered some of the worst conditions either of us had experienced and had survived. We were bowling along and for the first time in weeks, the scrub wasn't tearing at us. We were nearly half-way through the trip and we'd finally had some luck. Months later, with the expedition just a memory, Andrew would confide:

'You know, finding that seismic line up to the Mt Davidson outstation track really saved us. I don't know how we would've got those camels through there otherwise. We'd be still out there if we hadn't found it. We were very lucky.'

As I got used to the camels, I felt they were accepting me as one of the team. I looked at them plodding obediently along, gear just so, bending to their work. It's a very capable turnout, I thought. Andrew, the camels and I were working as a team, so my greatest fear seemed to be unfounded. My upper body strength had let me down, but I was having no trouble walking. I was backing up day after day, not needing a rest, and walking the same pace as Andrew and the camels. My fear that I would be left behind or that Andrew would have to continually stop and wait, faded. Barring an unforeseen disaster (and they were never far away), the expedition should succeed. If it failed, it would fail only because we lacked the resolution to complete it.

And the desert was seeping into my bones; slowly, inexorably, I was coming to terms with it. *This is a remarkable life, remarkable in its simplicity. Only have one shirt, one pair of pants, one pair of boots. No decisions to make. Only one priority: to stay alive. I will stay alive today & I will walk 20 kms. Drinking 6 L of water a day, eating dried food. Simple healthy life. But very hard. No decisions to make. Simple,* my journal recorded that day. I still felt that I was engaged in a murderous physical contest with the desert, a malevolent opponent determined to do me in. The contest, however, was producing surprising clarity of thought and peace of mind.

The desert life was devoid of the ordinary trials of raising a family, paying the bills, running a business, managing people and living in Sydney. I began to see why the Australian outback appealed so much to the pioneers like Gregory and Stuart, and why they no sooner finished one harrowing expedition than they were off on another. It also helped me to understand Andrew – this was his life. It's a life with its own particular stresses, but they are different from those I encounter living in a big city. Dominated by that one big challenge – the need to survive – desert stresses are manageable. As each day passed, I became calmer, more relaxed, almost tranquil.

Now that we were walking on a track, I didn't have to navigate and Andrew was freed from his recent weaving course. Neither of us had to concentrate on where to put our feet. We could walk and talk for the first time since leaving Mt Stuart. We talked of many things: his sharemarket investing, the grey nomad phenomenon in Australia, and time.

'Time's really precious in modern society,' I said. 'Look at us, one of the hardest things to organise was for us to get the time to do it. We're only out for 35 days – nothing, really. Gregory was out for almost two years.'

'They had a completely different concept of time then,' Andrew agreed. 'If they saw something interesting, but it was out of the way, they just went and had a look. If they found a nice waterhole, they could often stop and recover. I notice it particularly with guests coming out on tours. They have flights to catch, and they can't miss them under any circumstances, so there is always this pressure, even when they are out here trying to enjoy themselves.'

We walked along in the bright sunshine. Sometimes the conversation would stop for awhile and then start up again. Otherwise, the only sound was the *pad, pad, pad* of the camels' feet along the sandy track.

'Today, you have to be doing something constructive every day or you're considered to be wasting your time,' Andrew said, breaking the silence.

'I agree. But unfortunately, the only type of activity that's considered constructive is economic – making money. If you're not doing that, the activity's not considered worthwhile. This expedition would be considered by most people as a waste of time.'

'Yes, the early explorers had it over us in that regard,' Andrew said.

'Mate, the plagues of modern blokes: money, ambition and

time. Chasing the first two means you've never got enough of the last.'

A strange thing happened that afternoon: for the first and only time on the trip, my legs became very sore. We were walking quickly, but the change in action is what brought it on. For the last twenty days, I had been walking with a high knee action, stepping up and over, up and over, all day. Now I was walking in deep sand down a clear track with a long, loping stride and my muscles were screaming in protest at the shift in gears. Hamstrings twinged, calves ached and thighs burned. 'Tomorrow morning I'm going to wake up as stiff as a board,' I told myself. (And I did!)

We endured a forced march of 28 kilometres that day, determined to reach the first of the artesian bores east of the Granites mine. Late in the afternoon, the low thud of industrial machinery drifted towards us, an unusual sound in the desert vastness. I strode ahead, keen to see if there was respite for our thirsty mates.

'Bloody hell,' I said, on reaching a large clearing. Confronting me was a thundering diesel-driven, automated bore pump, a chunk of heavy industrial technology in the wilderness. In vain, I searched for a low-pressure outlet. Andrew halted with the camels about 50 metres away.

'No go?' he asked.

'No. Bloody thing's completely automatic, driven by radio signals from the mine,' I said, pointing to the mast rising above the bore shelter. 'There are valves we could open, but I wouldn't do it while the pump's going as the pressure's so great we probably wouldn't be able to get them closed again and there'd be water everywhere. Might also let air into the pump if we open one of the valves, and that could shut the whole thing down. Not a great way to earn a warm welcome from the Granites' management.' We could hear thousands of litres of water being sucked out of the desert and surging through the pump, but we couldn't get at it.

'I'll have a look,' Andrew said, leaving me in charge of the troops.

He spent some time examining the pump closely. 'You're right, I don't want to muck around with it. The boys won't get a drink tonight. No feed here, either,' he added, looking at the threadbare scrub with exasperation. We'll have some very cranky animals in the morning. Let's go and look for a campsite.'

We camped about 300 metres past the bore. For the first time, the camels showed some bad temper. Cooper fought with Andrew and resisted the hoosh. Andrew calmly tried to put him down, but the animal fought the pressure on the lead rope and bellowed furiously. We no sooner got him down and moved to the next camel in line, than he stood up again. Reluctantly, Andrew foreleg-tied him with his lead rope. As soon as they were unsaddled, the camels shuffled back to the pump and milled around, regarding it mournfully. We felt their frustration as we could all smell the water but couldn't get at it.

Andrew monitored his charges continuously, never taking his eyes off them even as we organised the campsite and built the fire. It increased his distress to see them huddled around the pump, and was heightened when, for their own safety, he had to take a stockwhip and drive them away from the whirring machinery.

'They're really thirsty, aren't they?' I said.

'No, not yet, they're not. They're like us with a beer – they'd *like* a drink, but they don't *need* a drink. All the same, I'll be glad to get some water into them.'

That day's march into the Granites bore from the God-forsaken Camp was the longest single day's walking of the trip to date – 28 kilometres in six hours, 38 minutes. Unknown to us, it was to be one of the longest distances we would walk in one day for the entire journey. Sore legs apart, the forced march left my feet unaffected. When my boots came off that night, I blessed the ridges of hard calluses that had replaced the red, bruised flesh of the journey's beginning.

A mob of dingoes surrounded the camp, yipping – a strange sound unique to them – all night. The camels were untied before dawn and headed straight for the bore. An enduring image of the expedition is of Andrew, cup of tea in one hand, stockwhip in the other, walking to the bore to drive the camels away as the sky was turning pink in the east. At first light, we wrestled the gear on to the animals. They roared more than usual as they were hooshed down, and some, like Cooper, became increasingly cranky and stood up before loading was finished, threatening to spill gear everywhere. Nevertheless, like every other day, the camels bent to Andrew's will and we loaded without too much aggravation.

We were under way at 9.09 am and only three hours later reached our resupply camp. Originally, with six camels we had planned to cross the desert with no resupply. I had hoped to avoid the giant Granites goldmine at all costs. However, with only five camels, we couldn't carry enough water unless we found some en route, so we had decided at Mt Stuart to meet Trevor and John on the Tanami track, south of Fiddlers Lake. Altering our course at Thomson's Rockhole, and our failure to find water for the camels, had meant a further change of plans, and Andrew had used the satellite phone to warn Trevor that we were being forced a long way north of our intended route and now had no choice but to go into the Granites to water the camels. We had arranged to meet Trevor and John east of the Granites later that day.

After we camped, Andrew decided to water the camels using our drinking water, presuming that we could replenish our supplies at the Granites mine, now only 25 kilometres away. A grey box was emptied of food and filled with water. Morgan was led in first. He attacked it with gusto, demolishing two full jerrycans' worth, amounting to 44 litres, in less than five minutes.

The sound of the water being poured into the box, the sight of Morgan slurping and the smell of the water drove the other camels nuts. They were securely tied to trees away from the campsite but fought lead rope and halter to get at the water. Thrashing around, they raised a fearsome cloud of dust. I thought that they might uproot the trees they were lashed to. If they had broken free, there would have been a pandemonium of spilled water, upended jerrycans, broken grey boxes and, possibly, injured cameleers. Anticipating this possibility we had tied them to the biggest trees available. Each camel was untied and, in turn, led to the watering point. Each drank about 50 litres, and in less than twenty minutes had demolished almost 300 litres of water – our remaining supply less one forlorn jerrycan.

Jammed full of water the temperament of the camels changed immediately. They stood, or sat dozing and burping, in the heat – a look of sheer bliss on each face. Soon they were up and attacking the acacia with an enthusiasm that had been absent in recent days. I could almost imagine them saying, 'Look out, I've got some serious eating to do.'

Their owner's mood also changed. 'This is great. This is great,' he said, standing quietly watching them, hands on hips. 'Filling them up and not asking them to walk anywhere with a belly full of water. Great. They'll feed well tonight.' The relief almost oozed out of him.

Our five camels had been our faithful companions for 370 kilometres and hadn't tasted water for seventeen days. I didn't begrudge them a drop. John and Trevor arrived mid-afternoon and jerrycans were loaded on to the truck for the trip to the mine. John had brought me a long-bladed sheath knife, which he insisted that I carry.

Camp 19, the Resupply Camp, as it was called in my journal, on the Mt Davidson outstation track, was the half-way point of the trip. We reached it on Saturday, 3 August 2002. With many small steps, we were slowly counting off the miles.

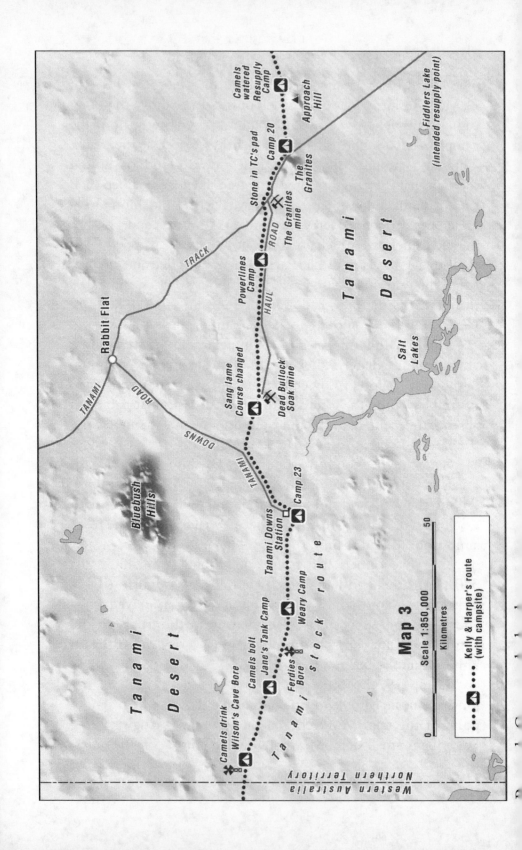

Map 3

Scale 1:850 000

Kilometres

0   50

Kelly & Harper's route
(with campsite)

Western Australia
Northern Territory

Tanami Desert

Tanami Desert

Tanami Desert

Bluebush Hills

Rabbit Flat

Fiddlers Lake
(intended resupply point)

Salt Lakes

Camels watered
Resupply Camp

Approach Hill

Camp 20

Stone in TC's pad

The Granites

The Granites mine

Powerlines Camp

HAUL   ROAD

TRACK

TANAMI   ROAD

DOWNS

TANAMI

Sang lame
Course changed

Dead Bullock
Soak mine

Camp 23

Tanami Downs Station

Weary Camp

Jane's Tank Camp

Camels bolt

Ferdies Bore

Tanami stock route

Camels drink
Wilson's Cave Bore

CHAPTER 8

The endurance test: The Granites to the border

Australia is the lowest and flattest continent on earth. Apart from Antarctica, it is also the driest. About 70 per cent of the mainland is arid or semi-arid, meaning its annual rainfall is less than 500 millimetres. That we found the Tanami hot, flat and dry was no surprise to Andrew or me. The Tanami Desert received its name from a rockhole in the ranges northwest of our position. The name is a corruption of the Aboriginal word *chan-a-mee*, meaning 'never dry'. The three-syllable word was originally *tan-ar-me* but it has been further corrupted through usage to the word we know today, pronounced with a 'my' as the last syllable, rather than 'me'.

Australian deserts are more *Mad Max* than *Lawrence of Arabia*. They are often stony plains, punctuated by flint-hard ranges and flat-topped mesas. We do have sand-ridge country, but the dune system and swales in Australia are usually clothed in vegetation.

Our deserts aren't like other deserts, as they do receive rain. There's not much of it, and it's sporadic, but it does rain. Blasted by fire and occasionally swept by flood, with soils depleted by a billion years of erosion, Australian deserts have evolved unique plants and animals to cope with their circumstances.

An interesting evolution is spinifex, first lieutenant to the mulga in our battle with the Tanami Desert. Spinifex, unique to Australia, is our most abundant grass, covering a quarter of the land mass yet most of the population, huddled in Sydney and Melbourne, never see the plant, let alone experience the joys of sitting in it or having its spines spear through their trousers or lacerate the backs of their hands. Spinifex only occupies the driest, most barren, most weather-blasted and drought-scorched country. It's the true symbol of Australia's deserts, yet it's seen by few of our people. First out of the ground after fire, seemingly surviving on no water, it is the only green plant in my experience that can be uprooted and immediately used as fire kindling. Spinifex will burst into flame if you stare at it too long; it's that volatile. Pete Warburton, whose tracks we would soon cross, called it a 'cheerless' plant. Not a bad description. It's a dismal plant whose texture is as alluring as the back of a porcupine. Nevertheless, after a couple of weeks, I was almost immune to it.

No plant or animal, however, captures the essence of the Tanami Desert like the mala – the rufous hare wallaby. I desperately wanted to see one. Michael Terry had seen many:

> These marsupials bounded away at an amazing rate, never
> slackening speed till they disappeared over the nearest
> sand-hill. Speeding away between the tufts of spinifex,
> their flight was marked by spurts of dust kicked up by
> their small but powerful feet. The way they kept to the
> tortuous fairway between the grassy islands was wonderful,
> and we do not recall having seen one, notwithstanding the
> high speed, hop over a tuft. Dodging here, dodging there,
> they flashed in and out of view with bewildering
> suddenness: sometimes hidden by the grass, sometimes
> tearing across the bare red sand.

Terry's words, written in 1925, are the best description of the mala I have seen. Unfortunately, it is only in books that I can now enjoy this creature. By the time we arrived at the Granites, we knew it was gone from the central deserts. We had seen not even a paw print, its traces lost among those of the feral cat and the fox, the animals that had destroyed it.

I felt the ground vibrating. It started as a subtle tremor which gradually increased until the earth shuddered under me. The noise was worse. I could hear them coming from about five kilometres away; just a gentle murmur at first. The noise would build and build, until it was right on top of us. With bull lights turning night into day, the road trains swept down on us with an ear-shattering roar and a billow of wind as they thundered past.

I leapt to my feet. Half asleep, I thought the monster would roll over the top of me. But with a clash of gears and a hiss of air brakes, the ore truck disappeared into the night. The noise receded, and in five minutes the desert was still. The pattern, however, was established and I knew that in about ten minutes the process would start again, with a full truck grinding up the rise coming in from Dead Bullock Soak to the Granites.

I looked at my watch. It was 1 am. 'Shit, I can't stand this. I've got to get some sleep,' I thought. I pulled on my trousers and wet shirt, found my boots and pulled them on, rolled my swag, strapped it and threw it over my shoulder, and started walking away from the haul road and the demon engines of the night. The scrub was brutally thick and I couldn't see a thing. I pushed blindly on through it, hoping that I wouldn't fall down a hole or tread on a death adder, which are active at night. When I'd achieved some distance between the mechanical monsters and me, I kicked the tufts of spinifex aside, rolled out my swag and was soon fast asleep, the ore trucks letting out a muffled boom as they roared by in the distance.

We were camped under the powerlines connecting the Granites mine with its partner, the Dead Bullock Soak mine, 40 kilometres further west. We had met Brian Fowler, the mine manager, when we came in to fill our jerrycans. An aerial photograph showed that there was only one way to traverse the huge industrial complex – straight through the middle.

'Beside the haul road there's a set of powerlines which run due west for about twenty kilometres. You can walk along them towards Dead Bullock Soak before heading off into the desert again,' Brian said. I studied the high-resolution photo again. The only alternative was a detour to the south, which would add about 60 kilometres to our journey. 'Before you commit, you should be aware that the biggest road trains in the world use that haulage road to bring ore into the Granites from Dead Bullock Soak. They then run back empty to reload. They do that every twenty minutes, and it goes around the clock.'

'What, 24 hours a day?' I asked.

'Seven days a week!' he confirmed. 'Also, the powerlines aren't fenced and run right next to the haul road in some places, so you'll have to be careful with the camels.'

It seemed that we didn't have any choice. However, I noticed a bore track about half-way to Dead Bullock Soak that would get us off the road and keep us pointing west. This was the route we would take, I told Brian.

Our campsite of Monday, 5 August, under the Dead Bullock Soak powerlines, was about 50 metres from the haul road. Brian hadn't been exaggerating about the road trains. With six bulk ore trailers, they were big enough to require an additional powered trailer pushing from the middle. Road trains weigh around 400 tons fully loaded and are the largest road vehicles in existence. Their twin diesels produce about 1000 horse-power, dwarfing our humble companions, who suddenly looked very small.

'Don't worry, Morg. I wouldn't trade you for one of those,' I said, walking beside him.

As we plodded along next to the road, the drivers gave us a wave and a salute with their air horns. The contrast wasn't lost on either of us. 'The old and the new way of moving stuff around,' Andrew said. I took some dramatic photos of the humps plodding along, roped end to end, doing their patient duty, while a vast road train, its carriages also coupled end to end, thundered by in the background.

The camels were bursting with water. Watered in stages so their bodies could adjust to the massive intake, each animal had drunk around 60 litres, about three jerrycans. Our jerrycans were also brimming, refilled at the mine. It was artesian water, raised from the underground river far beneath us by powerful bore pumps. The only surface water we had seen on the journey was the puddle at White Stone Well. Andrew was greatly relieved to get water into the camels, but I wasn't happy with the direction our journey had taken. As a city boy, I had come out here to see the wilderness, not the industrial technology of the Granites. Its noise and bustling human activity pitched me head-first back into civilisation. This part of the journey held no navigational challenges, with the haul road on the left and the featureless scrub on the right. It was an endurance test, walking towards the horizon beside a set of dead-straight powerlines – a form of endurance test, nothing more.

As usual, our routine began before daylight the following day, with Andrew already up and checking the camels. Forgoing our usual custom, all the camels had been tied securely to trees during the night, with none left free to graze; if one of them had strolled on to the haulage road, it would have been a disaster for animal and truck driver alike.

Andrew looked tired. 'Have a good sleep? I asked.

'Not bad. What about you? Saw you heading for the scrub in the middle of the night.'

'I got about five hours in. Had to move. I thought the things were going to come off the road and go right over the top of me.'

Worried that one of the camels might have broken loose during the night, Andrew had slept at the camp. Still, lack of sleep didn't dent his usual early-morning industry as he bustled around, attending to chores, before bringing in the camels. Methodically, he checked the boxes, tightened the jerrycan lids, packed away the food and ensured that everything was ready. We bent to the task of lifting on the saddles. I was buggered. The saddles felt like lead and I was breathless after we lifted each one. My condition was irrelevant, however. This was our now-familiar morning ritual and was performed regardless of how we felt.

'None of this makes you tired, does it?' I said as we heaved Cooper's saddle on board. Coop let out a bellow and honk.

'No, not really. I enjoy loading and unloading camels, making sure all the gear's right. Making sure everything's tidy and done properly.'

After the jerrycans were loaded and tied, the food boxes loaded and tied on, it remained only for the green boxes to go on. Andrew lifted these and I secured them with the double straps. These were the most important boxes and no chances could be taken with them. We moved to the front of the string and he bent down and slid his right hand through the small handle on the top of one of the boxes. Effortlessly, he lifted it with less exertion than a gym junkie doing a light forearm curl. This ritual, repeated every morning for over a month, still amazed me. Over 50 kilograms of metal box – the equivalent of more than two jerrycans of water – was lifted in one hand and gently dropped on to TC's saddle racks; I moved to secure it.

'Sorry I can't lift those boxes,' I said. 'I feel bad about it.'

'Don't worry. No one else can lift 'em either,' he replied.

'I'm buggered if I know how you do it so easily.'

'Muscle memory. I do it all the time, so my muscles are used to it.'

'I must have muscle amnesia,' I said.

'Different day jobs, remember,' he said, as we moved around the front of TC to tackle the other box.

'It's my day job,' was always Andrew's reply whenever I remarked on how easily some things came to him that were so difficult for me. His physical strength, lack of concern about sleeping dirty, his boundless energy, infinite vision and uncanny sense of direction were all things that I had noticed since leaving Mt Stuart. When I remarked on how well he managed the camels and what a great feel he had for animals, the reply would be: 'It's my day job.' But behind this glib retort was a much more complex individual whom I was slowly getting to know, not by what he said, but by what he did. Not only good with animals, he was also an astute observer of people and had been watching me to figure out just what I was capable of. I followed the Heyerdahl principle and tried to avoid asking Andrew about himself. The rigours of the journey meant that we only spoke to each other briefly during the day and this on matters of immediate need, such as our course. Nevertheless, two men alone together for over a month, sharing a campfire, a blackened billy and sinew-tearing toil, will get some picture of each other, if not by words then by some form of bush osmosis.

On the last Sunday in July, we had eaten lunch in the long grass north of Mac's Bump and, unprompted, Andrew had spoken of his life and family. He was the youngest of four children, the only son. His mother, Jean Gilchrist, a product of

North Sydney Girls' High School and, I would learn later, a strikingly attractive and popular woman, went to live in the bush and made her life with Ian Harper, the Deniliquin doctor. She had recently passed away. Andrew, his father and grandfather were former students of Melbourne Grammar and members of the Melbourne Cricket Club. The Harper family had been in Australia since 1856; of southern English stock, they were Australian pioneers. Having recently had their heraldry done in England, they had taken a boar behind a picket fence as their crest, with the motto: *Firm and True*. Andrew had already mentioned that the family still had some heirlooms that came over on the ship with his forebears in 1856.

'Gee, this's the bush aristocracy,' I thought, as we sat in the scrub that day. Our histories couldn't have been more different. We came from opposite ends of the bush totem pole. My parents were Irish Catholic farmers who fought the Australian scrub for generations and lost. My father toiled seven days a week, in harsh, thankless drudgery, stopping only to go to Mass on Sundays. He never had a holiday and was the hardest-working man I've ever known. Drought, the environment, overwork and the banks killed him, and we grew up knowing only poverty.

I marvelled at how two people as different as Andrew and me had come to be sitting under the same scrubby tree enjoying a cup of tea. I would have liked to share some of my childhood experiences with him, but the spirit of Thor Heyerdahl prevented me. Another time, another place, perhaps. But Andrew was no rural toff; he had fought every inch of the way and life had dealt him some tough cards. As he seldom indulged himself, I let him talk. And it was a story which turned surprisingly on the axis of the humble mosquito.

'A big problem for me was I got a dose of viral encephalitis in 1985, which knocked me completely flat for about eighteen months.'

'What? Meningococcal disease?' I was shocked. The

Sydney papers recently had been full of horror stories of this sometimes-fatal disease.

'Yes, I couldn't work and could hardly move. I was lucky as I could go home and Mum nursed me. I also had Ross River fever, although it wasn't diagnosed at the time.'

Ross River fever is a mosquito-borne disease that's rife along Australia's inland rivers. Painful, arthritic-like inflammation of the joints and crushing lethargy are the symptoms. There is no cure other than time and the body's own repair mechanisms.

'In 1989 I got another bout of Ross River fever, and had to have long periods off work. The heat and long hours at Boonoke aggravated the problem and in 1990 I had no choice but to resign from my job at the station.'

This explained the gap in Andrew's résumé when his life appeared to have stopped.

'My immune system was so weak it really flattened me, left me very debilitated. It took me a long while to get back into full-time work. When I did, I found that I needed constant rest. I went on a holiday with one of Rex Ellis's camel tours while I was recuperating, liked it and found I could cope with the work.'

'Catching those diseases; it's lucky you're not dead.'

'There are times when I thought I was,' he said.

I was shocked. Of all the things that I had guessed may have shaped Andrew's life, poor health wasn't one. 'So, you're fully recovered now?' I asked.

'No, not really. I get tired and need time off to rest. It will probably have some impact on me for the rest of my life.'

'You're not getting tired out here, as far as I can see.'

'No, but this is a long trip. I'll need to rest when I get home,' he said. 'I couldn't do the sort of work you do. I need the flexibility to have time off.'

'Mate, *I'm* not sure I can do the sort of work I do,' I replied.

Some mental arithmetic told me that Andrew was only 22 years old when he contracted viral encephalitis; a tough burden for a young person. I don't know Andrew all that well, but he certainly doesn't lack courage, I thought to myself, gazing out at the heat haze.

I had many questions, the main one being his motive for undertaking the Capricorn Expedition in 1999. Earlier in the trip, Andrew had mentioned that when he was working as a jackaroo on Kelso Station in Queensland, he was intrigued by the Tropic of Capricorn, which ran through the property. He dreamed of walking along it. Ill-health prevented this. Possibly the expedition was a celebration of health and life after his recovery from a succession of devastating illnesses; his mind and body saying, 'I'm still here. I can still do this.' I wanted to grill him further, but held my tongue. I'd had setbacks which I was struggling to overcome – in particular, a disability in mid-life which had lost me the partial use of one hand. Maybe Andrew and I were both out in the desert trying to prove something to ourselves.

Little things can go wrong on these trips and have to be constantly managed. Before reaching the powerlines, we had crossed the Tanami track. The track is surfaced by tailings from the mine's ball mill, and as we strode along TC began slamming his front foot down, trying to dislodge a stone caught in his pad. Unfortunately, a camel's leg, unlike a horse's hoof, cannot be picked up and checked. Their feet can be examined only when the animal is seated and can't strike out. Andrew hooshed him down in the middle of the track and gently probed his pad, but could find nothing. I watched anxiously. We had no spare or tag-along camels and a lame one, unable to walk or carry gear, would be a major problem. Andrew got the old camel up and we walked on. For the next couple of hours, TC continued to pound his foot into the hard surface of the track, but the problem then went away without our intervention.

As we left the Powerlines Camp on Tuesday, 6 August, my journal recorded: *At 0844 temp 18.9°C. Will be a hot one. O/night low of 8.8°C and hum 33% at dawn. 0855 left marching W along powerlines . . . 1250 lunch – one thing I have realised how the left over tea can be used to wash your hands. AH & I never throw the dregs of the tea away. Spent most of lunch trying to fix butane stove – no go – something wrong with it.* The miniature stove, designed for mountaineering, not for dusty deserts, was dying as we walked through the Granites. I couldn't fix it and we were faced with having no tea at lunchtime, a punishment no explorer should have to bear.

We pushed on through a blindingly hot afternoon, skirted the cavernous pit at Dead Bullock Soak, and weaved through towering mullock heaps of red earth. It was an eerie landscape.

'Mate, these blokes are covering themselves in glory,' I said, poking a thumb at the camels. 'Thundering ore wagons, horns blasting, air brakes hissing, gearboxes crashing, bore pumps roaring and mullock heaps that look like Mars, and the boys haven't batted an eyelid. I'm impressed.' I knew I would get no argument. 'If we'd walked horses through there, half of them would be back in Alice by now and the other half in Darwin, and we'd have gear all over the flat.'

'Yes, I wouldn't like to have tried that with horses,' Andrew replied. By late afternoon we were back in the desert. Camel feed was scarce as the country had been burned, and we didn't find a camp until 4.42 pm. For once, we camped in grass, not spinifex.

We had walked 53.5 kilometres in two days, clearing the Granites without mishap. One day we had averaged four and a half kilometres an hour, which is close to the maximum speed of a camel led through the desert by a man on foot. I was updating the map and journal and simmering the evening meal when Andrew walked in from tethering the camels for the night.

'Have a cup of tea? I worked out we're only 94 kilometres from the Western Australian border. We'll be there in four days, with any luck,' I said, pouring tea from the steaming billy into Andrew's pannikin.

'We'll *need* some luck. Sang's lame.' Andrew couldn't have stunned me more if he'd pulled out the rifle and shot me. This was the worst possible news. The third camel in the string had injured himself and couldn't walk.

'Bad?' I asked.

'Pretty bad. He's limping. Can't put any weight on it. I think he must've staked it on some burned mulga. He was fine when we came in and when I let them out to graze, so it must've happened in the last hour.' When mulga burns, it often leaves a snapped-off section of sharpened trunk sticking out of the ground, ready to impale the unwary. The underside of a camel's foot is composed of a toughened pad, designed to cope with sandy or stony deserts. They haven't yet evolved enough to cope with sharpened stakes. A camel restrained in hobbles cannot always choose where to put its front feet and is especially vulnerable.

We talked of the alternatives. Horses go lame for no reason and may stay that way for weeks. A moderately lame pack horse is immediately unsaddled and all the gear, including the saddle, is transferred to another, spare horse. We didn't have a spare camel. 'We could really use that sixth camel now,' I thought to myself. One option was to load up the other camels with Sang's gear, but he'd still have to carry his saddle.

'We could take some of the full jerrycans and food boxes off Sang, transfer them to the other camels and put empty ones on him,' I suggested.

'Yes, we could do that – on the assumption that he can walk.' A camel that couldn't walk didn't bear thinking about. We'd be stuck here waiting for him to recover, gradually running out of food and water.

It was a sombre camp that night, with not much chatter.

As I unrolled my swag, the lights of the Dead Bullock Soak pit lit the eastern horizon. The faint rumble of ore trucks and mine machinery carried on the breeze. The sound of intense human activity was disturbing. 'Over there, people are working, earning money and supporting their families,' I thought. I got a terrible attack of the guilts.

That night, at camp 22, on 6 August, looking back towards Dead Bullock Soak, I wrote: *That is my world where I should be, not sleeping out here in the long grass like a hobo. Their world seems like the real world, and it is carrying on without me, ignoring what we are trying to do, which is irrelevant to ordinary people's lives. This sort of exploration would have been part of the mainstream 150 years ago because society needed explorers to go out & map the country and see what is there. Today what we are doing serves no useful purpose to society.*

I wouldn't have believed that one day I would lie in a swag, deep in the desert and look longingly at a goldmine. I think my sentiments were driven by a couple of long, very hot days and a forced march of more than three weeks, sometimes through atrocious conditions. Fatigue was setting in, and lack of sleep the night before, combined with the stress of getting the animals through the mine, was making me sour. Moreover, I was missing my family and couldn't communicate it to anyone. Also, the prospect of managing a lame camel was crushing.

However, jumbled in with these emotions was the feeling that we were working hard, probably harder than anyone at the mine, and not being paid for the effort. Reward for effort is hard-wired into men's brains at conception. It's a hard genetic trait to toss. *I envy those people getting paid for what they do. The noise up there belongs to a world of clean clothes, vehicles to drive, air-conditioning, children and getting paid as a reward for effort*, I wrote. The realisation that the economy and society were careering along quite happily without me was unsettling. I felt like an outsider, like some mad eccentric.

With trepidation, I watched Andrew lead in the camels the next morning. Sang was still limping. When the string halted, he stood on three legs, his off-side foreleg bent at the knee, holding his pad slightly off the ground. That animal's not going anywhere, I thought. Before a camel can sit, it must first kneel, putting weight on one front leg, while bending the other. It genuflects, kneels, and then slides its back legs under, sitting on all fours. Sang had great difficulty with this reflex manoeuvre. Finally, he was down and Andrew carefully examined the pad. There was no sign of any injury, so we loaded him with his usual quota of water and food, and my swag.

'I don't know about this. The animal's as lame as a dog,' I said, when all was complete and the camels were ready to stand.

'We'll give him a try, see how he goes. *Ibnah*, boys. Up. *Ibnah*. C'mon, TC. C'mon, Sang,' Andrew said.

We held our breath as the camels lurched to their feet. Sang got his back legs underneath himself while kneeling on his front legs. Rocking back and forth, he got half-way up on one front leg, then tried to move his sore leg underneath himself but got stuck, as it couldn't bear the weight. 'C'mon, boy. C'mon, Sang. *Ibnah*, mate,' Andrew encouraged him. With a lurch, Sang pushed himself upwards. He stood on three legs, fully loaded, keeping his sore pad just off the ground. We were ready to go.

'We'll try it like this for awhile, and see if he can keep up,' Andrew said.

'Why don't we take all the gear off him, load it on the other camels and just let him tag along behind?'

'No, this way's best. The other camels will tow him along and help him keep up. If we cut him loose, he'll try to keep up, but he'll gradually get further and further behind and we'll lose him.'

I wasn't so sure. A horse as lame as Sang was wouldn't be going anywhere, although Andrew assured me it wasn't as bad as it looked.

Yet another course change was required. We had planned to head southwest around Tanami Downs cattle station, then due west to the border. Andrew didn't want to take Sang into the scrub in his present condition, though, so after consulting the maps I set a northwest course towards a track running down from Rabbit Flat to the station. It was the opposite direction we had hoped to travel in and increased the walking distance, but we had no choice.

'Well, let's give it a try,' Andrew said. We set off. To my astonishment, Sang stepped out gamely. I had to look hard to notice that he was putting the injured pad down very gingerly, but it didn't seem to impede his action. At best, I expected that he would walk slowly and his lead rope would continually tug on Cooper's neck – that Cooper would be towing him. It didn't happen. Andrew was philosophical. 'They're tough. He's feeling it, but he'll do anything to avoid being left behind.'

We found the station road before lunch and turned south. The outline of the Bluebush Hills on the horizon had been our morning guide. Because of the course changes, we were about 40 kilometres further north than I had planned back in Sydney. To protect myself from the merciless sun, I kept my hat pulled well down and usually rolled down my shirtsleeves during the hottest part of the day. There was no way to protect my hands, though, which were exposed to the elements. At lunch under a bloodwood as we approached the station, I wrote in my notebook of the phenomenon of swollen fingers from continual walking: *My hands are a mess. Fat sausage fingers, dirty broken nails, backs of hands sunburnt raw & dirty, cut and scratched. They look like someone else's fingers. Lit fire and boiled tea. Stove is buggered. Cannot make a fist, skin on my hands is so dry and tight.*

At lunchtime our camels, like us, enjoyed the break. TC, who sat only a metre or so away from me, closed his eyes and dozed even though his head was in the upright, alert position and he was loaded with gear. We didn't unsaddle at lunchtime. Cooper really relaxed, stretching out his neck and laying his head on the ground. He was soon fast asleep, completely immobile. The other camels closed their eyes and dozed in the heat.

'Hey, Andrew. I think one of your camels has died,' I said, pointing to Cooper.

'Cooper? He'll sleep anywhere.'

'Better not start snoring. I can't eat lunch with a snoring camel.'

A camel is said to be a horse designed by a committee. The Walpiri people of the Tanami, who saw horses before they saw camels, called the animal 'the emu-horse', combining the body of a horse with the long neck and head of an emu. In fact, they're a marvel of evolution. I examined TC's head – it had been designed to conserve water. The nostrils were slits, which are folded down to retain moisture as the animal exhales. The folds also keep out driving sand during desert storms. The eyes, recessed in the skull, were shaded from the fierce heat and came with long, thick eyelashes to keep out dust and flying sand. The ears were full of thick hair for the same reason. Thick pads on a camel's elbows, knees and stifle – the bony joint of the back legs – help to bear the animal's weight when seated. A camel's manure comes out as tiny square blocks, about the size of a seamstress's thimble, totally devoid of nutrients and moisture and as hard as a house brick when they are trying to conserve water. A camel's stomach and its ruminant eating method gives the animal the ability to extract every ounce of water from apparently dry vegetation.

I took a date – dates were part of our lunchtime dessert

menu – and walked out from the sparse shade to where TC sat dozing in the heat, holding the treat on the palm of my hand. I had read that the Arabs fed dates to their horses, and I wondered if camels also ate them. The old trooper barely opened his eyes as I approached. He sniffed the palm of my hand and with a flick of his lips the date was gone. I guess that answers that question, I thought. Cooper, seated just behind TC, didn't stir.

'Don't spoil that camel. They'll all want one next!' Andrew called out cheerfully from his spot in the shade next to the food boxes. I patted the top of TC's head and returned to finish my lunch. The old camel had already resumed his slumber by the time I sat down.

The Arabs called their magnificent horses *drinkers of the wind*. I wondered what they called their camels? If the Arabian horse is the Ferrari of the animal world, then the camel is the Mack truck. 'Yep, that's what you are, TC. You're a Mack truck,' I said in the direction of the dozing animal. 'You aren't pretty, but you sure get the job done.' TC partly opened his eyes at the sound of my voice, peered at me through his long eyelashes and immediately dozed off again. What he thought of my appraisal, or indeed what his opinion of the trainee cameleer on the expedition was, he didn't share with me.

As we headed south, the country began to change. Slowly, surely, although a traveller in a car wouldn't have noticed it, the desert was showing us a different face. First, the giant anthills returned; then the scrub receded. The ancient river channel was back. I realised that it ran from Thomson's Rockhole, south of the Granites and Dead Bullock Soak, and on towards Western Australia. It was sobering to reflect that we could have walked west from Thomson's Rockhole and avoided all the dreadful scrub around the Godforsaken Camp. If we had followed the channel, we would have cut kilometres off the journey and avoided the stress of traversing the minesite; it was an opportunity lost.

I saw my first saltpan that afternoon, a shallow depression that catches wet-season downfalls and then leaves behind a thick coat of mineral salt as the water evaporates. The sun bounces off the saltpans with a frightening brilliance. The saline soil underneath the saltpans guarantees that little vegetation grows there. The spinifex was in retreat and the scrub thinned out.

We reached the Tanami Downs Station homestead late in the afternoon. Andrew waited with the camels while I went to pay our respects to the managers and check on the status of the bores. It was a strange feeling walking up to the homestead. We hadn't seen a cattle station since Anninge on the second day of the trip. That seemed a long time ago. Also, Tanami Downs has something of a celebrity reputation, being the former home of the Mahood family when the property was known as 'Mongrel Downs'. It was the subject of Marie Mahood's book, *Icing on the Damper*, about her life there in the wilderness. The station staff came out to look at the camels. 'Where're your back-up vehicles?' they asked, echoing Clint Campbell's question at Anninge Station.

After photos were taken and we gathered intelligence on the bores in Western Australia, we headed towards the border. Finding a camp at 5 pm, we unloaded the animals and waited anxiously to see how Sang behaved. Still trying to understand camels, I feared that he might be too sore to get up and feed; that he would sit there and starve. He sat for awhile, watching his companions head towards a nearby bloodwood grove, and moaned quietly. Finally, he lurched to his feet and hopped off after them. He had a shocking limp, which nearly broke my heart, but I had feared worse. 'That's a surprise. He's no worse than this morning. I thought after that march today he would be properly buggered,' I said to Andrew.

'Yes. He's getting by. The other chaps are towing him, but he's getting by. Camels – they'll surprise you by how tough they are.'

'Too right! Walking a lame horse that distance would cripple him.' Despite the time on the track – almost seven hours – we had covered only 23 kilometres, a slow day. The old bush proverb that you can never walk faster than your slowest animal was proven that day.

It was three days to the border, three days that would test every fibre of my mental and physical stamina. It was time to dig for the inner grit, and I had to dig deeply. Whereas the eastern Tanami had confronted us physically, it now decided to test us mentally.

The desert west of Tanami Downs, ever full of surprises, became a wide black soil plain covered in waving Flinders grass. Gone was the mulga and most of the spinifex. We began walking up long sand ridges that would often take an hour to crest. My notebook for Thursday, 8 August, records: *1224 sand-hills and open grassland – spinifex starting to disappear, country definitely changing has a softer look. 1231 sighted first cattle since leaving Anninge Station also 6/8 kangaroos first since Thomson's rockhole. The views rolled out to an infinite horizon that receded as we walked toward it.*

'This country is amazing. We could be in western Queensland. Some parts of it even look like the back paddocks at Boonoke,' Andrew said, referring to the Murdoch property in southern New South Wales where he had once worked. The vista of the eastern Tanami, constrained by dense scrub, was replaced by a panorama of a long, straight horizon, uninterrupted by even the slightest bump. The vast distances we could see brought a new challenge – that of monotony. Often I would take a fix on a tree, walk towards it for an hour, and arrive to find a bush no bigger than myself. I then took a new fix on another distant tree on the next horizon and began the walk towards it. This process was repeated hour after hour, day after day. The mirage and heat haze writhed along the far horizon. It played havoc with perception of distance and the size of objects. Sometimes, I would pick a distant navigating point, which would slowly disappear in the boiling haze as I walked towards it. It was navigating into infinity and we never seemed to get anywhere.

Coming up from the Lander in the early part of the journey I had sung to myself to pass the time. I sang Hank Williams's 'Your Cheatin' Heart' and 'I'm So Lonesome I Could Cry' and Slim Dusty's 'Lights on the Hill'. Because Andrew and the camels walked about 100 metres behind me, in reality Andrew and I did the trip alone, each lost in his own thoughts, each concentrating and trying to summon up the tenacity to keep going while doing their jobs: mine was to navigate; Andrew's to pick the best way forward for the camels. I felt I was locked in a battle between my body and the bush and had to coax my body along. I concentrated totally on the compass, my notebook and the map that I carried permanently in the thigh pocket of my trousers. I looked either at the horizon or at my feet. Occasionally, I would stop, draw breath and stare back at the camels, but mostly I looked at the compass, which I checked continually. I was enveloped in complete silence. Sometimes I got lonely. I sang as many songs as I could remember from *Les Misérables*. Songs like Javert's 'Stars', which is a blokey song, lonely and inspiring and appropriate for a desert crossing. 'Drink With Me', from the same musical, played repeatedly in my head, like an audiotape on an endless loop.

My children loved *Les Mis*. Catherine played the music on the piano in our lounge room. Singing it reminded me of home and family. The lyrics from 'Drink With Me', about a toast to friendship, bygone days and a life that used to be, reminded me of a hike up the north wall of the Grand Canyon

23 years ago with two mates from New Jersey. Carrying full packs in sweltering August heat, national honour was at stake and it was soon a race – a race I was determined to win. I beat the Americans easily and was puffing hard at the top. We laughed about it as we admired the view from the rim of the canyon. How different it was now. I'd consider it a win if I just managed to keep up with Andrew and the camels.

'Where have all the years gone?' I asked myself more than once through the long silences of the afternoons. When I was really tired or it was very hot I cursed God and fate for relentlessly taking away the years and never giving any back. 'If only I was twenty years younger, I'd show Andrew a thing or two.' Irish author Jonathan Swift said that no wise man ever wished he was younger. I proved him wrong walking across the Tanami.

Walking in the mornings was okay. Through this part of the journey, a southeaster would welcome the early hours and the delicious feeling of a breeze hitting the back of my soaking-wet shirt was invigorating. I looked forward to scroggin and then, as the temperature started to climb, I looked forward to lunch and would begin to sing. The hours after lunch were tough; it was a matter of pulling my hat down over my eyes and just walking. Walking and singing.

I sang loudly and it seemed strange to hear the noise in the wilderness. I sang often and it seemed to drive away the loneliness. Walking and singing, hour after hour, the rhythmic swing of my arms and the metronomic crunch of my boots, took my mind off the ongoing trial and I entered a dreamlike trance. Walking with a measured gait, I became oblivious of the heat and fatigue that assaulted my body. I forgot that I was drenched in sweat and badly in need of a wash. It was marvellous how quickly the afternoon would slip away. It was like form of perambulating meditation.

Slim Dusty's song about a truck driver dying on a rainy night, or Hank Williams' about a midnight train whinin' low are strange hymns for an Australian desert crossing.

Why those songs? I don't know, but I sang them over and over every day for five weeks and managed to keep myself company and keep my body driving forward. And I recited poetry. Great slabs of it. Poetry was read to me every night as a child and, walking along in the silence, snatches of poems long forgotten started coming back. It was always the same verses and I wrote many of them in my journal at the end of the day's march. I never sang or recited too loudly while Andrew was in earshot, in case he thought I was becoming demented. Nevertheless, I realised that he too would also get lost in an inner space.

'Is it that time already? Gee, the time's gone quickly,' he would often say when I signalled the scroggin or lunchtime halt. Sometimes he would have the slightly dazed look of someone who has been dozing in the heat. He was in the zone.

Singing might seem like a strange desert pastime. However, months later I laughed when I read that Mike Terry and the tough-as-nails bushman, Ben Nicker, often sang as they rode their camels; to combat the monotony, to ward off the boredom and to allay the pangs of thirst. Moreover, Aborigines had sung themselves right across the country.

On and on we trudged. Indicative of my mood, I called camp 24, the second camp west of Tanami Downs homestead, the Weary Camp. We were 53 kilometres from the border. The camels were stately ships swaying across a red desert ocean, a caravan of the ages. Their rhythmic gait, mile after mile, added to my afternoon stupor. It was very different from their wretched, scrub-smashing scramble in the early days.

Sang had made it through his second day without incident. We had pulled the swags and full jerrycans off him early that morning and distributed them around the other camels. His load now comprised only his saddle and empty jerrycans. Incredibly, after we unsaddled him that night he ambled off, noticeably sounder than he had been in the morning. Don't ask me how.

I cooked a roast lamb and vegetables dried meal that night with Deb mashed potato. I tried endless variations to ensure that we had an interesting diet. I also cut up some dates and dried apricots to bulk out the scroggin and make it last longer. As dusk fell I went to get my head torch from a bag that was resting on my tarp. As I approached it, I saw about fifteen centimetres of reptilian tail disappear under the blue plastic sheeting. A lump over a metre long moved under the tarp, making a familiar rustling sound. The snake's head bumped into the bulk of my rolled-up swag sitting on top of the tarp and stopped. I decided that I could do without my torch for a while. I would let my new-found friend check out the shade under the tarp and hopefully he would then go back to the bush.

'Got a snake under my tarp,' I said to Andrew when I walked back to the fire.

'Better there than in your swag,' he said.

'Bloody oath.'

We had a plan for every emergency; for broken limbs, wounds, loss of camels, scrub fires and separation. In the event that we were separated, we would light a small fire, on a high point if possible, keep it going, then sit and wait. If we were caught in a scrub wild-fire, we would immediately light another fire on the lee side of the camels and move in behind the second fire as it caught. This would put us on burned country. We would hoosh the camels down, foreleg-tie them, get the gear off and wait for the original fire to reach us, safe on the newly burned country. The things we didn't have a contingency plan for were bad burns and snakebite. If one of us was very badly burned, he would die from shock long before the other could strap him to a camel and get help. If we were both burned and injured, obviously we were finished. In the event of snakebite, our only treatment was a pressure bandage to slow the spread of toxin through the lymph system and retard organ failure. The death adder and mulga snake are so poisonous that serious illness is the best possible outcome.

'You would be turning very blue after a snakebite and five days on the back of a camel trying to get into Balgo or somewhere with a Flying Doctor strip,' Andrew said cheerily. Some things in the wilderness defy resolution. However, I now had unshakeable faith in our teamwork. I knew that no matter what happened, Andrew wouldn't leave me to die in the bush and wouldn't desert me if we were separated, and I think he had the same confidence in me. There was a growing feeling of comradeship and trust. We had shared the same hardships, loaded camels together on mornings so freezing our noses ran, plodded behind each other through the still, burning heat of the day, and shared a billy of tea at day's end. We were realising the simple joy of struggling together to achieve a common goal. To make the expedition work I had anticipated that Andrew and I would have to work as a team, but in reality, it was a team of seven. I had a growing respect and admiration for our pack animals.

Late that evening I returned to my tarp and, using the shovel, gingerly lifted the sheet and peered underneath. The snake was gone; its slithering track disappeared into the long grass at the side of the camp. The wisdom of keeping a swag rolled up tight until you get in it was confirmed once again.

Morning at the Weary Camp. Camels loaded. Andrew waiting to stand them up. Everything as usual, as practised for weeks. He called them up. The last act was roping the five camels together, which I did with the quick-release bowline knot I had used every morning for the entire journey. Sang was last up, struggling a bit. He still avoided putting weight on his sore pad, took a small step to adjust his stance, and stumbled. Then, to my horror, and before I could move, the saddle slid off his hump and, with a crash, fell down his rib cage. Three hundred kilograms of saddle, jerrycans, food boxes and racks were hanging under the belly of a very confused and frightened camel, secured by the still connected girth. I was standing too far away to get to him. Andrew was at the head of the string. Alarmed, Sang instinctively pulled backwards, trying to flee, but was restrained by his halter rope which was tied securely around Cooper, the camel immediately in front.

'Here we go. In a moment he's going to start kicking out at the saddle and bucking, then the lot of them will start. There'll be camels and gear everywhere,' I thought.

Andrew was beside the animal in an instant. He pulled hard on the tail of the quick-release knot, as Sang began to buck and rear. Nothing happened. He tried again, looked at me and pulled repeatedly on the knot. It didn't snap open like it always had. He didn't say anything – just turned around, looked at me and pulled with all his might. Sang was straining, starting to rear, the saddle crashing and rattling under his belly. John Wilkinson's warning came back to me from the start of the trip: You don't want to be around camels trying to get knots undone. Just cut the rope.

That's what happened. Andrew drew his knife and, with three or four deft cuts, slashed Sang's lead rope, freeing him from Cooper. He then cut Char's rope, which secured him to Sang. Next the breastplate and crupper were sliced from the saddle. Finally, with a flick of Andrew's wrist, the rope cords of the girth went. With a loud crash, saddle and gear landed upside down, between Sang's feet, with a garland of cut rope. All this activity happened in a matter of seconds.

I grabbed the last two camels and Andrew had the front two. Sang, to his eternal credit, although shuddering with fright, simply stepped over the saddle and sat down next to it waiting to be reloaded. 'Oh, thank you, you wonderful camel. I hope you spend your last days in a paddock with long, green grass and a river nearby,' I thought, as we tethered the other camels to nearby trees before returning to assess the damage.

We pulled the gear off the saddle and then righted it. No

damage was done. None of the sensitive equipment – rescue beacons, cameras or navigational equipment – was on Sang. A new rope girth, breastplate and crupper were fitted, the saddle was lifted back on and the whole procedure was gone through again. Andrew said nothing except, 'Didn't you see the saddle start to slip?' I had, but there was nothing I could do; it was all over in an instant. Andrew was obviously frustrated, but to his credit and my great relief, he didn't take it out on me. My cherished roping technique hadn't worked, but there was no reprisal. I got the message. I picked up the rope from the ground with the knot still intact. The rope was coarse, thick hemp; I used smooth, nylon yachting rope for tethering horses. For the safety bowline to release, the rope must be able to slide. Sang's enormous weight pulling back on the rope, combined with the texture of the rope, made this impossible. His weight had locked the knot. From then on, I tied the camels each morning with a fixed bowline and the Harper template was complete. It was humble-pie time again.

Our march to the border was along the old Tanami stock route. Seeking an alternative market for Kimberly cattle, the pioneering pastoralists had sunk a series of bores between Billiluna on Sturt Creek and the Tanami track. They, like us, had realised that the Tanami provides no surface water and that if cattle were to be overlanded between the Kimberly and Alice Springs, bores were needed. We struck the first of these, Ferdies Bore, on the second day past the homestead. A tank held salty artesian water, which was fed into a long stock trough. It was too saline for us, although the camels needed no encouragement and topped up the water we had given them at the Granites. I splashed the cool, almost cold, water over my face and hands. It was refreshing beyond my powers of description.

The country was very different here, with different animals. To the south, low red sand ridges were clearly visible. Just before lunch, a family of five emus appeared, walking a parallel course, stopping occasionally to peer at us. They were

the first I'd seen in central Australia. The sand ridges we walked
up were extraordinary, often taking many hours to crest. We
reached Jane's Tank late in the afternoon after a long haul up
a sand ridge. It was to be the scene of a near disaster.

Complacency is the enemy of successful expeditions. I had
grown complacent. This far into the trip, I believed that we
were gaining the upper hand on the desert. It had thrown
everything in its arsenal at us and we were still going. But the
Tanami is cruel, confounding its opponents when they least
expect it. The camels, which up to now had shown impeccable
manners, were the unexpected source of the problem.

Saturday, 10 August, Jane's Tank Camp. Daybreak. The
loading was finished and Andrew was tidying up some last-
minute details. It was time to rope the camels together. The
humps sat chewing quietly, moaning occasionally. I waited for
Andrew to stand them up. It had been a morning like every
other, with one exception – Morgan had refused to sit in line
facing the same way as the rest of the camels; he had turned
and sat backwards, looking down the track we had walked up
the previous evening.

We got him up several times and turned him around, but
on the hoosh, he reversed direction as he sat. After several
attempts to get him down the right way, we finally gave up.
'OK, Morgan. If you want to look for Frank, go ahead,' Andrew
said. Morgan peered intently back into the bush, head up
sniffing the breeze, all his senses alert. We looked in that direction. Nothing.

'Must be a bull [camel] back there somewhere,' I said.

'Yes, or Frank the bunyip. He thinks Frank's back there
somewhere and he has to guard the camels.' Andrew explained
that Frank had followed Morgan across a lot of Australian
deserts creating noises in the scrub that only Morgan could

hear, and generally creating mayhem. This was the first time Morgan hadn't obediently sat down at the rear of the string facing the way he was supposed to. We were at our most vulnerable just after loading was complete. The camels were seated with their hobbles removed, but had yet to be roped together. At this point, they were a group of unfettered individuals, not a roped-together unit. For this reason, Andrew wouldn't tolerate any of the animals standing up until all the loading was finished and he'd issued the command.

It happened without warning. *Crash! crash! crash!* A mob of half-wild steers came thundering through the dense blood-wood scrub, burst into the clearing, took one look at us and the camels, and fled back into the undergrowth bellowing wildly. Cattle had recently reappeared for the first time since Anninge Station. They had fled on our approach and this close encounter was too much for the camels, who had grown accustomed to the desert silence.

Morgan, already on edge as he had obviously picked up the scent of the cattle, leapt to his feet and, despite the full load he was carrying, charged out of the camp. Cooper, always keen for some mischief, saw Morgan go and was off after him. Sang and TC, also fully loaded but unroped, rose as one and fled. Poor, nervous Char was left standing in the middle of the camp, quaking in fright and torn with indecision. He looked at us, looked at his fleeing companions, then bolted. He literally galloped out of the camp. In the blink of an eye, we were standing in a deserted campsite. Our water, food, satellite phones and emergency beacons were disappearing on the backs of the escaping animals.

This had been my wife Prue's greatest fear. 'What happens if you lose the camels with the water and the emergency communications equipment at the same time?' We were about to find out.

Broad grassland spread away to the north in the direction the camels were heading. 'Our only hope is that they run into a fence out there,' I thought. The scene was reminiscent of

Harold Bell Lasseter's experience in the desert west of Alice Springs many years ago. The prospector's loaded camels bolted and he chased them waving his pistols, faced with a terrible choice: shoot them and recover the food and water, but be left with no transport, or let them go and hope to catch them. He let them go and died of thirst and starvation weeks later.

Then a funny thing happened. Andrew shouted, '*Oodoo*, Morgan! *Oodoo*, TC!' This is the Afghan word for 'stop'. Thundering along at a full gallop, Morgan suddenly stood on the brakes and looked around to see where Andrew was. Cooper then cannoned into Morgan. The others pulled up, and there was a melee of camels trotting in circles and bumping into each other. The saddle racks of one collided with the racks of another, setting up a fearful racket.

'*Morgan*, you dickhead! Where d'you think you're going?' Andrew shouted. The big camel looked at him anxiously over the intervening space, as Andrew approached him with a very purposeful stride.

'Have a good holiday, dickheads?' Andrew said, as we reached the confused-looking group and gathered their lead ropes. This was the closest Andrew ever came to rebuking the camels, the closest he came to swearing at them. And it was said more in jest than anger. I had several comic minutes being dragged around in circles holding on to one end of a long lead rope with almost a ton of frightened camel and gear on the other end of it. I got a feel for how heavy a camel really is as I tried to make TC stop jogging. There was no chance if they didn't want to stop. To our great relief, the saddles hadn't come off and no gear had been damaged. We were lucky.

'Why'd they pull up?' I asked.

'They're so used to the routine and to me telling them which way to travel that when they get in a situation like that, they become confused. They know they've got their saddles on and are supposed to be walking, but the boss camel – me – isn't there to tell them what to do. I didn't think they'd go far.'

We led them back to camp, sat them back down to check all the gear and were soon on our way.

While crossing Tanami Downs, we saw the last of the poplars. They had been scarce since we'd reached the Granites and this solitary specimen looked forlorn. Nevertheless, the camels dragged Andrew towards it and demolished it. We were still uncertain as to the tree's exact identity.

'I don't know what tree it is, but exotic or native it's not killing the camels,' I said.

As we crossed the desert, whenever feed was scarce, Andrew constantly checked that the humps weren't feeding on poplars alone. Months later I identified the mystery tree as the desert poplar (*Codonocarpus cotinifolius*). Andrew was right – it is a *Gyrostemon*, a cousin to the poison camel bush, but a harmless member of the family. *Codonocarpus* means 'bell-shaped', referring to the fruit. The desert poplar is the fastest-growing tree in central Australia and exists hand–in–glove with spinifex, racing the spiky nightmare out of the ground after fire.

It is found only in Australia and attracts biologists from all over the world. Why? Because it may hold a cure for cancer. In the 1940s, a Western Australian Aborigine, Albert Neebrong (or Nibberong), walked into Dalwallinu hospital and was diagnosed with cancer of the tongue. Albert absconded, fearing that his tongue may be cut out. Three years later, he was re-examined and the disease had vanished. Albert claimed that an Aboriginal medicine man had cured him using ashes from the desert poplar mixed with an extract of maroon bush (*Scaevola spinescens*). This traditional cure involved making a bitter-tasting 'tea' from the root bark of the maroon bush.

I also found reference to Aboriginal use of the poplar as a painkiller. If I had known its value, I would have treated the plant with greater respect. What treasures await us in inland

Australia – if the feral animals don't get there first! We saw no more poplars once we crossed the border.

A cameleer to the end, Andrew said months later, after it had been positively identified, 'I still don't trust that plant.'

We reached the Western Australian border on Sunday, 11 August, my wife's birthday. We had camped the previous night at Wilson's Cave Bore, the last on Tanami Downs Station. In front of us the stock route continued into Western Australia, but we knew that all the bores were abandoned. Although we couldn't drink the water at Wilson's Cave, the camels relished it. I had a welcome wash, ladling water out of the trough with my quart pot. Refreshed, I climbed the side of the tank which fed the trough. In the green water the dismembered remains of a large bustard floated in serene disarray. The native bush turkey had died in the tank some days previously. Ahead lay a waterless stretch similar to that encountered during the first part of our journey. My next wash would be in Lake Gregory.

There was a mood of quiet excitement as we approached the border.

The country we had crossed in recent days was black-soil grassland. I had almost forgotten spinifex. We had struck some turpentine scrub, but otherwise it had been beautiful walking. Andrew was in raptures about the country, describing it as some of the best cattle-grazing land he had ever seen. It was an oasis of fertility in the midst of a desert. He remarked repeatedly how it reminded him of parts of Boonoke.

However, the country changed again as we approached the border. Stone and sand replaced the black soil underfoot and the grass faded. We wouldn't see mulga for the rest of the journey. Hakea, dry and withered, began to appear in thickets and the spinifex returned. Our pace increased as the border loomed.

We saw a tall steel post sticking up out of the plain, about a kilometre in front of us, then a gate. 'That'll be it,' I shouted back to Andrew, pointing ahead. 'Mate, there's Western Australia – big billabongs, date palms and a pub right on the border,' I said, as he arrived with the camels. Alas, it wasn't to be. We crossed that great imaginary landmark, longitude 122° east, at 11.11 am, just west of Lake Alec. I filmed Andrew and the camels leaving the Northern Territory.

The crossing was an emotional time for me. The border was an arbitrary, invented line, not bound by any features. The gate was a wreck; on both sides, the fence marking the border had fallen down. It was a scene of desolation and human defeat. The bare red country stretched away to a limitless horizon in every direction. It was a deserted landscape. The words of the English poet, Percy Shelley, came to mind. In 'Ozymandias' Shelley writes of a traveller who discovers an imposing statue in the desert whose regal visage speaks of the power of command. Across the pedestal of the statue is written:

My name is Ozymandias, King of kings
Look on my works ye mighty and despair!

But the statue is broken and scattered around the flat. Around the wreckage, Shelley writes, *boundless and bare the lone and level sands stretch far away.* I used these words to welcome Andrew and the camels to Western Australia. We stopped for scroggin just over the border. 'The desert sure mocks human endeavour,' I said.

'What do you mean?'

'Well, imagine the arrogance of drawing a line across a place like this and saying it's the Northern Territory on one side and Western Australia on the other; looks just the same to me. Lines out here are meaningless. This country was here thousands of years before white fellas arrived and I'll bet it looked just like this,' I said, looking around. 'And the country'll still be here brooding away, lost in time, when all those lines are blown off the map by history. The buggered gate and fence symbolise it all – how the desert always wins. Long-term, the desert always wins. I reckon Shelley nailed the Tanami. He summed it up better than Lawson and the other Australian blokes.'

Andrew pondered this bit of bush philosophy, probably thinking he was shepherding a lunatic, while quietly munching on his scroggin. We gathered the camels and walked into the afternoon heat heading westward. *Boundless and bare the lone and level sands stretch far away*. I said those words over and over as we walked through that hot afternoon; west into the sunset, west towards Lake Gregory. We were entering the expedition's final days.

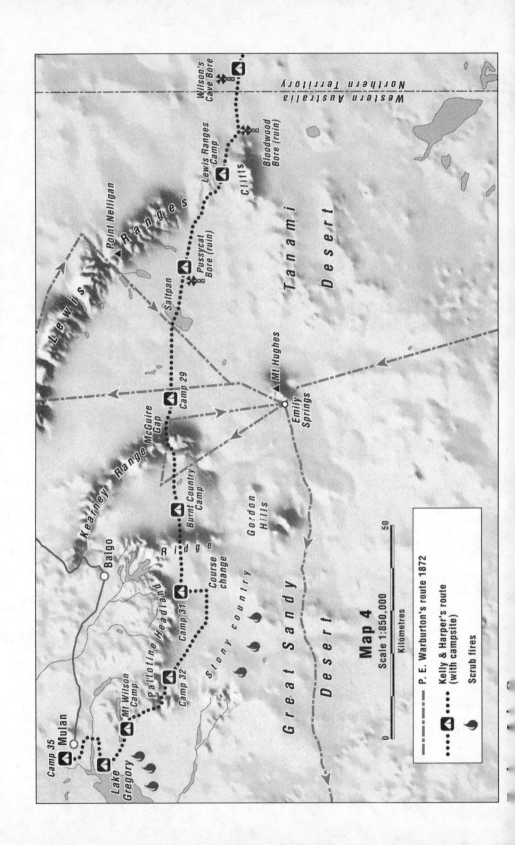

Map 4

Scale 1:850,000

Kilometres

0   50

P. E. Warburton's route 1872

Kelly & Harper's route
(with campsite)

Scrub fires

CHAPTER 9

Walking with giants: The border to Mt Wilson

The border was a milestone. Crossed on the 28th day of the expedition, it marked 550 kilometres of walking. Lake Gregory was only 182 kilometres away. We were exactly three-quarters of the way through the journey. The doubts that had assailed me early in the journey – Would we make it? Is it possible to walk across the Tanami? Could I keep up? – were still there. But now they were matched by a grim determination.

'Think we're going to make it?' Andrew asked in jest during the afternoon.

'Mate, having come this far, I'm going to see Lake Gregory even if I have to get there on my hands and knees.' I wasn't joking. I resolved to climb Mt Wilson and see Lake Gregory no matter what it took. I was elated to be part of a team; buoyed by the *esprit de corps* of the seven-member exploring party and our shared endeavour. As the other camels towed Sang, so did the group drag me along; there was a feeling that *all* of us were going to Lake Gregory. The only thing that would stop me would be if Andrew held the .308 Remington to my temple and pulled the trigger.

The route before us had many challenges. The desert was

yet to capitulate. We knew there was no water between the border and the lake and that even the lake may be dry; most years it was. We planned to follow the old stock route into Western Australia, walking northwest as far as McGuire Gap, a break in the Kearney Ranges about three days away. The course was then west, passing under the Pallotine Headland, before visiting the Gunawarrawarra Rockhole, then on to Mt Wilson. This route anticipated approaching Mt Wilson from the east, but like many things in my life, this was easier to dream about than to accomplish. We weren't destined to approach Mt Wilson from the east.

We headed for the Lewis Ranges, dead ahead. This would be a day with a difference, ending in a camp mutiny. I had recorded the minimum overnight temperature as 7.9°C, which meant it was going to be hot. During loading, I was sweating profusely and said to Andrew that it would be a scorcher. He nodded. The days had been getting progressively hotter as we crossed Tanami Downs and, although I was acclimatised, I felt a rising level of exhaustion. At lunchtime, not long after the border crossing, I placed the thermometer on a bag in the sun.

'You're supposed to measure temperature in the shade,' Andrew said, watching me while he ate his lunch.

'We're not walking in the shade. This feels like a bloody hot day and I want to find out just how hot.' The thermometer clocked 39.4°C – by far the hottest day of the journey.

We pushed on and shortly after lunch reached Bloodwood Bore, a set of wrecked cattle yards and an abandoned windmill. As expected, there was no water. It was a desolate scene. The country was desert bloodwood trees, with spinifex in the understorey. Unlike most of the country we had walked through, it had been burned – and burned hard. Only the blackened tufts of the spinifex showed where once the plant had flourished. In between the tufts was red desert sand. Late in the afternoon, I took a drink from my water bottle and it was empty; I sucked hot air. The water bottles were always filled at lunchtime and for the first time I had emptied mine.

We trudged along with the long red cliffs of the southern Lewis Range on our left. If I hadn't felt so thirsty and exhausted, I would have marvelled at the change of scenery – cliffs and ranges; finally, a break from the infinite nothingness of the Tanami horizon. I concentrated on just putting one foot in front of the other. The sun radiating off the bare red desert was blinding. At 4.05, when we decided to camp, I was stumbling.

After unloading the camels I sat on a green box and had some magic fruit drink. It didn't help. I felt numb and crook. Andrew got up and started to collect firewood, which was my job. I stood up, but my knees buckled and I sat back down heavily. 'Get up and help, you prick,' a voice said in my head. Again, I struggled to my feet, tried to take a step and sat back down again. 'Get up. Get up,' the voice said, but my body wouldn't comply. There was a rebellion under way, with my body refusing to obey my brain. I finally lurched to my feet, wobbled to my tarp, pulled off my boots and collapsed. I was dimly aware of Andrew lighting the fire and asking, 'Cup of tea?'

'No thanks, mate.' For the first time on the expedition, I passed on the afternoon cup of tea. The short distance from my tarp to the campfire could have been the distance to Sydney – I couldn't have made it. The camels were feeling the heat and all stuck their heads into the scant shade provided by one of the small scrubby trees at the camp. I fell asleep.

The tinkle of camel bells on the quiet, desert air penetrated my stupor. It was cool. Through the fog of sleep, I realised that the sun had set; evening was drawing down. I looked at my watch – an hour had passed. I pulled on my boots and stumbled to the fire. Andrew was tethering the camels for the night, about 50 metres from the camp. The firewood was stacked in neat bundles; small and large kindling, tonight's fire and the breakfast fire. I coaxed flame out of the hot coals using a handful of spinifex, filled a billy and began to boil water for dinner.

'Sorry I didn't help get the firewood. Think I must've got a touch of the sun,' I said sheepishly.

Andrew didn't say anything. He didn't have to. It was another black mark, which I look back on with great regret. Like my failing to lift the green boxes, it was a sign that the partnership between us wasn't an equal one, which I had so hoped it would be. Unfortunately, my fellow traveller never required my assistance or fell down in his duties, so it was hard for me to square the ledger.

The Lewis Ranges Camp marked one of the most difficult days of the expedition; the exhilaration of finally reaching Western Australia crushed by the exasperation of increasing fatigue. It was also the first time in all our years of marriage that my wife and I had spent her birthday apart.

A cool southeaster blew as we left the Lewis Range Camp the following morning. 'You know, even though the temperature got up to 39°C yesterday in the sun, the humidity was only 28 per cent. Imagine what it must be like out here in the summer,' I said to Andrew.

'I can imagine, and it wouldn't be good.'

'Some of the early explorers, like Gregory, did travel in northern Australia during the summer and the wet season. They must've been so tough,' I said. 'I feel like we're walking in the footsteps of giants.'

'Don't forget that they were doing it all the time.'

'Yeah, but look at all the technology we've got: dried food, UV sunglasses, high-tech boots, insect repellent, sophisticated navigational gear, sunscreen, dried fruit for the scurvy, and watertight plastic cans for the water so that it doesn't leak or go off. And with all that I have a day like yesterday, which reminds me of the human element. I take my hat off to them.'

While I'd found it a challenge to successfully operate in business, I realised as we walked away from the Lewis Ranges Camp that nothing is as demanding, challenging or draining as the battle to stay alive in a hostile environment.

People ask me, 'What did you talk about?' 'All manner of things,' I reply – mostly practical, and seldom about ourselves. Nevertheless, it was sometimes difficult. After walking separately for hours in complete silence, we would come together at scroggin or lunchtime and often we were too tired to talk. In addition, after concentrating on a compass for hours on end, day after day, saying nothing, I found it difficult to switch on my brain and start talking. Our unwritten list of banned topics of conversation was a long one, so our exchanges were usually brief, matter-of-fact and unembellished. To many people, they would have seemed unnecessarily stiff and formal, but we found that we could communicate with few words and both of us valued silence.

A typical 11 am scroggin stop in the Lewis Ranges: camels standing roped together in a line, looking around; Kelly ladling scroggin into Harper's cupped hands from a zip-lock bag; both men concentrate intently on this undertaking.

KK: 'That enough?' looking at the pile in Harper's hands.

AH: 'Thanks.'

KK: 'Warm morning.'

AH: 'Sure is.'

KK: 'Breeze is nice. Makes it a lot cooler.'

AH: 'My word.'

KK: 'Camels okay?'

AH: 'Yes, stepping out well.'

KK: 'Good stand of bloodwoods back there.'

AH: 'Too right.'

Sounds of eating. Camels and men motionless, gazing at the horizon.

AH: 'How far this morning?'

KK: 'About thirteen kilometres, maybe fourteen. Want some water?'

AH: 'Thanks.'

Kelly reaches up, takes the water bottle out of its scabbard, and hands it to Harper. Long silence. Harper walks around the camels checking gear, and then replaces his water bottle on the camel saddle.

KK: 'Sang's leg seems to have healed. Amazing.'

AH: 'Yes.'

KK: 'Happy with this course?' Kelly studies a baseplate compass in his right hand.

AH: 'Yes. Let's go, boys. *Ibnah. Ibnah*, boys.'

It was not all serious, however, and when we had the energy, there was often banter and laughter. I had lost a lot of weight; just how much, I wouldn't find out until I arrived back in Sydney. Nevertheless, I knew it was a considerable amount, as I had drawn my belt in four notches and had none left. Even though I was feeling weary, I decided that I had earned the right to give Andrew at least a little stir. His one weakness seemed to be a sweet tooth, and maybe a little personal vanity, so I thought I would poke him in his weak spot with a pointy stick and observe the reaction. As he nibbled his scroggin, savouring each chocolate-coated almond and sultana, I asked: 'Hey, Andrew, have you seen those Austin Powers movies, the ones with Mike Myers?'

'Sure have,' he said.

'You know that big Scottish bloke, Fat Bastard?' One of Myers' characters is a grossly obese Scotsman who thinks he is irresistible to women.

'Yes, he's funny,' Andrew replied.

'Well, you're the spitting image of Fat Bastard. Mate, I hate to say it, but those chocolate almonds have had a terrible effect on you.'

Andrew stopped dead and looked at the small pile of scroggin cupped in his hand. 'What?'

'Yeah, put a kilt on you and you're Fat Bastard. I don't know what your father's going to say when you get back to Deni. He'll say, "That big, fat bloke isn't my son; my son's a skinny fella." He won't know you, mate. Sorry,' I said.

He laughed. '*You* shouldn't talk. You don't mind the chocolate almonds yourself.'

'But, mate, *I'm* fading away. You'll be the first explorer in Australian history to come back from the desert fatter than when he left. Your only hope is to give up the scroggin from here on and let me finish it.'

He thought for a while before replying. 'No, this is a team effort. I have to help out.'

N W—◇—E S

Despite my weariness and the oppressive heat, we really cracked on that day, covering the 29.5 kilometres to Pussycat Bore in six and a half hours, for an average speed of four and a half kilometres an hour. It was the longest day's march of the trip. Broken troughs, tanks and the remains of an upended windmill signalled that we had arrived at the bore. To the north-northeast, the magnificent navigational landmark of Point Nelligan stood out from the Lewis Ranges. We camped among the debris of failed dreams. There would be no water here. Although we had adequate supplies and were rationing it carefully, there wasn't a day we didn't look for water, not an hour that passed that I didn't think of it. We always hoped that one of these bores would be operational.

For a change, I cooked Thai vegetable soup with a tin of corn kernels and pasta. *Very good*, my journal recorded. With a pair of dividers, I worked out that Mt Wilson, Augustus Gregory's furthest point east, was 126.5 kilometres distant. Only five days' walking, but crossing those plains would require all my tenacity. I wrote: *I can hardly put one foot in front of the other. Tomorrow will be a shocker. Long straight course and where will we end up; Lake? No. Shady forest? No. Mountain pass? No. Not really anywhere – just somewhere that looks a lot the same as this.*

I found this part of the journey very hard – hard to keep walking, hard to confront that terrifying red horizon every day, and hard to stay mentally alert and positive. The twenty-kilometre days didn't bother me, but slogs of almost 30 kilometres were hard, especially when we did a couple in a row. I longed for a day off, just a rest – however brief – from walking, but I would rather have cut off a leg than ask Andrew for a break. If Andrew and the camels kept walking, then so would I. The terror of the western Tanami and its wide-open, endless horizon tormented me. Dorothea Mackellar was wrong; it isn't the *wide brown land*, it's the wide *red* land, and these words rolled endlessly through my head as I walked and watched the red desert coat my boots.

Someone, somewhere, had pity on me. I awoke the following morning before daybreak. Sirius, the morning star, fairly blazed in dawn's early light and would soon escort the sun over the horizon. Its appearance heralded the start of summer down south and the oncoming wet season up north. Winter was passing. I looked at it in wonder as I did each morning, and marvelled at how much we city dwellers missed by sleeping inside. As I came fully awake, I realised what had disturbed my sleep. Melodic birdsong was emanating from a bush about a metre behind my head. I lay still, listening to the songbird greeting the dawn. It was the first birdsong I had heard since the start of the desert crossing. The bird's trilling invaded the silence of the solitary camp. Beethoven wrote three birdcalls into his *Pastoral Symphony*, but this Australian bush soloist humbled even *his* music. The ruins of Pussycat Bore and the music that morning emphasised just how puny are man's efforts alongside nature's mighty works. Suddenly the music stopped. I looked around and could see nothing. Silence once again prevailed. It was time to get up.

Mid-morning that day, I stopped and waited for Andrew and the camels. 'We're in Warburton country,' I said, pointing to a blue bump that disturbed the flat horizon, about 25 kilometres to the south. He looked where I was pointing. I'd been expecting to see this landmark at some point in the day's march. 'That's Mt Hughes. Pete Warburton camped there at a waterhole he discovered called Emily Springs.'

The discovery of that waterhole by the desperate explorer represented everything in Australian history I didn't like. On 16 August 1872, Warburton wrote: *We had scarcely travelled five miles to-day before a thick smoke arose close before us. How the blacks let themselves into this trap I don't know; they never would have set fire to the country had they seen us so close. Of course, they paid the penalty for their carelessness, for we soon invaded their camp and took possession of an excellent well.* Gregory's journals are free of this aggression. He was a good-enough bushman to find his own water; he didn't need to steal it from others. I wonder about the fate of the people Warburton chased off that waterhole into the desert. He did this frequently, and I don't number myself as a member of the Warburton fan club.

'After setting up camp at Emily Springs,' I continued, 'Warburton and his son rode up here around the Kearney Ranges looking for Lake Gregory. We'll cross his tracks after lunch.'

'Why'd he come up here?' Andrew asked. 'Lake Gregory's over to the west.'

'His longitude was out by about 80 kilometres. Chronometer might've been wrecked or he might not've had one. Maybe he'd damaged his sextant. He was looking for broken, uplifted country, because that's where Gregory said the lake was. So, from down there,' I pointed to Mt Hughes, 'he must have thought the Kearney Ranges were the lake's location.' We looked towards the outline of the Kearneys on the north-western horizon.

Andrew pondered this, then turned to look north. I showed him the Lucas map, the last in the series that I had laid out on my lounge-room floor all those months ago. Four pencil lines arced out from Mt Hughes, representing Warburton's frantic search for the lake and its water.

'I wouldn't have come up here. I would've gone west from Mt Hughes,' he said. 'It's obvious that the country is breaking to the west. He should've looked there.'

'Well, he was desperate. The camels were beat up and the blokes were beginning to starve by the time they got here. A camel calved just south of Mt Hughes and they'd eaten it before it touched the ground,' I said.

I told Andrew the Warburton story as we walked along. Peter Egerton Warburton was born in 1813 in Cheshire, England. He saw naval experience before serving for 24 years in the Indian Army. In 1853, following his retirement, he arrived in Adelaide with his family.

'See, that's one of the problems with these blokes. Warburton didn't even *arrive* here until he was about 40 years old. Then he was a copper – he was South Australian Police Commissioner for the next fourteen years. That's why he and Stuart couldn't cut it against guys like Gregory, who grew up here.'

In 1872, Sir Thomas Elder chose Warburton to lead an expedition into central Australia to look for grazing land. It would be the first Australian expedition to be equipped wholly with camels – seventeen in total. *No horse could have lived with us. Camels alone can travel over any but boggy ground. Horses alone are useless where there is no feed and little water, but excellent where both are abundant. I, however, have never found any such country,* Warburton's journal records.

Warburton's expedition left Adelaide on 21 September

1872. With the benefit of both Gregory's and Stuart's previous incursions into the area, they headed for Alice Springs, following Stuart's route north. Like us, they paused in Alice, getting organised and hoping for rain. On 15 April 1873, Warburton took his party west, aiming for the coast but, finding no water, decided to strike out for Lake Gregory. Like us, though we came from different directions, he had to battle the Tanami. He had four riding camels, twelve baggage camels and one spare camel. With him were his son Richard; John Lewis, an experienced bushman; Sahleh and Halleem, Afghan cameleers; a cook, Dennis White and Charley, an Aboriginal boy.

On one of the rare occasions of the journey, Andrew and I walked together and talked through that long afternoon. I was conscious once again that this arid expanse of desert had storylines running across it. It was an eerie feeling to be crossing Warburton's tracks going north–south while we headed inexorably west, and yet both Warburton and ourselves were looking for the same thing.

'Why were they in so much trouble by the time they got here?' Andrew asked, looking perplexed. 'They had camels, and they hadn't come all that far from Alice.'

'Because Warburton was a dud,' I replied. Andrew was really taken aback at this and thought about it for a while.

'No, that can't be right. If they left Alice in April and arrived here in August, then his camels should've had plenty of condition. It was the cool time of year. They must've had trouble with the mulga belts north of Alice.'

One of Andrew's engaging qualities is that he would never join me in sticking the slipper into Australia's explorers. He never really bought my criticisms of Stuart, nor would he hear a word against Warburton. As a bushman, he regarded them as kindred spirits despite their failings. I was interested in excellence and compared all of them to Gus Gregory and, to a lesser extent, to James Cook and Matthew Flinders. Just coming into the bush and surviving wasn't enough for me. Similarly,

237

Andrew wouldn't discuss Chris Richards' failed expedition along central Australia's Dingo Fence, saying we didn't have the facts.

'They had a bit of trouble with the mulga and the spinifex,' I said, 'but so have we, and we're making better time on foot than they did riding. His big problem was he kept losing the camels and spent a lot of time looking for them, and he backtracked a lot looking for water.'

Warburton's other problem was lack of planning. 'He only had six months' rations and they'd already been on the go for four months when they got here. He'd hoped to be almost in Perth, and here he was stuck up in the Tanami,' I said. Warburton, like Stuart, had no provisioning contingency, a precaution that even the greenest bushwalker takes today.

We walked along with the camels pacing evenly behind while I talked and we examined the landmarks. 'Warburton brought his son Richard on the ride up here. There were just the two of them. Everyone else was back at Mt Hughes,' I said. As we strode along, I wondered what father and son had talked about. Even today, I wouldn't bring one of my children into a wilderness like the western Tanami.

'Possibly, Warburton wasn't a good manager of camels,' Andrew suggested. 'A lot of them weren't; they brought the Afghan cameleers along and then refused to listen to them.'

'Maybe. He was pushing the camels to do very long distances each day; much longer than us. They probably carried heavier loads, too.' It appears that Warburton's Afghans weren't great managers, either, as they allowed a couple of the animals to just run away. 'Warburton was about 60 years old, which wouldn't have helped,' I added.

✦

Lunch that day on the plains between Pussycat Bore and McGuire Gap is one I will long remember. Lunchtime found us in the middle of a vast saltpan. These depressions in the desert collect the intermittent rainfall which evaporates and leaves behind a residue of pure, white mineral salt. This one was ten kilometres wide.

'Now, *this* is a cheerful place,' I said, laughing. Not a tree or plant higher than my knees could be seen. Underfoot was a crust of dried mud and salt which cracked and broke as we walked on it. Salt-tolerant samphire grass stretched in every direction. The camels relished the plant as we stood deciding what to do.

'Struth! These animals will eat *anything*,' I said.

'They love the fresh samphire grass – must be the salt in it,' Andrew replied. 'We could keep going to the other side of the saltpan, but that may be several hours away and it may be no better.'

I checked the map. The pan wasn't marked.

We hooshed the camels down where they'd stopped walking. A plume of dust and dried salt puffed into the air as each animal flopped down. I dragged the shovel off Morgan's saddle as Andrew topped up the water bottles with a siphon hose from the day's jerrycan. We brought the lunchboxes over and sat them in the salt.

'Mate, sit anywhere you like. At least it's not crowded, I'll say that for it,' I said.

Andrew moved off to take some photographs of our lunch spot on the saltpan. I burst out laughing.

'What's so funny?' he asked.

'Mate, the turnout's buggered. No shade, no firewood, no cup of tea and we're arse-deep in salt.' For some reason our situation struck me as hilarious. Because no trees grow in the saline soil, there was no firewood; hence, no cup of tea. This is precisely the situation I had hoped to avoid with the small fuel stove. The stove, unfortunately, was deceased.

Andrew's photograph, developed months later, shows the camels hooshed down and me making lunch. Around us stretched the reds and yellows of the samphire. The grass looked like gorse or heather from Stuart's country far away. 'It looks like bloody Scotland or the North Yorkshire moors,' I said to Andrew. The photograph is one of my favourites from the trip. It shows the beauty of the Tanami; a savage beauty, but beauty nonetheless. It occurred to me that a few weeks ago this sort of desolation would have frightened me; now I found it funny. Slowly, surely, this desert was seeping into my bones. I was becoming part of it.

We sat and munched on dry biscuits, washed down with water. I licked my finger and stuck it into the salt between my boots. 'Tastes just like table salt,' I said, sticking the finger into my mouth. 'Better not let it go to waste. Might just put it on the tomatoes.' I sprinkled it over the dry biscuits.

Still, it was a desolate scene. The heat roiled along the horizon and the glare was ferocious. I slipped my sunglasses off just to see what it was like. 'Ouch. Not such a good idea,' I thought, as the sun slashed the back of my retina with a hard white light. 'Imagine what it'd be like dying out here with no water,' I said to Andrew. Not taking any chances, I retrieved my water bladder from TC, who was sitting contently in the salt about ten metres away. I rested the precious water at my side against the food boxes. The sun continued to pound down mercilessly.

We finished lunch in record time and moved off – there was no point in sitting there in the open. Whirlwinds, the cockeyed bobs of the desert, blew across our path like mini-tornadoes sucking up dust and dried salt in long columns as they raced across the country. My boots were covered in salt.

'You know, Warburton ended up eating seven of his camels – that's almost half of all the animals he brought with him,' I said to Andrew as we walked into the afternoon. 'He even had a recipe in his journal for how you cook up camels' feet to make 'em edible.'

'How'd he do that?' Andrew asked, shocked.

'Burn 'em in the fire, smash 'em with a tomahawk and then boil 'em for two days,' I replied. I happened to be beside the camels at one stage during the afternoon and looked at their big flat pads as they ambled along. Imagine how hungry you'd have to be to eat a camel's foot, I thought. The *slosh, slosh, slosh* of the water in the jerrycans next to my ear was a comforting sound, our guarantee of survival.

'What about you, Morg? I think I'll stick you in the cooking pot, you old bastard. What d'you think about that?' I asked his lordship that afternoon as I undid his girth, breast-plate and crupper.

Roar, roar, bellow, honk, honk, honk, chew, chew, chew, came the reply. Guess he didn't much care for the idea of being turned into chops. Then again, I didn't much care for the idea of dining out on his very large feet.

Our camp that night was in the shadow of the Kearney Ranges. McGuire Gap, our route though the mountains, was clear in the fading light. That camp, number 29, of 13 August, I called, possibly unfairly, the Not Particularly Anywhere Camp. It would be our last on the Tanami stock route.

That evening, I read Warburton's journal. Nothing much has changed. He called it *a most desolate, burnt country.* Tormented by small black ants, he complained: *We could get no firewood, so altogether had a pretty miserable time of it.* In the coming days, as he marched north and in frustration retreated to Mt Hughes, he described it as *a vile country . . . Not a drop of water!* After a week of fruitless searching he gave up and headed west, concluding correctly that there must be an error in longitude and surmising incorrectly that he was sixteen kilometres east of the lake. It was 80 kilometres distant. Warburton's frustration and despair radiate out of the pages of his journal. His party was placed on short rations of flour soon after. Within weeks, they were starving.

Our trail the following day was over the Kearney Ranges. At sunrise, McGuire Gap was clearly visible. Two hours of brisk walking brought us to the ranges, where we took scroggin at the peak of the gap. The views were enormous. 'Look at that, you can just about see back to the border,' I said, looking at our route of recent days.

'Yes. Warburton would've been able to see that there was no Lake Gregory north of here. Did he come through here?'

'Yes, he was the first white person to come through here.'

'How're you travelling?' Andrew asked. It had been a very hot morning.

'Not bad. I was walking with my mate again this morning. He always shows up on hot days when I'm really tired.'

'What? There was someone else out here? I didn't see anyone. Who was it?'

'Didn't you see him? Bloke with a long beard, good walker; we've had some long chats on this trip, particularly in the last week or so.' I munched on my scroggin, keeping him in suspense. I let the silence hang. I'm sure Andrew didn't have a clue what I was talking about. 'Said his name was Time – Father Time. He often comes out of the scrub and walks with me. I say to him, "Go and talk to Harper," but he said he doesn't want to talk to you, he only wants to talk to me. Been meaning to catch up for a while, apparently.' Andrew seemed to find this very funny.

'Country's been burned hard here. Good for walking,' I said.

'Yes, but there's not much feed for the camels.' The ridges of the Kearneys were bare red stone – not a blade of grass, not a tree, broke the hostile surface. It seemed devoid of life. We moved off, cresting the ridge and crossing the flat plateau on top.

'So, what did you and Father Time talk about?' Andrew asked.

'Turns out he's a Bob Dylan fan, too.' Andrew had mentioned one day that Dylan was his favourite musician.

'Is that so?'

'Yes, you know those words from the Bible, something like "To everything there is a season and a time for every purpose under the heaven". I think it was made into a song by Bob Dylan.'

'You mean "Turn, Turn, Turn",' Andrew replied.

'Yeah, that's the one. Old Father Time thinks it applies to me.'

'How's that?'

'Well, I think my time for doing expeditions is coming to an end and this will probably be the last one. Old Father Time's definitely caught up with me on this trip. I don't think I'll ever be able to walk this far again, and I'd hate to end up being a burden on one of these trips.'

Andrew pondered this for a while. 'By the way, Dylan didn't write that song,' he said. 'It was a female. I think it was that girl out of Peter, Paul & Mary.'

'Well, the Byrds made it a hit, but it was Dylan who wrote it, I'm sure,' I said.

'Don't think so,' he replied.

That's how easily arguments start. The Heyerdahl wisdom was never more apparent. We had spent a lot of time together under trying circumstances without there being a breath of conflict, but instinct told me that a poisonous argument could start over something as trivial as the author of a song. I let the matter drop immediately.

I wondered what Warburton and his son had discussed as they rode through McGuire Gap – not Bob Dylan, obviously.

Bush tucker abounds in the Tanami if you know where to look. After we crossed the border, we found that bush tomatoes grew in abundance in the sandy soil. I plucked handfuls of them as we walked along, looking forward to adding them to our dinner pot. They were about the size of a passion-fruit – green when raw, white when ripe.

'Be careful with those,' Andrew said, when I sliced one open and examined the flesh. 'One of the varieties is really toxic.'

'Do you know how the Aborigines prepared them?' I asked.

'They just ate them when they were ripe, but they knew which were the right ones to eat,' he replied.

I opened one of Andrew's reference books that night. The common bush tomato (*Solanum chippendalei*) is high in vitamin C and an important food resource for local Aborigines. The dog-eye bush tomato, or bony-fruited bush tomato (*Solanum quadriloculatum*), had a red skull and crossbones next to its photo in the book and the word 'toxic' in bold red letters underneath. Both varieties looked pretty much the same to me. Only an expert can tell the different varieties apart, the book warned. Disappointed, as I had collected a decent pile, I chose not to add this bush vegetable to our food supply.

We turned off the Tanami stock route just past McGuire Gap and headed west into trackless, burned country, towards Lake Gregory. Western Australia was throwing up challenges. The ground turned from sand and clay to stone the further west we travelled. Evidence of recent fire was everywhere. Some days we would walk from dawn until dusk finding nothing alive for the camels to graze on. Herbage was often black and charred. Spinifex inhabited the stony ranges but it, too, was burned to stubble. I called camp 30, our first west of McGuire Gap, on Wednesday, 14 August, Burnt Country Camp.

Fatigue was causing me to make mistakes. One day while siphoning water out of the lunchtime jerrycan into Andrew's canteen, I let the plastic siphon tube slide out of the can and the two cupfuls of water in the tube spilled on the ground. We stared at the small puddle evaporating before our eyes. Wasting water in a desert – a mortal sin.

Another day I got the shovel blade tangled in one of the saddle girths while Andrew was tightening it around a camel. It could have been disastrous if the camel had stood up and started to charge about with the long shovel handle swinging wildly about. I wasn't feeling sore, my muscles didn't ache, and my body was obeying instructions from my brain – but I was very tired, almost as if I hadn't slept for several days.

Andrew wasn't immune, either. I was packing gear at the Burnt Country Camp while he was about 400 metres to the south, bringing in the camels from their morning graze. The sun was just coming up. I watched him rope the camels together and then looked away, attending to the camp. When next I looked, he was walking, not towards the camp, but away to the northeast.

Presuming that there must be a gully between us which was preventing him returning directly to the campsite, I wasn't overly concerned. But as I watched him walking further to the northeast, I suddenly became alarmed. Hang on, mate. You'll end up in Darwin if you keep going in that direction, I thought. I was confused as to what he was doing; he appeared to be wandering off. I realised that he'd missed the camp! He was in burned country and I was standing in unburned scrub, the saddles buried in spinifex. The fingers of shadow clinging to the bush in dawn's first light didn't help him. He couldn't see me or the gear, and for the first time on the journey, his sense of direction let him down. I walked quickly towards him, waving my hat. Soon he would be out of the burned country and would disappear into the bush.

'Hey, Andrew!' I sang out and waved my hat. 'Andrew,

mate!' He heard me, stopped and looked. He must have thought the camp was still in front of him, so he ignored me and resumed walking. I yelled again. He stopped, looked around. I continued walking towards him. Standing motionless with the camels, he finally realised his mistake and began walking towards me. When I turned around to retrace my steps, the camp had vanished! Confronting me was a landscape of grey scrub and bare, red and black burned country. Of the camp, there was no sign. That jolt in the guts hit me again. Unlike the walk away from the camp at Mt Leichhardt, there were no towering landmarks here. As I had walked towards the rising sun, I simply turned around and walked on my shadow. This led me unerringly back to camp. It reminded me that for all my carefully planned contingencies, I hadn't considered what we would do if we had the camels but lost the camp with its food and water. Even now, I don't have a ready answer for this eventuality which would have been a grave mistake.

Ahead were some significant obstacles. A long ridge running north–south blocked our path and we debated how best to tackle it. I wanted to go up and over; Andrew preferred to go around. I thought it faded to the north; Andrew wasn't so sure. Our differing opinions started to grind against each other. I had set all the courses so far and Andrew had never contradicted them. However, on the other side of the ridge was probably the most significant obstacle of the whole journey, the Pallotine Headland.

One of the joys for me of exploration and of travelling in the bush is studying topographic maps and visualising how the country will look, and then going out and seeing how close I was to interpreting them correctly. I had studied the 1:250,000 scale maps, which were very short on detail, for countless hours and had let my imagination run riot. I had identified the

Pallotine Headland as a major obstacle, but because of the lack of topographic contour on the maps, it was impossible to work out exactly what sort of a challenge it would present. Its washed-out gullies and plateaus could be impassable for camels.

We crested the ridge just before lunch. Ahead were gnarled cliffs dropping down on to a broad plain. Warburton had sought this high country in vain. Gregory would have crossed the same country if he had continued travelling east into the desert past Mt Wilson. Like Stuart, he was never to discover what lay before him. We had a great advantage as we saw the country that had been denied to them both. Looking down on that arid plain, I now knew that the landscape would have consumed Gregory and all his party, as surely as the eastern Tanami would have destroyed Stuart. Both men made the only sensible decision, it was now clear. Andrew, however, still struggled to exonerate Warburton.

'I don't understand Warburton,' he said, as we considered the view. 'You could tell from back near Mt Hughes that the country rose over here towards the west. I can't believe he made a mistake like that and didn't at least come this way and have a look.'

'We'll never know, but it was a mistake that nearly killed him, so the desert made him pay,' I replied. Our recent experiences had convinced me that deserts are ruthless exploiters of mistakes, inexperience or excessive pride. Gus Gregory had been free of those flaws; Robert O'Hara Burke had possessed them in abundance. The Australian wilderness had dealt with each man accordingly. Burke, with his companion William Wills, died a lonely death from malnutrition beside Cooper's Creek. Only one of his party survived and none of his animals.

As much as we admired the view, we had a problem: somehow we had to get the camels down the cliffs in front of us. To the north was the jump-up or escarpment of the Pallotine Headland, running parallel to our route of march.

'We can't take the camels down there,' Andrew said, looking at the cliff face.

I wasn't so sure. 'What about the spurs running out on to the plain from up here?' I asked, pointing to the long stony ridges that projected from the cliff top on to the plain. 'We could travel down one of those spurs, if we could find one that wasn't too steep.' Descending spurs is the traditional method of taking horses off high country in the southern highlands of Australia. On foot, it would have been an interesting challenge. With horses, it would have been only marginally more difficult – steep, but manageable if care was taken. Andrew wasn't prepared to risk it with the camels.

'No, these animals are far too top-heavy.' He was referring to the camels' packsaddles, which sit on their humps and make the animals unstable when asked to negotiate anything other than flat country. The packs on a horse are carried lower, straddling the animal's rib cage. This lowers its centre of gravity and makes it more sure-footed and stable in steep country.

'If the camels stumble and fall, we've had it. We'll go south and walk around this cliff face,' he said.

I agreed to the detour begrudgingly, as it might add up to 30 kilometres to the journey. We headed south. Luckily, a faint track crossed our path before we had marched more than a few kilometres. It disappeared down one of the spurs. We followed its faint impression and the camels slowly picked their way down the cliff face. Half an hour of this found us out on the plain walking southwest below the towering rampart of the Pallotine Headland. A chance discovery had saved us many extra kilometres. Lunch was taken on the plain, with the Pallotine cliffs dominating the northern horizon. To the south, the rolling red sand dunes of the Great Sandy Desert put in their first appearance.

'You know, it's my wedding anniversary today,' I said. 'When I was walking down the aisle of the Beauty Point Catholic Church in Mosman, I couldn't have imagined that 21 years later

I'd be spending my wedding anniversary with a bloke I don't know all that well and five camels, under a scrubby bloodwood tree in a remote part of the Tanami Desert.'

'You never know where life will lead,' Andrew said.

'True, but I've missed my wife's birthday and our wedding anniversary for the first time in two decades. Big year.'

We had agreed on a westerly course skirting the worst of the deep ravines around the headland. This would take us too far south, which frustrated me; I was keen to head northwest, directly towards Lake Gregory, as soon as the country allowed. Mid-afternoon I judged that the escarpment to the north of us was fading and changed course to the northwest, aiming directly for the lake. Unfortunately, I failed to tell Andrew of my change of plans. Normally, I set the course in the morning and we discussed any changes then. I was tired, and possibly my concentration was failing. I don't know. Late in the afternoon, Andrew pulled me up. 'You've changed course?'

'Yeah, Mt Wilson is northwest of us now, about 36 kilometres, and the escarpment's starting to fade. I think we should set a more direct course.'

'I don't agree. I don't think you're reading the country. The escarpment's still there even though we can't see it. We'll hit it soon on this course. I don't think it's fading, I think it's just changing direction.' He was obviously irritated that I hadn't consulted him.

We were at an impasse. The maps couldn't help, as there wasn't enough detail. Instinct, gut feel and experience were required to read what lay ahead. Andrew was sniffing the wind. We were like two old gunfighters facing each other down on Main Street at high noon. Someone would have to give way.

Shortly afterwards, I was walking a long way ahead scouting the route. Without warning, and just as Andrew had predicted, I hit the edge of the escarpment. I was standing on top of a cliff just like the one we had encountered at lunchtime, only much steeper. Again, it blocked our path. To the northwest, our preferred direction of travel, was a jumble of broken ranges riven by deep gorges. In order to get directly to Mt Wilson and Lake Gregory, we would somehow have to get the camels down off this escarpment.

Andrew was also worried during the afternoon about the animals. We hadn't seen a forage tree for nearly two days and I could see him looking around desperately for somewhere to tie the camels for the night. The lack of camel feed was weighing him down. Even I could tell that the animals were getting hungry. I walked back towards the group.

'You're right,' I told him. 'There's a big cliff about a kilometre ahead.' He didn't say anything.

We camped under two lonely gums below the escarpment. My journal recorded it as the Anniversary Camp. *Cooked honey soy chicken – last two packets of it. Put last of apricots and dried peas in mixture. Cooked pasta as we had plenty of that left, however, sun dried tomatoes, dried bread, Prue's soup and sultanas are all gone.* The beef jerky was also finished, so we were getting down to the basics, but our supplies of rice, pasta and dried meals were more than ample to finish the trip.

About 665 kilometres were behind us; only 38 kilometres now separated us from Mt Wilson, but it seemed an impossible distance.

In the pre-dawn, I lay in my swag collecting my thoughts. Something was different. I thought about it for awhile. No camel bells – the camels hadn't yet been untied. I hadn't heard Andrew go past. The sound of his boots pounding by on his way to untie the animals in dawn's first light was usually my alarm clock. I pulled on my boots, laced them and grabbed my sticky shirt. By now, I ran my personal camp just the way Andrew did. Gear bag on one side of the tarp, boots and journal near my head, torch next to my boots and hat, map-case, compass and utility belt arranged along the top edge of the tarp. Clothes were hung over a saddle to dry. Even though it wasn't light, I knew exactly where everything was. I raced to the fireplace. Last night's fire was cold ashes under a mound of sand. I looked for Andrew; I could see the camels still tethered about 50 metres away. In the pre-dawn gloom, Andrew was a barely discernible lump, still in his swag at the other end of the camp.

Hope nothing's wrong, I thought. A sudden irrational fear ran through me that he had died in his sleep. Normally, his swag would be rolled neatly on his tarp and he would be tending the camels while I passed by on my way to light the morning fire. Not this morning. He didn't stir. I quickly had the fire going and filled the two billies. Maybe I'm not the only one who's getting tired, I thought. But you'd never know it; he never shows it. At least he's human.

At the clash of the billies, Andrew sat upright and in less time than it took me to blink had his swag rolled and was away, untying the camels. Mate, I'd cook you some bacon and eggs if we had any – you certainly deserve it, I thought.

Fatigue was affecting the animals, too. All the camels had lost weight, evident in the hump shrinkage that had occurred since Mt Esther. A camel's hump is an energy tank where reserves of fat are stored. Char, the smallest and youngest of the camels, had practically no hump left and it became difficult to keep the saddle on him. He was beginning to resemble a horse. Old TC, our lead camel, had also lost a lot of weight and, after being unloaded in the evenings, would often sit for a while and just stare at the sunset while his mates ambled out of the camp. He would moan quietly, sometimes not much more than a whisper. It was a mournful sound.

'Bit tired, mate?' Andrew would give him a friendly pat after we had finished stripping him of gear. 'He's getting towards the end of his career, this fellow. I'll gradually start putting lighter and lighter loads on him in the next couple of seasons. Then he'll be retired.'

During breakfast as we stood silently eating porridge and watching the sun rise, a pair of white corellas greeted the dawn with a noisy screech. These birds are a symbol of life in the far north and teem along the rivers and billabongs, wherever there is water. 'Hello, maybe there *is* water in Lake Gregory?' I said to Andrew.

'Yes, we're only 40 kilometres from the lake as the crow flies, so you might expect to start seeing some bird life soon,' he replied. The corellas' racket was a change from the silence that had prevailed for most of the journey.

We headed to the top of the escarpment for a look as soon as the camels were loaded. I hoped to see Mt Wilson and journey's end from the cliff top. We were greeted with an enormous panorama of valleys and broken country, with a flat plain at the bottom, much of it still cloaked in shadow. It was similar to the view from the ridge the previous day.

'Well, we can't take the camels down there,' Andrew said.

'What about having a look for a spur? We might be able to pick our way down to the bottom, like we did yesterday.'

'No. If we get caught in one of those gullies, we may never get out.' He looked to the south. 'We can't go north, over the headland, so we'll go south, around all this,' he said, sweeping his hand around the plain, hundreds of metres below us.

My heart sank. Our two ideologies clashed. I thought like a bushwalker. If I was alone on that ridge and wanted to go to Mt Wilson, I would draw a straight line on the map and start walking. The worse the country, the better; I'm always drawn to ranges, canyons and rugged places.

Andrew took a more considered view. He thought of his camels first. He looked at the country, considered the difficulties, factored in his camels' capabilities and came up with a decision that accommodated them. He never thought about his own requirements or his own fatigue, even if it added extra distance to the journey. His animals came first.

'We go south, right around this stuff,' he insisted.

'That's a big detour, mate. A long way out of our way. Mt Wilson's northwest of us.'

'No choice. We can't take the camels down there,' he said again.

We were at another impasse. I was grumbling to myself: Jesus Christ, why won't Andrew have a go at the country? Chance his arm a bit? He's so bloody conservative – never takes a risk. I stepped from one foot to the other in frustration. 'There *must* be a way. There's a way down every spur I've ever seen.' I was still fixed on the idea that we were in a brawl with the desert and I hated to back off, to give it a victory. I thought we should tackle it head-on. 'Why don't we have a go?' I said, but Andrew was unshakeable. Someone had to give ground. In 'The Gambler', Kenny Rogers sings about playing poker and advises how important it is to know when to hold your cards and when to fold 'em and walk away.

I looked north, then along the cliff face for any welcoming spur that we could get the camels down. I'm sure I could get horses down here, I thought . . . *know when to hold 'em.* Andrew looked at me; I looked at him. We stood staring at each other on a cliff top in the middle of the Tanami. Someone had to give in . . . *know when to fold 'em.* I folded. We headed south.

Explorers and bushwalkers know well the frustration of walking *away* from your destination at the end of a long journey. We were walking south – our destination was northwest. We were walking in almost the opposite direction to where we wanted to go. Gee, Andrew's a stubborn bugger! I grouched to myself as we walked along. The irony of me wanting to risk the camels, while Andrew wanted to take the more conservative route, was lost on me at the time. Hadn't I criticised Stuart for being too much of a punter? Hadn't I criticised Stuart for not reading the country? Now, I wanted to have a punt; I was playing John Stuart to Andrew's Gus Gregory. It emphasised the differences between us – I'm interested in the battle, and he's interested in the outcome, and that's probably what makes him such a good bushman.

On reflection, the Pallotine Headland showed the wisdom of combining Andrew's detailed knowledge of camels with my willingness to give him the final say. Unlike me, he didn't consider our expedition as a form of mortal combat with the landscape. Unlike me, he had the ability to think like a camel, having a deep understanding of their capabilities and short-comings. While I grumbled to myself, not for a moment did I seriously consider contesting Andrew's judgment. And while I grumbled, I kept it to myself and didn't sulk. One of the great strengths of our expedition was that neither of us lost our temper when things didn't go our way. Despite differences in our age and upbringing, we managed to communicate and resolve what was best for the expedition.

By scroggin time, we'd walked out to the fringe of the Great Sandy Desert, south of the broken country. We were further from Mt Wilson then than when we'd camped the previous night. The huge loop meant that we would pass a long way south of the Gunawarrawarra Rockhole, which I'd hoped to visit. Maps couldn't help us now – there wasn't enough detail to decide whether we could or couldn't descend that cliff face. We would have been as well served to throw the maps away. It was all down to skill and experience now.

Our campsite that night was a Tanami special. No shade, no grass, no trees – not even any spinifex. I was getting concerned for the camels. As on many recent nights, they would have slim pickings. We had looked all afternoon for forage trees without success. The place looked like the end of the earth. 'Hey, Andrew. Have you heard of that book *The Restaurant at the End of the Universe*?' I asked as we unloaded.

'Yes, I've read it.'

'Well, this is the carpark,' I replied.

I called the campsite Camp Frustration. Why? We had trav-elled twenty kilometres that day for a net gain on the ground of only fifteen kilometres, and at sunset I still couldn't see

Mt Wilson, even though by my reckoning it was only eleven kilometres away. We had walked 685 kilometres; the remaining distance seemed infinitesimal, yet we couldn't bridge it.

'Robert Scott of the Antarctic was only about this far from base camp when he died. I know how he felt,' I said to Andrew.

'He probably felt a bit colder than this,' he replied. A huge fire was setting the southeastern horizon aglow as I turned in. The fire front may have been 100 kilometres long; a spectacular scene. I went to bed that night knowing that by the next time I rolled out of my swag, I would have climbed Mt Wilson.

I'll never forget walking those last kilometres to Mt Wilson. As we loaded the camels, I said, 'You know, by the end of today we'll have connected Stuart's journey with Gregory's journey right across the centre of Australia. That's quite something, when you think about it.'

'Well, we're not there yet,' Andrew replied. 'We've got to get off this plateau and down on to that plain so that we can start walking north.'

Warburton had been looking for a lake buried high on a plateau. We had walked along the edge of the plateau in recent days. Now we needed to find the lake. Would there be another impassable cliff face in front of us? The map gave no answers.

In less than two hours we had an answer – a gentle incline led down the escarpment. It was no trouble for the camels, and the country changed dramatically. We had found the country that had eluded Warburton. Gone was the blocking headland to the north; instead, flat-topped hills were scattered at random around a wide stony plain. To the south, the rolling sand ridges of the Great Sandy Desert were starkly in evidence.

I scurried up a ridge to check the views. All my fatigue

was gone. I felt as I did on the first day of the journey. It was a spectacular scene. After having looked at grey scrub for weeks, the stony red ramparts and flat-topped mesas were a revelation. To the west, a long, strikingly blue line of mirage blended sky and desert. I looked hard at the mirage. Surely that's not Lake Gregory, I thought. The thin blue line ran from the south as far to the north as I could see. Surely the lake's not full of water? Of Mt Wilson, there was no sign. I had expected to see it stark on the lakeshore. Instead, dozens of flat-topped hills fitting Gregory's description studded the landscape. Careful navigation would be needed to ensure that we climbed the right mountain.

I bet if we started walking towards that blue line, it would fade away, I thought as I walked off the ridge and made my way towards Andrew and the camels.

'See Mt Wilson?' Andrew asked, when I reached him.

'No, it must be behind some of those other hills further north. Remember, it's only about 30 metres high, according to Gregory, so we won't see it until we get quite close to it.' I didn't mention the mirage.

We started walking. Soon I was holding the camels while Andrew took a turn to climb a ridge. I felt a gentle tug on the brim of my hat, then it was whisked away. I turned to see my Akubra dangling from TC's lips as the big camel looked at me with an expression that seemed to say, 'Hat? *What* hat? No, sorry, I haven't seen your hat.' And that was about as close as I came to being savaged by a camel during the entire journey.

'See the lake over there?' Andrew's voice drifted down from the ridge top and I saw him pointing west. 'Looks great, doesn't it?' he shouted.

So, it *was* Lake Gregory and it was full of water. It was enormous; it must have been many times larger than Sydney Harbour. Gone was the fatigue. Gone was the loneliness. Gone were all the doubts about whether we would ever get to see this sight. I had never walked with such eagerness as I did that day – even the camels sensed it. The sound of boots crunching on stone was music to my ears. Each small ridge climbed gave a new vista. Each held a promise of a small flat-topped mountain – Gregory's Mt Wilson – our journey's end.

Never beaten, the desert played it hard with me right to the finish. I was looking at Gregory's map of the area and comparing it to the coordinates noted in my field book. The compass sat on the book, which was in my right hand. There were numerous hills dotted about the landscape and I was concentrating furiously, determined to find the right peak. Andrew and the camels were about 50 metres behind me. I walked along looking at the surrounding hills, rather than at the ground. Suddenly, my right boot landed on top of a spinifex tuft and slid off, turning sideways, before ending up in a crack in the rocky surface: my right foot was turned so that it faced my left instep. I felt myself falling. My ankle locked solid, began to bend, the knee to twist.

'Just relax, don't fight it. Fall and roll. Keep the weight off your ankle,' a voice in my head said. 'Don't break the compass.' It all happened in slow motion. As I fell, I realised that I was going to land in a large clump of spinifex. I couldn't use my right hand, which held the compass, so I took all the impact on my right forearm. The spinifex spines lanced into the soft underside of my arm as I landed with a crashing thud. I lay sprawled on my back in the spiny plant. 'Bloody terrific. Break my ankle on the last day,' I thought, as I lay there.

Andrew reached me with the camels. He was laughing hysterically. TC peered down at me over Andrew's shoulder, curious to see what I was doing.

'That's the funniest thing I've ever seen! One minute you were there, the next you were gone. It was like you'd fallen down a big hole. Gee, that was funny!'

'Ha ha,' I said, as I slowly got to my feet, gingerly putting weight on my ankle. It was sore but not sprained or, worse, broken. I was lucky. I pulled spinifex spines out of my arm. Several dozen had gone in and broken off – the deep ones showed as red punctures.

Spinifex comes in many varieties. In the sandy country of the Northern Territory, we often encountered feathertop spinifex (*Plectrachne schinzii*). Its wavy tufts gave the appearance of walking through fields of wheat, but disguised the spiny misery beneath. We also encountered clumps of soft spinifex (*Triodia pungens*), some up to two metres high. This spinifex merged to form the bristling battlements that I hated and I often pondered the strange sense of humour of the person who named it.

In the bare, rocky desert of Western Australia, we met porcupine spinifex (*Triodia irritans*), discrete clumps of needle-sharp plants resembling thorny beer barrels. Luckily, they were easy to walk around, but were murder if you happened to stumble into one. But it was hard spinifex (*Triodia basedowii*) into which I had pitched myself. These plants die in the middle, leaving an outer halo of bristly, spiky grief. 'Evil doughnuts', I call them.

'Now, *that* would get the media's interest. "Sydney explorer disappears on last day of expedition." The *Herald* would love that,' Andrew said.

'Yeah, good. Well, I'm still here.' I was laughing now. I felt like such a goose. How things had changed. As a teenager, the thought of being laughed at had been unbearable. Blows would have been exchanged. Even at the start of this trip, as I chafed under Andrew's directions, I couldn't have accepted his laughter at my expense. Now, we had endured too much together for me to take offence. Besides, he seemed to be laughing *with* me and not *at* my misfortune. Anyway, I thought it was funny, too.

We pushed on. The scenery was magnificent, the photo opportunities endless and our speed slow, due to the constant stops to enjoy the views. Our stops for water breaks were now very enjoyable excuses to contemplate the landscape and share our sense of wonder.

'Will it be fresh?' I asked, looking towards the lake.

'Probably not. Most of them aren't. But this one's got so much water in it, we may be lucky. After a very good season, when the lakes are full, you'll often find the water is fresh, but it becomes really salty as the lake dries up.'

'Guess we'll soon find out,' I said.

At lunch we were less than two kilometres from Mt Wilson, but still it was hidden. Lunch was now a meagre affair. The dried tomatoes and beef jerky were finished. Biscuits, cheese, Vegemite and jam sustained us.

Half an hour after lunch, I crossed a small ridge and suddenly there it was – looming ahead of me, across a gully, was our destination. The easternmost point of Augustus Charles Gregory's drive into the Tanami Desert was a barren, red, rocky hill – flat on top, blasted by sun and erosion, magnificent in its isolation. At 2.45 pm on Saturday, 17 August 2002, we stood under the brow of the mountain, two men and five camels. After walking for 33 days, we had linked Gregory's expedition with that of Stuart. We had arrived.

CHAPTER 10

Gus Gregory and the inland sea

Our tracks had crossed those of three seasoned explorers, John Stuart, Mike Terry and Pete Warburton. All were raised in Britain and came to Australia as grown men. None had professional training in navigation, surveying or the sciences. Brave, resourceful men, they each made a contribution to our understanding of the Australian interior and each survived its rigours. Towering above all of them, however, is a leviathan figure of exploration. We were now entering the country that made him famous.

The Duke of Newcastle, Secretary of State for the Colonies and one of the most powerful men in the British Empire, began planning in the early 1850s a grand expedition to unlock the secrets of northern Australia's geography. Many hats were thrown in the ring to command the prestigious undertaking. It was the largest and most expensive land exploration ever planned by the empire. At its core, this expedition, if successful, could link the settled areas of southern Australia with the big Indian market. It was also hoped, finally, to settle the vexatious question of whether an inland sea occupied the

Australian centre. Wealth and acclaim would certainly attend the commander of such an expedition. The leading lights of the day pressed their claims. Major Thomas Mitchell, Captain Charles Sturt and Lieutenant Edward John Eyre had their hands up. These were the most distinguished explorers of Newcastle's generation – military men who were lionised in British society. However, Newcastle had heard a whisper from Swan River about a brilliant Australian surveyor, aged in his mid-thirties, who was revolutionising the way inland exploration was undertaken.

This unheralded Australian, when not long out of his teens, had led two pioneering expeditions into the desert wastes around the Swan River colony – the area known today as Perth. In 1854, Newcastle gave the young surveyor his shot at a place in the record books by appointing him commander of the North Australian Exploration Expedition. Newcastle had looked past his celebrated English colleagues and given the job to an Australian, a young colonial with a colonial's experience of the bush. The surveyor's name was Augustus Charles Gregory.

Gus Gregory had arrived with his parents and four brothers in the fledgling Swan River colony in 1829. He was ten years old. Raised on a farm hacked from the scrub, he was by his late teens a seasoned bushman, happy with the heat and waterless wastes of his new home. He was an expert horseman, a good navigator and familiar with indigenous Australians. Schooled by his mother in the European traditions of the Enlightenment, he showed a great flair for mathematics and was accepted into the ranks of the colony's busy survey department, under John Septimus Roe, Phillip Parker King's able assistant and a product of the Enlightenment traditions which produced Captain James Cook. From Roe, Gregory learned surveying, astronomy, cartography and celestial navigation. He was probably the best-educated land explorer ever to take the field in Australia.

He soon demonstrated that he was a naturally gifted explorer. In his early twenties Gregory led the first major expedition into the Western Australian interior. The Irwin River Expedition of 1846 was extraordinary at the time. Covering 1533 kilometres in 47 days at an average speed of 33 kilometres per day, through some of the worst deserts in the world, Gregory didn't lose a man or a horse, never got lost, and mapped all the major features on his route in the positions we know today.

Several years later, he followed that feat with the Settler's Expedition up the Western Australian coast into similarly waterless terrain. Carefully planned and brilliantly executed, this expedition covered 2500 kilometres in ten weeks, averaging 36 kilometres a day. This was the equivalent of riding a horse from Sydney to Mt Isa, a distance beyond the comprehension of explorers on the east coast of Australia only 30 years earlier.

Showing great skills in the modern sciences of planning, logistics and management, Gregory assembled his team in Sydney in early 1855 before sailing for the Victoria River on the remote northwest shore of Western Australia. He had to overcome all the problems of transporting animals and men in two windjammers with only rough charts. His difficulties were compounded by the drunkenness of the ships' commander. Despite a near shipwreck and shortages of water on the high seas, by November 1855, Gregory had successfully established a camp on the Victoria River, near Timber Creek in today's Northern Territory. In spite of the difficulties of the Top End wet season, he was ready to attempt something never tried before – the exploration of the interior of Australia from a base camp on its northern coast.

Gregory brought many innovations to Australian exploration. Two, in particular, are noteworthy. During the voyage up the Queensland coast, he summoned the senior members of his party together. These included the botanist, Ferdinand Mueller, the artist, Thomas Baines, and the geologist, James Spottiswood

Wilson. As expected, these men were appointed the officers of the party. Gregory's brother, Henry, a superb bushman and seasoned explorer, was appointed second in command. But to the dismay of some – Wilson, in particular – Gregory announced that his officers would have no special privileges. Like the men, they would be assigned horses to load and tend, and would have to share the camp duties. This was revolutionary. Until then, the English explorers who had graced Australia's shores had brought their country's class system with them, so that often the officers had the tents while the men slept exposed to the elements. Sometimes, the officers rode, while the men walked. Sometimes, officers and men sat at different fires. Gregory reflected the temperament of his country and, recognising that its harsh environment was a great leveller, introduced egalitarianism into Australian exploration. It has since become a cornerstone of our culture.

Gregory not only changed the method of exploration, he also changed the manner. Previously, exploration had been a slow, ponderous affair. In the early days, the explorers didn't even have horses to ride and proceeded on foot. When horses became available, they were teamed with bullock wagons, which hauled heavy and often superfluous equipment, such as tables and whaleboats, through the wilderness. In black-soil country after rain, these wagons would bog to the axletrees and a week might be spent to gain a few kilometres. In dense scrub or rocky country, they were often abandoned. Other gear, especially riding saddles and packsaddles, was often inappropriate for the heat and long distances encountered in Australia. The privations suffered by horses in the outback meant that saddles that fitted at the start of the trip never fitted at the end and ruined many animals' backs. Gregory changed all this. He invented light, rapid-transit exploration based on pack horses. Rejecting all heavy and unnecessary equipment, he redesigned the clumsy English packsaddle so that it could carry more weight, 'breathe' in the extreme heat

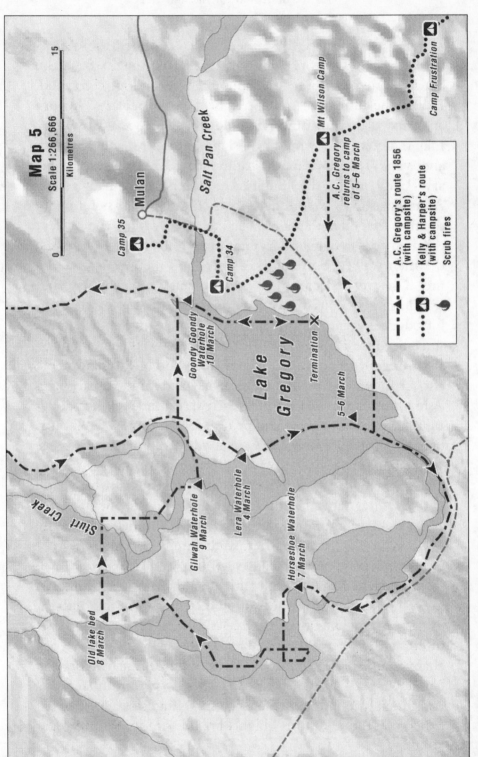

Map 5

Scale 1:266,666

Kilometres

0   15

Mulan

Camp 35

Salt Pan Creek

Camp 34

Mt Wilson Camp

A.C. Gregory returns to camp of 5–6 March

Camp Frustration

A.C. Gregory's route 1856 (with campsite)

Kelly & Harper's route (with campsite)

Scrub fires

Sturt Creek

Goondy Goondy Waterhole 10 March

Lake Gregory

Old lake bed 8 March

Gilwah Waterhole 9 March

Lera Waterhole 4 March

Termination X

5–6 March

Horseshoe Waterhole 7 March

and be adjustable as the horse's weight fell. It became known as the Gregory Pattern packsaddle and the design is unchanged to this day. He also invented a new form of compass useful in dense scrub, and experimented with ways of baking meat and flour into biscuits to preserve the nutritional value.

Because of his rapid transit method, Gregory passed quickly across Aboriginal land, often departing before his presence had time to become an irritation. Given the distances he travelled and the remote regions he explored, his lack of conflict with indigenous Australians sets him apart from many of his peers.

In January 1856, Gregory left his Victoria River principal camp and headed south. His expedition was as different from Stuart's as is possible to imagine. While both Gregory and Stuart were born leaders of men, the comparisons of exploring technique end there. With Augustus Gregory, a professional surveyor and seasoned explorer, went his equally experienced brother, Henry, as second in command. He also took with him three hardened bushmen, Robert Bowman, John Fahey and George Phibbs; the specialist harness maker and farrier, Charles Dean; as well as the expedition supernumeraries artist, Thomas Baines; botanist, Ferdinand Mueller; and the collector, James Flood – in all, a party of nine men.

If Stuart brought a 'no worries', amateurish enthusiasm to exploration, which has endeared him to Australians, Gregory brought a 'leave no stone unturned', clinical professionalism, as shown in his provisioning. He packed five months' supplies on his pack horses, including: flour, 1470 lb; pork, 1200 lb; rice, 200 lb; sago, 44 lb; sugar, 280 lb; coffee, 28 lb; tobacco, 21 lb; and soap, 51 lb. He had a total of 3330 pounds (1500 kilograms) of food – 1.1 kilograms of food per day per man. By a strange coincidence, this was the exact same amount that Andrew and I allowed on our trip.

Possibly most importantly, Gregory took 27 pack horses, six riding horses and three tag-along horses. If Stuart's expedition was doomed to fail before it left, Gregory gave his every chance of success.

Probing into the interior, he formed a forward base camp on a permanent waterhole on Depot Creek, near today's Mt Sanford cattle station. Leaving a detachment of horses and men under the command of Thomas Baines, he continued south with a highly mobile, lightly provisioned party, which included his brother, Henry, and the botanist, Mueller.

A week's ride brought them to the source of the Victoria River in hills on the edge of a fearsome desert. In words that I could have written 146 years later, Gregory said of the desert which he had just discovered: *A vast and slightly undulating plain extended to the horizon, with scarcely a rising ground to relieve its extreme monotony . . . The country became a perfect desert of red sand, with scattered tufts of triodia* [spinifex] *and a few bushes of eucalypti and acacia.* And so, on 7 February 1856, a white Australian gazed for the first time on the northern Tanami Desert and stimulated all that was to follow.

Undaunted by his first look at Australia's central desert, Gregory headed west, skirting the top edge of the Tanami. Reaching Western Australia, he found a creek, which he named the Sturt, and followed it south for a month, eventually arriving at the large salt lake that today bears his name. However, no balm greeted the weary traveller, no sound of waterbirds enriched his morning, and no blue line on the horizon signalled water. The lake was dry. I know how he must have felt. On 4 March he wrote, while riding down the dry bed of the lake: *The country passed was of a worthless character, and so much impregnated with salt that the surface of the ground is often covered with a thin crust of salt.* The following day he climbed Mt Wilson, a small hill to the east of the lake, naming it after his troublesome geologist who had been left behind at the Victoria River Camp. The lake itself he didn't honour with a name. His chart records simply: *Dry bed of Salt lake 900 feet above the sea.*

My feelings as we scrambled up the last few metres of rough hillside are difficult now to describe. I felt that a part of Australian history had come alive. The terrain was flat and rocky on top, with not a stitch of vegetation. I was breathless with excitement, and speechless with wonder. The views defied description. The lake, a sparkling blue sheet of water about fourteen kilometres distant, dominated the western horizon. Everywhere else was desert – bare, red, stony desert. It was so different from the country between the Lander and the Granites that it was difficult to believe we were still in the Tanami. We could see our camels tethered about a kilometre away in a stand of bloodwoods by a gully coming out of the hills. We said nothing for the first few minutes, and just stood looking at the view, gobsmacked.

'Well, this is it, mate,' I said, finally breaking the silence. 'This is where it was proven that there isn't an inland sea in Australia. This is as far as Gregory got before he turned back.'

'Reckon anyone's climbed up here since?' Andrew asked.

'Probably not. Impossible to know,' I replied.

We took many photographs. I spread Gregory's maps and sketchbooks out on the rocks and checked his compass bearings. I read aloud the entry from his journal, written on top of the mountain in 1856, while Andrew filmed.

> *5th March . . . As some low rocky hills were visible to the east we steered for them. At 2.10 halted half-a-mile from*

the hills, and then ascended them on foot. They were very
barren and rocky, scarcely eighty feet [twenty metres]
above the plain, formed of sandstone, the strata horizontal.
From the summit of the hill nothing was visible but one
unbounded waste of sandy ridges and low rocky hillocks,
which lay to the south-east of the hill. All was one
impenetrable desert, as the flat and sandy surface, which
could absorb the waters of the creek, was not likely to
originate watercourses. Descending the hill, which I named
Mount Wilson, after the geologist attached to the
expedition, we returned towards the creek at the south end
of the lake, reaching it at 9.30.

I pointed to each of the features Gregory had named. The low, rocky hillocks to the southeast were the hills that Andrew and I had walked through that morning. 'He was right in calling the country an impenetrable desert. That country we came through couldn't be crossed with horses,' Andrew said. 'He was a good reader of country. The only reason we got through was because we had camels.'

'You know, the amazing thing is that it hasn't changed one bit,' I said. 'We can come out here and see it looking just the same as it did when Gregory climbed up here.'

We buried a plaque recording our Tanami journey under a pile of stones.

'Well, was it worth it?' I asked Andrew.

He thought about it for a while. 'I guess I have to say yes,' he laughed.

'You *sure* do,' I said. We sat quietly marvelling at the view.

'Just imagine,' I said. 'Gregory, Stuart and all the others were paid to come out here and explore. Now, a century and a half later, we're doing it for nothing. In fact, we're prepared to *pay* to have the same experience they did.'

'Shows you how much life has changed. Would you have liked to live back then?'

'Too right, mate!' I replied. 'They had such exciting lives! New worlds to explore, mentally challenging stuff to do, all the science they had to know, the navigation, botany and geology. I know so little of that stuff.'

'Parts of it must have been tough, though.'

'Sure, parts of today's life are tough, too. But those guys were paid to do something that was dangerous *and* exciting *and* mentally stimulating. How good is *that*? And look at the environment they did it in,' I said, sweeping my hand around the views. 'Beats sitting in the traffic on a wet Monday morning. This trip's answered the question for me about why they made one expedition after another.'

'So, what about you?' Andrew asked. 'I suppose I don't have to ask if you thought it was worthwhile.'

'Mate, walking 700 kilometres off the clock, seeing all this new country, sitting here reading this journal where it was written, and looking at all the maps and sketchbooks Gregory drew here – life doesn't get any better for me.' We lapsed into silence again.

'This is special. No monuments or anything man-made, just a mountain and a lake with a wealth of history. You wouldn't see anything like this place anywhere else in the world,' I said. 'So, yes, even though we didn't get paid for doing it, I still think it was really worthwhile.'

I thought of the lines across the landscape. We could trace from Gregory's sketchbooks his route from the lake to Mt Wilson. It wouldn't have surprised me to see, through the shimmering heat haze, a group of bearded men burned black from months of tropical sun, driving pack horses across that plain towards us. We traced Gregory's journey down the eastern side of the lake, and his retreat north to Sturt Creek.

'Tough trip out here on horses,' I said. 'Gee, he must have been a good horseman.'

'Yes,' Andrew replied.

'Especially when you consider it was bone dry when

Gregory was here. He rode right down the middle of the lake; it was just a giant saltpan then. Two of his campsites out there,' I said, indicating the lake, 'are underwater at the moment. It's amazing what a couple of good seasons can do, isn't it?'

'Yes, it may have completely changed his impression of the area if he'd found the lake full like this,' Andrew said. 'He might have ridden further out into the desert, or he might have recorded the country as being magnificent grazing land with plenty of water.'

'We'll never know,' I said. We sat looking at the view. I was greatly relieved to stop walking, if only briefly. To sit and just stare at the view, with no camels to attend to, meal to cook or journals to update, was a tremendous luxury. This was one of the few times that Andrew and I had sat down and just talked.

'You know, Gregory's journey from here back to Brisbane was amazing,' I said. 'They rode back to the Victoria River depot, across Arnhem Land and the Gulf country, then down the Great Dividing Range in Queensland to Brisbane – about 4000 kilometres in nine months. Even if he did nothing else, getting all those horses and men back to Brisbane from here is a bloody remarkable Australian story.'

'It's a long way on horseback,' Andrew agreed.

'Mate, it's a long way in a car. Makes me tired just thinking about it,' I said. 'And he didn't lose a man, no one even got sick – incredible story, really.' This time we were in complete agreement. We sat and watched the sun sink slowly into the lake; it was one of the most peaceful, contented afternoons of my life.

'Well, there's a project for you. You should try to get the Gregory story better known,' Andrew suggested.

As we prepared to leave Mt Wilson, a feeling of melancholy settled over me. Maybe it related to the ages of the players in this story. Gregory, when he stood on that mountain, was 36. Andrew was only slightly older at 38, and Stuart had been 44 when he reached his furthest point west. I was relatively senior at 49. I spared a thought for Warburton, who was about 60 when he undertook his desperate search for the lake. I had a feeling that I wouldn't see this country again. 'You know, in years to come when we're a pair of cranky old bastards, we should come back here, dig up the plaque and check out the view,' I said.

'But you're already a cranky old bastard,' Andrew replied.

'No, seriously. When we've both got grandchildren, we should load 'em in a four-wheel drive and bring 'em out here camping. Walk them up this mountain and show them the history. Tell them about the explorers and show them the sketch-books and maps and stuff, and talk about what we did when we were young.'

'Well, if we're bringing grandchildren here, I'd better get home and get busy. I haven't even got to the children stage yet,' he said.

We walked off the mountain as the dying rays of the sun played over the lake and turned the surrounding hills a riot of red and orange. I felt a tremendous sense of achievement in what we had done. The fact that we had come in on foot, with no one to help us and no vehicle support, added to my satisfaction.

The gulf between explorers like Gus Gregory and Pete Warburton is demonstrated in their cartography. Gregory arrived at the salt lake that now bears his name, with a defective chronometer. Moisture had snapped the winding chain of his Arnold timekeeper and he had to strip it in the field for repair, in itself a remarkable achievement. Without knowing Greenwich time, correctly placing the lake's longitude on his chart would have been difficult, if not impossible. Nevertheless, he did it. His camp of 4 March 1856, on the western shore of the lake, is marked at longitude 127° 30'. It's actually longitude 127° 25' – he was out by only five minutes of longitude. His positioning of the lake is therefore eight kilometres too far east – about two hours' walk – an extraordinary performance with a sextant and faulty chronometer. I tried to match his achievement with my own sextant on the lakeshore the following night and couldn't. I didn't have the right stars in the early evening and was too tired to wait up. Despite having accurate charts showing the lake's position and Gregory's detailed description, the closest that Warburton got was about 80 kilometres to the east. This error represents about three to four days' walk with camels – an eternity in the desert.

Gregory's exploration is for those who enjoy watching Tiger Woods hit a golf ball, or Tony Lockett snatch a flying mark, or who delight in hearing Daniel Barenboim play Chopin. It's for those who are interested in the pursuit of excellence, where pleasure comes from knowing that no human being can do it better. He is the yardstick against which all Australian exploration must be measured.

That night around our campfire, in the shadow of Mt Wilson, the pressure was off and we yarned for quite awhile. I agreed with Andrew that we had succeeded where Gregory and Stuart had failed, only because we had camels and they had horses. A camel's ability to carry weight and go without water amazed me. To see an animal survive in a desert with absolutely no grass was a revelation. Despite all their bad publicity and my initial fears, they didn't stink, didn't bite, didn't kick and didn't spit – well, not very often. Overwhelming at first, they proved to be obedient and easy to load and lead. That they required no shoeing was an absolute bonus.

Andrew and I were fortunate to have visited the places where both Gregory and Stuart had turned back and to see the conditions that had prompted those decisions. The men and horses of both their expeditions lived to tell their tale, confirming the wisdom of the choices made by these outstanding explorers. We had demonstrated, in the most practical way, the superiority of camels over horses for desert exploration. As a horse lover, I was forced to concede that they just can't compete in the desert with animals like TC and Morgan, which can carry three times as much as a pack horse, can survive for weeks on limited water, and don't need grooming or shoes. That Gregory and Stuart had horses and lived, and Burke and Wills had camels and died, is a reflection not on the endurance of camels, but on the respective skills of the explorers.

For me, a city boy and horse lover, to reach these conclusions about camels without any prompting from Andrew, seemed to give him enormous satisfaction.

N
W — ◇ — E
S

Despite the overwhelming emotions accompanying our arrival at Mt Wilson, Andrew's routine was unbroken and we were up an hour before dawn the following day, preparing for our journey to the lake. That morning at the Mt Wilson Camp, I mentioned to Andrew that this would be one of the last times I would load a camel. 'You'll miss it when you're back in Sydney,' he said.

'Don't know about that,' I replied, as we moved to Morgan to begin lifting the saddles.

There was a question that I had been wanting to ask Andrew. I hadn't quizzed him too deeply about his Capricorn Expedition, but something intrigued me.

'Mate, you took three camels across Australia, so you had to load them by yourself every day for eight months?'

'Yes, that's right; unload them, too.'

'What I can't work out is how you got the saddles on without any help.'

'Simple, I just picked them up and put them on.' I looked at him and my scepticism must have shown. 'Do you want me to show you?' he asked.

'Wouldn't mind.'

He walked to Cooper's saddle, the heaviest in the string. He flipped the racks up and bent over the saddle like a golfer picking up his ball, getting an awkward hold through the racks to the ribs on the far side. 'No way you'll ever lift it like that,' I thought.

'Wait on, wait on. I've got to get some film of this.' I raced over to TC's saddle, where the video camera was stored. I began filming and commentating. Andrew leaned over the saddle once more.

'Ladies and gentlemen, Mr Andrew Harper of Deniliquin will attempt the packsaddle clean and jerk. Think this could be an Olympic event?'

Andrew grunted, taking the first weight of the unwieldy saddle. He rocked back and forth several times, then with neck muscles bulging, he lifted the saddle off the ground. Just a few centimetres at first.

'Aargh, no! I don't believe this. I'm getting a sore back just watching.'

Because of the shape of the saddle, he couldn't bend his knees and lifted it as dead weight. He raised it waist-high using his knee, then he rolled it shoulder-high and carried it to Cooper and placed it lightly on his back.

'Hey, Andrew. What box is the hernia truss in?' I asked. He laughed as he settled the saddle down on the camel's hump.

'Why?'

' 'Cause you're going to need it, pal. Actually, I didn't get that; camera wasn't on. Could you do it again? On second thought, why don't you load all the other saddles and I'll go and sit under a tree and watch,' I said.

'No, you need the exercise. Can't have you getting lazy at this late stage.'

'Mate, that was amazing. Suppose you're going to tell me it was muscle memory.'

'That's right,' he said. 'Now, we'd better get this gear loaded.'

Not long after we began walking, a large fire sprang up to the west. It burned along a broad front between Lake Gregory and us. The huge plume of black smoke boiled out of the bone-dry spinifex. We were in no immediate danger. Yet. The fire was travelling northwest pushed by a strong breeze. Men, camels and fire were travelling in the same direction. We were in no danger as long as the wind didn't change direction or drop suddenly.

'That'd be the Mulan mob out burning, chasing a goanna or kangaroo, I expect,' Andrew said.

Despite the inferno, I waxed philosophical as we walked along through the hot morning, all cares and doubts about the expedition's success behind me. 'You know, I think the most important tools for an Australian historian are a dusty pair of boots and a well-worn swag in the cupboard. I would love to come out here one day and see a history professor with a Toyota Troopie full of students and find them sitting around the campfire discussing how Australia's geography impacted on Gregory's and Stuart's expeditions. I'd love to see students out here arguing about who was the best explorer.'

'Well, that's a project for you,' he replied. 'You should challenge a couple of Australian history professors to a debate on radio.'

'I doubt they'd do it,' I said. 'Anyway, I think Australia's history and geography are inseparable. If we'd been a well-watered country with vast rivers and lakes out here, our history would've been completely different. We'd be another superpower.'

'Yes, that's true,' he said. 'I think it's interesting that 146 years after the first expeditions came out here, you still need camels to explore this country properly.'

'Yeah, and it's such lopsided development in Australia. In some parts like Sydney and Melbourne there are so many people you can hardly move. Yet there are fewer people living out here now than when Gregory discovered the Tanami in 1856. So there's a greater wilderness out here now than when white people first saw it.'

'Yes, that's true,' Andrew said. 'And you probably can't say that about any other place on earth.'

We were walking over an area between Mt Wilson and Lake Gregory that Gregory's journals described as the *Starvation Plain*. Often stony ground, sometimes bare even of spinifex, then giving way to dense patches of dry scrub, it was an apt description. We stopped for what would be our last 11 am halt.

'I wonder what Gregory's reaction would be if he knew that 146 years after his trip, people would be retracing his steps and feasting on chocolate-coated almonds, dried apricots, sultanas and mixed nuts in a concoction called scroggin,' I said to Andrew.

'Maybe that's why he called it the Starvation Plain. Maybe Mueller ate all the sultanas and they ran out of scroggin,' he said. Ferdinand Mueller, a thorough city boy who was hopeless with horses and renowned for getting lost, was the botanist who, despite his failings, built his reputation during Gregory's expedition.

'Possibly. The scrogg's been good, though – still fresh after five weeks. I only eat it because it stops scurvy,' I replied.

By late morning, the fire covered the western horizon, its front within 500 metres of us. Savage red and yellow flames spiralled into the sky. It made a roaring, smashing sound, as if it was tearing at the bush, demolishing it. It was a pitiless, inanimate sound – the cry of the dying bush. Black clouds of smoke boiled skyward as the flames incinerated spinifex, blood-wood and anything flammable – nothing was spared. If the wind changed, we were dead. The desert was having one last desperate fling at us, and one of my worst fears, being trapped in a spinifex fire, was there for stark consideration. We ate lunch standing up, watching the fire. We looked at each other. No words were needed. We couldn't flee. In that dense scrub and tethered to five camels, we couldn't travel quickly enough to get away. Instinct would tell us when to put emergency measures into play and start a back-burn. We weren't taking any chances and were ready to act at a moment's notice.

Suddenly, life became very complicated. To our considerable shock, two Toyota four-wheel-drive vehicles nosed through the bush about a kilometre away. Loaded with local Aborigines, they were heading south into the desert. In this wild place, vehicles were the last things we expected to see. They stopped and the passengers got out and started to move around. We shouted to try to attract their attention.

'Crikey, that must be the Mulan mob that's out burning,' Andrew said. 'They're upwind of us.' Andrew didn't need to spell it out. A fire lit to the south would race towards us on a following wind, and we'd be caught between their fire and the fire already burning to the west. 'We've got to stop them,' he said. We had no idea if anyone knew that we were on foot in the scrub travelling up the eastern side of the lake.

With enormous haste, the lunchboxes were thrown back on the camels and secured. I tied the shovel on Morgan. All thought of lunch ended. We hurried the camels to their feet and, for the only time on the trip, I saw Andrew exhibit something close to genuine anxiety. We practically ran towards the Toyotas, hoping that we didn't see the tell-tale puffs of smoke start to come out of the spinifex. We would be in desperate trouble if they lit a fire. To our great relief they saw us and started to wave. As it turned out, members of the Mulan community were out looking for us, tracking our progress on the radio.

'Hello, I'm Mark Sewell,' a tall, fit-looking man about Andrew's age said, walking towards us. 'I'm the Mulan administrator. Welcome to Lake Gregory.' We shook hands. 'Which one of you is Andrew?' he asked.

'He's the clean one,' I said.

That morning, Andrew had produced out of somewhere in his gear sack a clean shirt for the march to the lake. Experience told him that we might encounter a welcoming committee and he was determined to be suitably dressed. Unfortunately, I was sartorially challenged that day, still wearing the same pants that I had left Mt Stuart in five weeks earlier. Ragged and dirty they had acquired the nickname of 'the party pants', and my blue R.M. Williams shirt was now brown. There were many photos taken, handshakes and smiles as we met some of the locals and introduced the kids to the camels.

Those last couple of kilometres were difficult. We skirted the fire before the turpentine and spinifex on the unburned sections of the plain made one last attempt to frustrate us. Like every day in the desert, the afternoon was boiling hot, but we wouldn't be denied. At around 3.45 pm a herd of wild horses thundered up, looked curiously at our camels and fled. Then a flight of brolgas wheeled overhead, screeching raucously. We knew that soon we would see water. Then it happened. Topping a sandy ridge, we saw through a sentinel stand of ghost gums, the glint of the lake. We had arrived at one of the largest bodies of water in inland Australia. We made our camp on a grassy flat beneath a peaceful, spreading white gum. After 34 days of walking and about 720 kilometres, we had reached Lake Gregory. We had crossed the Tanami.

The number of waterbirds astounded me. The lake surface was covered in brolgas, ducks, magpie geese, corellas, black swans, and other birds that I couldn't identify. Zebra finches were thick in the sky. It was a haven of wildlife of all descriptions. Animal tracks criss-crossed the area between our campsite and the lake.

'I know why we never saw any animals on our way across the Tanami,' I said to Andrew in awe.

'Why?'

'Because they're all here.'

On seeing the lake, the camels needed no encouragement. No sooner had we stripped the gear from them than they practically galloped to the water's edge despite the hobbles restricting their movement. Not content to drink, they wallowed in the ankle-deep water at the edge of the lake, lying in the mud and kicking up their heels. Typically, Morgan and Cooper were the ringleaders and 'dived' in without a thought. Char, the young, small camel, timid to the end, hung back to see what it was all about, then carefully stepped into the lake while trying to stay out of Cooper's way. Cooper, 'the Monaro driver' as Andrew described him, was thrashing about with unconcealed glee.

'The boys are having quite a party,' I remarked.

'My word,' he said, relishing the sight of his animals covered in mud, enjoying their first swim for many months. These animals had been with us since we left civilisation. Most days, they were all that stood between us and a horrible death. At first, they had scared me; then their individual characters had emerged. I had found them faithful and enduring through all sorts of adversity. John Wilkinson was correct when he said at the start of our journey that they are the desert traveller's best friend.

The camels were having such a good time, I decided to join them. With my Speedos on and a quart pot, soap and sports towel in hand, I headed resolutely for the lake. It was only about 30 centimetres deep, so I waded out 100 or so metres until the water was just under my knees. It was clean and cold, and as there was an unlimited supply, I stood there pouring it over myself. The quart pot worked feverishly and I fulfilled my aim of having a swim in Lake Gregory – well, almost.

For the first time I took stock of how much the trip had taken out of me. My legs were like two drinking straws with feet attached, or a pair of chicken legs. The softness, courtesy of years of deskwork, was gone. I had no spare fat anywhere. I rejoiced that I had walked the distance without a whisper from my hips, knees or ankles, areas that plague many men my age. Prue's fears about my back had been unfounded, although not having to lift those green boxes was a blessing.

Standing in the lake surrounded by the breathtaking desert scenery, I felt the contest we had been engaged in was coming to an end. We had played a tough opponent and achieved an honourable draw. No one beats a desert, and I felt it threw out a challenge: 'Come back and play me anytime, boys. I'll always be here, always ready to accept any challenge. Ultimately, if you play me enough, I'll win.' The journey wearied me – it didn't weary the desert, which at the end was as strong as ever.

'You know, this desert is laughing at us,' I said, as I arrived back at the camp clean and refreshed.

'How's that?' Andrew asked.

'The only water we saw for the whole journey was a bucketful in the bed of the Lander River, and now that the journey's over, on the very last day, the Tanami gives us Sydney Harbour.'

He looked thoughtfully at the lake. 'It's a desert. You've got to expect nothing, because most of the time that's all you'll get. You just have to be thankful for the things it does send you,' he said. After my experiences of the last five weeks, I agreed with him.

No sooner had I arrived back at the camp than a convoy of four-wheel-drive vehicles appeared from the scrub. They pulled up a polite distance away, having been alerted by Mark Sewell after our chance morning meeting that we would be at the lake by the afternoon. How they found us, I'll never know. A mob of Aboriginal children tumbled out of the vehicles, eager to see the camels. Unfortunately, the camels became unsociable and fled. This didn't dent the children's enthusiasm. There were kids everywhere. Barefoot kids doing somersaults around the flat, kids chasing each other, kids shinnying up trees looking for bush tucker – a happy riot of colour and movement where before all had been quiet. Everywhere, flashing dark eyes and perfect teeth were on display. Laughter and the shrieks of delighted children rent the silence.

Mark Sewell had earlier introduced us to Rex and Julie-anne Johns, the traditional owners of Lake Gregory, who had formally welcomed us to their country. They were a wealth of information, explaining that Lake Gregory was known as Paruku before Gregory arrived. They presented us with a book of traditional stories of their Walmajarri and Kukatja language groups. Rex was keen to see the camels, as he had worked them along the Canning stock route as a boy. I showed him several varieties of bush tomato that I had collected. He explained which ones were good to eat and which ones were poisonous. He showed me how to cut them open and scoop out the edible pulp. Several of the older women in the group were digging on the sandy lakeshore, helped by a group of enthusiastic kids.

'What are you digging for?' I asked. On an upraised palm, I was offered a small pile of miniature onions.

'Bush onions; great favourite around here,' Mark said. 'They're digging where the brolgas have been scratching in the sand. Brolgas like the onions, too.' The bush onion or yalka (*Cyperus bulbosus*) normally occurs along watercourses or around the edges of saltpans. The Tanami botanist, David Gibson, later told me that the yalka was a good drought food for Aborigines and sustained mammals such as burrowing bettongs and brush-tailed bettongs. Gibson believes that rabbits devastated the plant when they entered the Tanami in about 1910. Rabbits tend to follow watercourses, and saltpan systems are one of their favourite habitats. Lake Gregory is probably far enough north to have escaped the main rabbit invasion, hence the availability of yalka.

Several children grabbed me by the hand and showed me the brolga scrapes. One of the digging women popped one of the onions in her mouth and laughed shyly. I did the same. It tasted like an onion, and several went in the cooking pot that night. 'Tastes better than bloodwood apple larvae,' I thought, 'and at least I got to see it before it became extinct like the mala.' I had acquired a wealth of information about bush tucker in half an hour with Rex and his community. It pays to be coached by experts.

The sun was dipping to the horizon and, too soon, our guests had gone. As the burning, orange ball touched the surface of the lake, it highlighted a scene of unbelievable serenity. Here was shade, grass and shrubs aplenty for the camels, and water everywhere. I couldn't remember camping in a more beautiful place. The desert had finally let up on me.

Our campsite was close to Gregory's final point of capitulation. After climbing Mt Wilson, he had returned to the lake and circumnavigated it in a clockwise direction, ending up very near our campsite. Throwing in the towel, he wrote:

> *10th March: As the whole country to the south was one vast sandy desert, destitute of any indications of the existence of water, it was clear that no useful results could arise from any attempt to penetrate this inhospitable region, especially as the loss of any of the horses might deprive the expedition of the means for carrying out the explorations towards the Gulf of Carpentaria. I therefore determined on commencing our retreat to the Victoria River while it was practicable, as the rapid evaporation and increasing saltness of the water in this arid and inhospitable region warned us*

that each day we delayed increased the difficulty of the
return, and it was possible that we were cut off from any
communication with the party at the depot by an
impassable tract of dry country, and might be compelled to
maintain ourselves on the lower part of the creek till the
ensuing rainy season.

And so the legend of an inland sea died on the shores of the lake where we were camped. Dispelled finally, not by an Englishman, but by one of our own, a man raised in the furnace of the Western Australian desert. After the expedition, Gregory wrote with great insight: *We now have sufficient data for assuming that the remainder of the unexplored interior is a desert.*

'You know, if Gregory had seen the lake like it is now, he may have thought for one fleeting moment that there *was* an inland sea,' Andrew said, as we sat by the campfire that night.

But it wasn't to be, and Gregory turned around and rode back to Brisbane and into the history books.

Dawn. Lake Gregory Camp. The noise was deafening. It started while I was still in my swag. Whistling, honking, hooting and quacking, the birds greeted the dawn with a thunderous din. Flotillas of birds wheeled overhead, most prominent being the brolgas, which wheeled and swooped in stately squadrons. Corellas, screeching, infested the trees; birds beyond counting splashed down in the lake. There were birds *everywhere*. I joined Andrew at the fire, but we were too mesmerised to get organised and stood watching the show.

'This is amazing!' I had to shout to be heard.

'Shows what a bit of water will do in the desert. What a paradise for birdwatchers.'

'I don't believe that,' I said, as a flight of pelicans touched down on the lake. 'Here we are, in the middle of a desert, and there's a mob of pelicans.' An hour after sunrise the show was over and all was quiet again. I learned later that Lake Gregory supports over 73 species of bird life and is a major drought refuge for waterfowl. It supports the largest breeding colony of little black cormorants in Australia.

'This partly makes up for not seeing a mala,' I said, as we began loading the camels.

Mark Sewell arrived with Rex Johns just as we'd finished loading and were about to leave for Mulan. There was one final job. Rex gave us permission to nail a small plaque to the ghost gum that marked our camp. The ceremony was performed and more handshakes, smiles and photographs were exchanged. I recorded the latitude and longitude in my journal, noting that our camp at the lake was only three kilometres southeast of Gregory's final camp at the head of the lake.

CENTRAL AUSTRALIAN EXPEDITION 2002
ARRIVED HERE ON AUGUST 13, 2002
KIERAN KELLY ANDREW HARPER
5 CAMELS

I asked Rex if, in the old days, Aborigines could have walked over from the east, from the Lander or the Granites, the way we had come.

'No. No water there,' he replied, pointing east.

'What about the bush foods like tomatoes and parakeelya that have a lot of water in them? Could they have survived on those, or other stuff we don't know about?'

'No. You need water. Bush tucker's okay, but you still need water,' he said emphatically.

'So, they couldn't have walked across from Central Mt Stuart?'

'No,' he said again, shaking his head.

I looked at the plaque and at the lake and found it difficult to tear myself away. 'I'll definitely come back here with my children – somehow, sometime,' I vowed. We turned away and began walking north towards Mulan. I paused several times for a last look back through the trees. It was a magnificent sight.

As we walked along, I checked the shovel, my special responsibility, and was heartened that it was still in place, secured by three half-hitches on Morgan's saddle. Emboldened, I asked Andrew, 'So, mate, am I still a cob?'

He laughed and didn't answer for awhile. I was picking bush tomatoes and sucking on them as we walked along. I handed him one.

'No, you're not a cob.' He paused for a moment. 'You're only half a cob,' he said, smiling.

I thanked him very much. I suppose it could have been worse. If I was half a cob, that means I must be half a cameleer.

'At least I didn't lose the bloody shovel.' We laughed and walked into the morning for the last time.

Maybe that was one of the great achievements of our trip – two people from vastly different backgrounds, almost complete strangers, could endure five weeks together in the wilderness and still share a joke and a laugh at the end. Interviewed months later on radio, Andrew said that one of the most important things about our adventure was that we were still sitting around the same campfire at the end of it. I agree.

Our 35th and last camp on Monday, 19 August, was at the stockyards of the Mulan Aboriginal community. With regret on my part, I helped to unsaddle big Morgan and the other camels for the last time. I gave his lordship a pat. 'Thanks, mate, for carrying the water all that way. And thanks for not spitting at me or kicking my brains out.' I now knew why this aristocratic animal was such a favourite with tourists. As usual, all I got was a honk and a couple of moans as he eagerly eyed the nearby acacia thickets.

Finally, the saddles, food boxes and jerrycans, many still full of water, were unloaded and lined up in rows on the ground. This time, they wouldn't be going back on the camels.

I had learned much from Andrew. He regards a bush camp as partly office, kitchen, workshop and lounge room. For it to function properly, rules have to be followed. These rules are based largely on courtesy, common sense and a need for privacy, even when alone in the bush with just one other person. We had discussed these rules many times during the journey – what makes a camp function and what makes it fail; what makes it safe and what renders it dangerous. That night at the Mulan camp, I wrote a summary of what I had learned on the journey about how a camp should be run.

My journal entry that night recorded that we had walked 732 kilometres in the 35 days since leaving Central Mt Stuart at an average of 21 kilometres a day. And except for the day spent exploring at Mt Leichhardt we had done it non-stop.

'Well, Kelly. You've done it. Walked across the Tanami,' he said, before we headed for our swags. 'Easy, eh?'

'Mate, the 732 ks were no problem; but if it was 733 ks, I would've been face down in the mulga with the dingoes arguing over the choice bits,' I replied, only half joking.

CAMP RULES AND BUSH COURTESY
A. HARPER   K. KELLY

1. The camp has one boss whose say is final on all matters, including selection of campsite and route.
2. No one to sleep near fire or camel camp.
3. Last person to bed banks fire.
4. All fires to be as small as possible and if spinifex is dense or it's very windy, to be built in a pit.
5. All fires to be lit downwind of camp. Lunchtime fire not to be built in the shade.
6. No one to sit between cook and campfire. Don't leave billy in no-man's-land between swags and fire. It's at the fire or at the food boxes.
7. Nothing to be thrown into the fire. Cook decides what will be burned. Unburned rubbish is packed on camels.
8. Firewood to be collected and stacked as soon as camels unloaded. Fireplace to be cleared immediately. All firewood to be sorted into different sizes before stacking. A pile of firewood to be stacked for morning fire before sundown.
9. All human waste to be buried. No going to toilet near camp.
10. Respect other people's privacy – don't sit on someone else's swag, use someone else's quart pot, pannikin or cooking utensils. Don't walk or sit on someone else's tarp.
11. Don't shine your torch in other people's eyes. Remember to switch head torch off.
12. No one to leave camp without telling someone else.
13. Don't touch or sit on saddlecloths.
14. Don't unroll swag until you are ready to get in it. (Exception for airing.) Swag to be rolled up as soon as you get out of it.
15. Cook must always wash hands before preparing food.

16. Only water to be used is nominated drinking or wash jerrycan. Don't touch other jerrycans.
17. Remain in swag if rifle fire heard at night.
18. Don't stand around fire while meals being cooked. Don't let fire go out.
19. Tea billy is sacred. Nothing to be boiled in tea billy but tea. Waste tea to be used to wash hands, utensils, etc.
20. Camels/horses come first and campsites are selected primarily for feed and tether trees. Camels unloaded as soon as campsite selected and before drinks or food taken by expedition participants.

CHAPTER 11

Homecoming: The shower's cold!

Dawn, heading east. East towards the border, east into the morning sunrise for the first time since the start of the journey. East in a truck with five camels and all the gear. For the first time in five weeks, we were moving without walking. Battling the flu, the ever-reliable Trevor Shiell had driven the truck 900 kilometres from Alice Springs to meet us. Our gear was loaded, goodbyes were said to Rex Johns and Mark Sewell, and we left Mulan behind, taking with us fond memories of the warm welcome we'd received there. After a brief stop in the Balgo Aboriginal community, founded by the Pallotine monks who left their name on the rocky crags that had recently blocked us, we drove back towards the Northern Territory border.

As we bumped over the rough desert track to the humble border marker, I felt nostalgic about crossing that imaginary line. A fortnight earlier, I had filmed Andrew and the camels crossing the same line while snatches of Shelley rattled around in my head. We were going in a different direction then. We turned on to the relative civilisation of the Tanami track and headed south. The journey offered familiar scenes. Dense groves of acacia scrub, sun-blasted desert bloodwoods and native orange hemmed in either side of the road. Spinifex filled every spare space. Fires trailed us all the way down the Tanami track. Some were just small spinifex fires; others were raging infernos devouring the bush right up to the edge of track.

'Where do all these fires start, I wonder?'

'Could be started hundreds of miles away,' Trevor replied. 'Could've burned all the way from the Queensland border. Could be a lightning strike.' We were in no danger in the truck as we sped by; and I watched the fires for miles, enthralled by their raw, destructive power. Nevertheless, I carried home with me a vision of central Australia as a land of fire and no water, where life is uncertain.

We passed the mullock heaps of the Tanami mine, a piece of history. We passed the turnoff to remote Rabbit Flat. Barrelling south, we crossed again the Tanami's ancient river channel and the scrub died to reveal the wide, spinifex-covered plain and towering termite mounds. This was travelling with a difference. This was travelling without sweat, without fatigue, without mulga clutching at your clothes and spinifex piercing your shins. This was travelling sitting down, travelling with the air-conditioner on. Travelling in a cocoon, we were shielded from the harshness outside.

'Not the same doing this in a vehicle,' I said to Andrew, who was handling the driving. 'The four-wheel-drive mob sure miss a lot.'

'That's right. You can *see* the country in a four-wheel drive, but you can only *know* the country by walking through it,' he replied. 'Still, it's better to come out here in a four-wheel drive and at least *see* the country, than to stay at home and have no idea.'

Looking out through the truck's wide windscreen was like watching a film called *The Tanami Desert*. Previously, I had been a player; I was now just a spectator. Irrationally, I felt that the desert was taunting me: 'Don't sit in that truck, you pussy. Come out and fight.'

As we swept down on the Granites, I saw where Andrew had led the camels across the track heading for Dead Bullock Soak. Flashing past once more were the landmarks that I had sought so eagerly a fortnight before, the tumbled boulders of the Granites, Mt Ptilotus and Approach Hill.

Evening saw us camped by the side of the Tanami track just north of the Aboriginal settlement of Yuendumu, made famous by Peter Garrett and Midnight Oil in their song, 'Beds Are Burning'. We drove about 700 kilometres that day, the same distance that our expedition had covered in five weeks. Ironically, after suffering only minor muscle soreness and stiffness on the journey, I was as rigid as a board when I alighted from the truck that first night. Everything ached.

Dawn saw us racing past Tilmouth's Well and soon the MacDonnell Ranges rose above the horizon. The colours in the morning sun were magnificent, the range a glorious mixture of purples, reds and blues.

'Albert Namatjira country,' I said to Trevor and Andrew, referring to the pioneering artist whose watercolours had put the Macs on the artistic drawing board. 'Gee, he really nailed the colours, didn't he?' Shortly after, we reached the point where Andrew had crossed the Tanami track in his 1999 Capricorn Expedition. I pestered him to show me the exact crossing spot, even the gate he had walked through. Typically, he was modest about his achievement. To me it was another explorer's storyline on the map, albeit a modern explorer and one that I knew. The crossing was on Anburla Station, made famous by Troy Dann, the outback television personality. Andrew had rested his camels on Anburla while preparing for the second leg of his journey.

We were soon in Alice Springs, unloading the camels. I said goodbye to the boys. Morgan, like me stiff from the journey, was supine in the yards at the Frontier Camel Farm the last time I saw him. Everyone commented on how much weight the camels had lost. Alice was a shock. As we hit the town's outskirts, cars, buildings and people filled the windscreen. The noise and activity were overwhelming, as were the number of people. My world of late had comprised only one other person and five animals. I had adjusted to the isolation, the walking and the desert. Now I would have to adjust back again.

With unrestrained glee, I stripped off trousers and shirt, soiled from the track, took off boots battered by spinifex, saltpan and stones, stripped off ragged underwear and piled everything in a smelly mound in the middle of my motel room. Grabbing soap, razor and shampoo I was desperate for a hot shower. I turned the tap on full pelt and held my hand under it, waiting for cold water to turn to hot. I waited. It was still cold. Thinking I had made a mistake, I turned on the other tap. I waited. It was cold, too. I turned both taps on full blast. They were both cold.

Mournfully, I retreated to the smelly mound. On went the shirt, the dirty trousers, the smelly socks and boots. No traveller has exhibited a more determined air than the one I exuded as I crunched across the gravel to the motel office.

'I want to see the manager,' I said.

'I'm the manager,' said the well-scrubbed, gentleman behind the desk. His appearance contrasted sharply with my travel-worn clothing and shabby, dusty boots.

'My shower's cold!'

'No, it's not.'

'Yes, it is.'

'No, it's not. You just have to let the water run for a while.'

I experienced exasperation for the first time in weeks. We looked at each other. Here in Alice Springs, deep in the Australian outback, I was having a Monty Python moment and this was John Cleese. I was reminded of the scene where he went into a cheese shop and the owner said that he could have anything he wanted, *except* cheese.

'Tried that,' I replied.

'Well, you'll just have to go back and try it again. There's plenty of hot water.'

'I realise now why John McDouall Stuart got on the grog after his exploring trips,' I said.

The manager and his receptionist looked at each other. I was beaten and retreated to my room. Stripping off again, I accepted the inevitable and broached the cold shower. I tried to convince myself that it was as good as a hot one, but this notion was soon dispelled as cold razor was drawn over old stubble. Here in my motel, I couldn't even light a fire for a tiny quart pot of hot shaving water. I already missed the bush.

Like Stuart just returned from the outside country, a drink was on my mind. That night, I met up with Andrew at Bojangles bar, an institution in Alice Springs where locals and ringers from stations in the desert mingle with German backpackers, coach tourists returning from Ayers Rock, and the ubiquitous grey nomads. Everyone looked so clean. Even Andrew was transformed. I was shocked. The sun-blasted cameleer of my recent experience, in shorts and sleeveless shirt, black from spinifex resin, was staying with friends and arrived refurbished into a scrubbed, well-dressed personage who blended anony-mously into the Bojangles hubbub. Thankfully, he hadn't discarded his battered Blundstones, although they'd had a meeting with the boot-polish tin.

Ellie, a friend of Andrew's and an Alice Springs local (one of the few people I'd met who had been born there), joined us. Peanut shells littered the floor, the beers were cold and the steaks were big – and therein lay the problem. I demolished two cold beers, but the steak was beyond me.

'Aargh, this is too big and fatty for me,' I said. 'My stomach can't take this.' The weeks of living on dried food and dry, lean jerky made rich food a problem it would take me some time to resolve. 'You know, despite the hardships, we never went to bed hungry or thirsty out there, and we were working much harder than any of the people in here wolfing down all this rich food. I think people in Western societies eat too much.'

Andrew agreed. Strangely, while there were things I did miss out in the desert, food and alcohol weren't among them. I listened with considerable envy as Ellie and Andrew planned a trip to Glen Helen Gorge in the western Macs. I was sorry that our trip was over and would like to have gone with them, but my thoughts were firmly turned to home.

We said goodnight outside Bojangles and our adventure ended. It was something of an anticlimax, as it was an early night. However, unlike Stuart, we wouldn't both have *sair heads the morn*. I lay in bed looking at the ceiling of the motel. The air-conditioning clanked, so I got up and turned it off. The bed was so soft I sank in the middle, and my routine of having hat, boots, journal, compass, utility belt and bag in their appointed places – all just so – was disturbed. I got up, pulled pillow, sheets and blankets off the bed, and lay on the floor. At least that was comfortable. The ceiling seemed to be perched right on the end of my nose. It was oppressive. During the night, I awoke and looked up into the dark sky. 'Gee, the stars have gone.' I sat up with a start thinking I should be lighting the fire. But there were no stars. I was looking at the ceiling. The room felt claustrophobic.

Andrew and Trevor picked me up in the morning and we said our goodbyes at the airport. In what seemed like no time, I was watching the beaches of Sydney slide by beneath the aircraft, then the harbour, then the giant glass towers of the city. When we touched down, I was jumping out of my skin, as I knew that my family would be there. It was almost six weeks since I had seen them. I was full of apprehension. Had anything changed in the past six weeks? Had anything bad happened that I hadn't been told about? Would I be able to fit back in? The last was a great concern.

Of course, I needn't have worried. There was great excitement at the airport. 'You're so thin!' my wife exclaimed. I was to hear this comment often in the coming weeks. When I stood on the scales at home, they showed that I had lost ten kilograms – about twelve per cent of my body weight – and this despite eating heartily for the entire period in the desert. Despite the weight loss, I had never felt fitter or more relaxed.

Still reeling from Sydney's overwhelming size, I was back at work a couple of days later. My journal of Monday, 26 August records: *Today put suit and tie back on and head into work. Suit pants way too big. Rainy day Monday.* The ride into the city on the Jetcat was a shock: the people looked so clean – women in smart dresses, men in sharp suits – clean clothes, clean hair and clean faces. I looked at my hands coming out of the cuffs of a crisp, freshly pressed white shirt. The backs of my hands were burned black from the sun, and my palms were stained brown from weeks of washing them in waste tea. Ingrained dirt and sweat, which defied scrubbing, clogged my pores. All the hair was gone from the back of my right hand, a souvenir of many campfires when I dived for the billy with a pair of pliers as it came to the boil. Spinifex punctures had left marks that were still healing, and across my left palm was a deep scar from a razor-sharp camel knife. All my fingernails were broken. My hands looked like they belonged to a different body.

My wife said that she had never seen me so calm in the entire time we had been married – almost serene. I felt great that first morning going off to work, super-fit and relaxed, almost euphoric. By contrast, many of my fellow male commuters looked sad. A rainy Monday morning on a big city commuter boat isn't a sea of joy. Still, we city males have it laid on. Just turn up at 7.05 am and transport will take you to the city. We don't have to acquire skills to survive, just skills to prosper. There is absolutely no risk. The nerve-tingling, gut-wrenching excitement that had recently been a part of my daily life was now gone. Perhaps that's why many of the blokes looked so grim. Possibly what they needed was to be deposited in an isolated environment, where they would be forced to look after themselves under conditions of extreme physical pressure and extended periods of silence. It would certainly change their outlook, and put every stress management guru and weight-loss program out of business. As the Jetcat pulled into Circular Quay, I looked up at the harbour bridge, where the rain-bound traffic was already gridlocked.

'All those Mercedes and BMWs are going slower than we did with the camels,' I thought, as I walked down the gangway and headed for my office.

N
W ◇ E
S

'Here's Moses returned from the desert after 40 days and 40 nights,' Steve Williams, one of my business partners, said when I walked into the office. He seemed to find this analogy highly amusing and has stuck with it ever since. So, 'Moses' became my new nickname.

'Learn anything about the markets while you were out there pondering?' John Parker, my other partner and a stock market tragic, asked.

'Yes, buy low, sell high,' I replied.

'Gee, you don't have to go out into the desert to know that,' was the general sentiment.

Much had occurred while I was out in the desert. World stock markets had collapsed, recovered and were crumbling again, mired in a swamp of corporate fraud and failure in America. Billions had been wiped off the value of shares, and fortunes had been lost while I was away. And that was the *good* news. A Palestinian family had been killed in an orchard by an Israeli tank firing shells containing fléchettes – finned nails that shredded people and fruit trees; the HIH Royal Commission provided a vision of corruption and incompetence on a grand scale; the Commonwealth Games had opened and closed; Kylie Minogue had toured Australia; and the Democrats had self-destructed – and Andrew and I had missed the lot. George W. Bush was grouching about Iraq when I left and he was still grouching about it when I returned. Most of the news made me feel like returning to the desert.

I made a cup of tea and realised that all we had in the office was Earl Grey, which tastes nothing like billy tea and comes in tea bags. How I missed the handful of bulk tea expertly measured from the cotton sack and flung into the boiling, blackened, tin billy on a tiny fire under that endless, burning-blue vault. I laughed at the memory of how carefully I made the tea to forestall feral twigs, fearing the wrath of the coach. Now I had a gleaming, white electric jug.

'Back in the biggest city in the country and I can't get a decent cup of tea,' I grouched to anyone who would listen. 'This stuff tastes like . . .'

We lunched at Wildfire that first day, a new restaurant at Circular Quay, near our office. One of the difficult things to adjust to was eating when I wasn't hungry. I hadn't exercised or done anything strenuous during the morning and the thought of sitting down to a huge meal made me feel sick. The restaurant specialises in huge slabs of grilled meat that repelled me when they were brought to the table. The desserts were worse.

I felt strange during those first few days back in Sydney. I had been obsessively focused for so long on just staying alive, that it was hard to change gears and shift back into city mode.

Less than a fortnight later, Prue and I attended a Saturday evening dinner organised by Paul and Barbara Dillon at their home in the leafy Sydney suburb of Roseville. The dinner was a get-together for the parents of girls in the Loreto College, Kirribilli, First VIII rowing crew of which my daughter Hilary is a member. Veterans of many pre-dawn drop-offs at Mosman boatshed or the Sydney International Regatta Centre at Penrith, everyone knew each other well. We were bound together by children of the same age and by a love of their sport. As evenings go, this was as Sydney as Sydney gets – with an important exception. Sydney dinner-party conversation is normally dominated by property prices, home-renovation horror stories, and fights with architects and builders. That Saturday, the discussion centred on camels, deserts and the differences between women and men.

I told everyone about Andrew's marathon expedition across Australia in 1999 and I was plied with questions about him.

'Doesn't he get lonely, walking in the desert on his own?' Belinda Grant, one of the mothers, asked.

'No, he seems very happy with his own company. Out there, there's plenty to keep you occupied.' I didn't even try to explain how you have to hypnotise yourself with the compass and zone out in order to get through the afternoon heat.

'Why hasn't he ever married? Has he ever been engaged?' Lexie Polin, another of the women, asked.

'Don't know. I didn't ask him.'

'Why not?'

'It's none of my business and it's not relevant.' I didn't go into the history of our great land explorers – few of them were married.

'Does he miss not having any children?'

'Don't know. We didn't talk about that sort of thing.'

'Why not?' Susie Swift asked. Susie, a plain-speaking person, was always quick to get to the point.

'Well, you have to respect the other bloke's privacy. You can't sit around asking personal questions or talking about yourself.'

'Then, what did you talk about?' she asked.

'It's hard to say. He's not an overly talkative bloke, like a lot of fellows who spend their life in the bush. We talked a lot about the camels, and food and water, and the route. We talked about the course we were travelling and what lay ahead. We walked separately, so the only time we got together was at night around the campfire. Most of the time, I was too stuffed to talk.' In truth, rolling into our swags not long after nightfall left little time for talk. When tired, Andrew looked at the fire and said little; when tired, I looked at the fire and said nothing.

'So, you're saying you spent five weeks in the bush with another man and you don't know him all that well?' Susie said.

'That's right. He's a private person and I had to respect that.' I thought of Shakespeare's line from *Henry V*: *men of few words are the best men* . . . This philosophy is accepted lore in the bush, but it's a hard concept to explain in town.

'What's he think about you? Does he think you're just another city person?'

'No idea. Never asked him.'

'Well, see, that's the difference between men and women. If I'd been out in the desert with another woman, I'd have known everything about her by the second day. *Everything*,' Susie said emphatically. Everyone laughed, but no one disagreed.

'Yes, you probably would have. But your expedition might've collapsed at the end of the first week and you might've placed yourself in danger.' I explained that I learned everything I needed to know about Andrew by watching him during the trip, by what he did, not by what he said. 'He's fit and tough and doesn't crack under pressure. I learned that he doesn't quit half-way through something and that he's good with animals.' Everything else was irrelevant to me.

'Yes, but you must've been curious about his history, his family, his girlfriends?' Susie said.

'Not as curious as finding out whether he would leave me in the bush if I was injured. That's a lot more important to me.'

'Do you think you'll remain friends, that you'll ever see him again?' someone asked. I'm often asked this question.

'I hope so, but I don't know what he thinks about me. He didn't share that with me. He's a great diplomat and may have been relieved to put me on the plane at Alice. I hope we remain friends. I think he's a good bloke, and we share a lot of common interests.'

Prue was asked her opinion, which I think carried more weight with the women than mine. 'Well, I think he's a very nice bloke. I think you'd all like him,' she said, as a postscript to the conversation.

'Sounds like a good catch. A shame he's too old for our girls,' Belinda said.

The conversation moved on after a spirited debate about whether a group of women could successfully mount a cross-desert expedition. I'm a city person and understand how urban people think, but it was difficult to explain to them the stresses and strains we'd been under, how we had struggled to stay alive, and how we had battled each day to take kilometres from the desert. There were never any easy kilometres. The desert gave up each metre begrudgingly. I still believe it's more important to trust and respect your companions on an exploring trip than to know every detail of their lives, but it's a difficult concept for some people to grasp.

It was with great sadness that I folded and packed away the maps. Across each one was a series of dots marking our route. Large dots with numbers indicated our campsites. The maps had the battered look of working maps that I love.

The navigational instruments went back in their box. The leather journal case was cleaned, oiled and stored. My study echoes still with memories of late nights spent poring over maps by Stuart, Terry, Warburton and Gregory. Five old hardcover books from Mosman library with the name 'M. Terry' on the spine sit on the end of my desk. Another book, with *A Journey across the Western interior of Australia. Warburton* on the spine, is near my elbow.

From the doorknob of my study hangs the leather utility belt made by Trevor Gibson, the Tenterfield saddler, now freshly saddle-soaped and oiled. From it hang a sheath knife, clasp knife, Silva baseplate compass, match case and Garmin GPS pouch. Instruments that I relied on every day in the desert are now redundant in my city life. I look at those bushman's tools with great regret.

My Tanami journal joined its two companions on the bookshelf. I open it frequently and catch a delicious smell of wood smoke and sweat. Its pages chronicle our journey and contain sketches of packsaddles and proposed routes and mountains that we saw. In places, a smudged brown thumbprint shows that I wasn't always successful in cleaning my hands before sitting down in the evening to record the day's activities.

My house faces northwest and I often sit and look over the harbour to the suburb of Castlecrag. The blue harbour, with its stately yachts and ring of lawn-shrouded houses, disappears and I see the country that lays beyond; the sand ridges, saltpans and the dazzling blue mirage. I see the kangaroos flee through the spinifex, their tails *thump, thump, thumpi*ng. I see again the regal bustards, watching our progress with haughty disregard. A vision of camels walking in single file in the afternoon gloaming, cresting a red ridge, stirs my memory. I see Andrew hooshing down TC, Cooper and the rest, near a grove of bloodwoods, their faces pointing to the west. Morgan would be the last to go down, checking the lay of the land before dropping to his knees with the inevitable groan. I only remember the good bits now.

I have promised my wife that it's over, that it's now time to enjoy the great indoors. But beyond the harbour, beyond the sandstone curtain of the Blue Mountains, that northwest country is lurking, brooding. It whispers to me and it's a siren's song and a call to battle. I stare at maps and unconsciously reach for the dividers, walking them up Sturt Creek and tracing Gregory's retreat from the dry salt lake. Up to Inverway Station, then across the Nicholson River and the headwaters of the Ord, up to the camp at Depot Creek, then into Mt Sanford Station. A 520-kilometre adventure.

We could do that in three weeks, even with rest stops, I catch myself thinking. I scribble calculations: two riding camels, three pack camels and one spare camel. About 45 kilograms of food. Easy. Wouldn't have to take as much water; probably only 200 litres – half what we hauled across the desert. There'd be good holes in Sturt Creek. Wonder if they'd hold during the dry season . . .

It would be a good trip. Wonder if Andrew would be interested? How could I talk Prue into it? Wouldn't it be great to link Mt Wilson with Gregory's retreat to the Victoria River? I ponder. That would mean I'd have walked or ridden all the way from central Australia to the Victoria River. Wonder how hard the permits would be? It's more closely settled, so a lot of it would be cattle country. We'd have to get permission from the pastoralists.

Suddenly, I'm off again. But I have to stop myself; it must remain a dream. It's over. *To everything there is a season and a time for every purpose under heaven.* Still, every man must have a dream

CONCLUSION

This is a story about men. About men and deserts. About men and adventure. About men and struggle. The story is about men who lived in three different centuries and came from a cross-section of cultures – English, Scottish and Australian. They are men from professions as diverse as the military, surveying, the tourism industry and corporate finance. They are, however, bound together by certain traits: all loved the wilderness, all returned to it time after time, all were baffled and led on by the far horizon, all struggled to overcome the primitive forces of nature. All the men featured in this story survived – some only just. All saw and recognised the great beauty of inland Australia, the place we know today as the outback. Their motives differed: Gus Gregory was doing his job; John Stuart and Pete Warburton did it for the glory; Mike Terry was looking for gold; and Andrew and I went looking for traces of all of them and for the adventure.

So, what happened to everyone? We left Stuart at the Lander after his perilous push into the Tanami and desperate retreat to water. Sick from sandy blight and scurvy, his horses were in dire straits and Ben Head suddenly took ill, but Stuart's courage remained undimmed. He returned to his camp at Mt Leichhardt, where Andrew and I had supped on blood-wood apples. He began to probe north and was almost killed near Mt Peake when he was dragged upside-down through the scrub by a tearaway horse, his foot stuck in his stirrup iron.

He returned to the Centre Camp near Mt Stuart and his wretched condition is reflected in his journal. Sending Kekwick to look for water, he wrote:

> Yesterday I rode in the greatest pain from the effects of my fall, and it was with great difficulty that I was able to sit in the saddle until we reached here. Scurvy has also taken a very serious hold of me; my hands are a complete mass of sores that will not heal, ... I am rendered nearly helpless. My mouth and gums are now so bad that I am obliged to eat flour and water boiled. The pains in my limbs and muscles are almost insufferable . . . I suffered dreadfully during the past night.

Why he didn't quit and go back to Adelaide, I'll never know. Stuart and his companions continued to probe north. By the end of June, the men were starving and complained to Stuart of weakness from lack of food. Even Stuart admitted that 2.3 kilograms of flour per week for each man wasn't enough for a long expedition, conceding that he hadn't brought enough food. Still he wouldn't retreat. Incredibly, he managed to travel a further 350 kilometres to Attack Creek, north of present-day Tennant Creek. Frustrated by Aboriginal attacks, Stuart was finally forced to retreat. Starving, sick and short of water, he, Kekwick and Head faced a 2400-kilometre ride back to Adelaide.

When finally he capitulated, Stuart had been out for his planned four months and still had to get back. Head was desperate: his weight had halved, and he was ravenous. Stuart accused him of stealing food from the stores and was unsympathetic to the greater dietary needs of a man of Head's size. He grumbled about Head all the way back to the settled districts, but Head paid the price. Despite being selected by Stuart for his second transcontinental bash, his health was broken and he withdrew. He never explored again.

While Stuart went on to great things, Head spent the rest of his life in obscurity, working as a guard and porter for the South Australian Railways. He died aged only 43. The shredding of Head's young life in the service of Stuart's ambition and lack of planning is one of the great tragedies of Australian exploration, and yet is largely unknown. Despite Head's suffering, he appeared to bear Stuart no ill will.

Unbeknown to Stuart as he rode south, Burke and Wills had left Melbourne in an attempt to overtake him in the race to the north coast. In January 1861, Stuart was off again in a desperate race with the Victorian party. This time he made it as far north as Newcastle Waters, before turning for the long march to Adelaide. Burke and Wills had almost reached the north Australian coast and died on the return journey before Stuart reached civilisation.

Undaunted, he set out a third time. After a nine-month-long, heroic journey on horseback, he planted the Union Jack on the coast east of present-day Darwin. He wasn't to know that John McKinlay, out searching for Burke and Wills, had beaten him to the north coast, although McKinlay, unlike Stuart, had not travelled through central Australia. Stuart barely survived the return journey of 3400 kilometres. Nearly blind, he was carried on an improvised stretcher between two horses for almost 1000 kilometres. He owed his survival entirely to the superb bushmen, Kekwick and Frank Thring, who accompanied him.

Shunned by Adelaide society because of his problems with the drink, the battered explorer returned home to Scotland in 1864. While it's impossible to think of Gus Gregory as anything but Australian, I cannot think of Stuart as other than Scottish, despite his length of stay in Australia. He came, challenged our deserts and had some success, but they sent him home 25 years later, a broken man. The deserts took Stuart's courage and resolve, and then bludgeoned him with them. He was a man battered to death by his own determination. As the Tanami whispered to me, so the deserts whispered to him: 'Come and challenge me and I'll beat you and break you – and ultimately I'll kill you.' Stuart's life proves that this is no idle threat.

Despite Scotland's softer climate, the damage was done and Stuart survived the expedition by only four years, dying in 1866 at age 50. As I approach that age, I am saddened that he didn't live longer to see his great achievement celebrated in the Overland Telegraph Line that followed his route. Still, his was a full life and I hope that he was content. Only seven people attended his funeral, which is a tragedy given the contribution he had made to the exploration of inland Australia.

If Stuart's mates knew him best, then Ben Head, the youngster on Stuart's 1860 expedition, should have written his epitaph: *He had the instincts of a bushman. However foolish he may have been in town, there is not a man in Australia can say a word against him as a leader in the bush . . . He was a born leader of men; the sharpest little fellow you would find in a year's march. He was a born explorer.*

Only Stuart, of all the men who explored the Australian outback, can aspire to that lofty position occupied by the four unquestionably great Australian explorers: James Cook, Matthew Flinders, Augustus Gregory and Phillip Parker King.

And what of Warburton? We left him at Mt Hughes, deep in the western Tanami, after his unsuccessful hunt for Lake Gregory. Enduring unbelievable privations, Warburton and his men reached the headwaters of the Oakover River, near the west coast. Starving and near death, Warburton couldn't go on. He sent Lewis and one of the Afghans on the expedition's two surviving camels, in a desperate lunge to the coast for help. In one of the remarkable stories of Australia, Lewis and his companion rode a further 280 kilometres and organised a successful rescue. Warburton's journey was undeniably ambitious, but it was also a shambles of bad navigation, reckless disregard for men's lives and poor management of animals. Of the seventeen camels in his care, seven were killed and eaten, one was too exhausted to continue and was abandoned, four fled, three died of *gyrostemon* poisoning and two survived. This statistic would doubtless trouble Andrew Harper. That Warburton survived was a tribute to Lewis's bushcraft. Lewis, like Kekwick and Thring, was the key to his group's success – an unsung hero.

Warburton returned to England after a 40-year absence, but lasted there little more than a month. Complaining of the English climate, he returned to South Australia. He died on 5 November 1889, aged 76. Warburton was the first man to travel from the centre of the country to the Western Australian coast. While he was a game man, his journey recorded little of scientific or commercial value.

And Michael Terry? We left his tracks behind near Dead Bullock Soak. He remains one of the great forgotten figures of Australian exploration. His 1928 trip across the Tanami took him over the Studholme Hills, where I shot the bull camel, then down the Lander River. He visited White Stone Well where, 74 years later, Andrew and I would attempt to water our camels. He arrived in Alice Springs having completed the first motor-vehicle expedition across the Tanami.

In all, Terry undertook fourteen expeditions using both motor vehicles and camels. His journeys through central Australia produced a significant legacy of books, magazine articles, papers published in scientific journals and newspaper articles. He is estimated to have written two million words on the outback between 1926 and 1967. Possessed of a keen eye for people, landscape, plants and animals, Terry was a pioneering outback photographer, recording some outstanding expedition scenes.

Terry, like many of the English explorers in Australia, brought with him a cultural and racial haughtiness that is apparent in his books. Also, he was a man of his time. His attitudes to Australian Aborigines combine curiosity and fear, admiration and contempt. When 'Jacky' was about, Terry's hand was never far from his pistol, which he wore habitually when in the bush. Terry's fear of Aborigines, borne of unfamiliarity and recent exposure to frontier violence, is in stark contrast to the attitudes of Gregory and Stuart, who came from Enlightenment and Christian backgrounds. Gregory also had the advantage of having grown up with Aborigines and of understanding their culture and habits. His journals reveal respect, not fear. Despite his failings, Terry did attempt to record the language and habits of Aborigines he met, including the Tanami's Walpiri people.

His books will jar on many modern readers, which is a shame as they glow with descriptions of the outback in pristine health, when the hand of the white man lay only gently on her. His contribution to the understanding of Australian mammals is outstanding. To him we owe the best field descriptions of the mala. Terry was probably the last white man to see alive the central hare wallaby (*Lagorchestes asomatus*), cousin of the mala. He collected a specimen of this small desert wallaby in 1932 and presented its skull to the South Australian Museum. It is the only proof that this species ever existed. Biologist and Tanami expert, David Gibson, and Terry researcher, Adrian Winwood-Smith, believe that Terry documented the existence of at least seven species of desert-dwelling, medium-sized mammals, an impossibility for modern-day desert scientists, due to extinction and habitat destruction.

Michael Terry died in Australia in 1981 aged 82 years, unheralded despite his successes. His exploring career spanned more than 60 years. Terry was the only explorer mentioned in this book to have lived during my lifetime. I would like to have met him.

Andrew Harper met the spirit of Augustus Gregory when he stood atop Mt Wilson looking at the lake named in his honour. His ear, however, had been bashed senseless about this explorer and the North Australian Expedition for the previous five weeks. He was probably glad to reach Lake Gregory so that I would shut up.

The North Australian Expedition of 1855–56 was the largest and most expensive expedition undertaken by the British Empire up to that date. It was a resounding success. It mapped the Victoria River Valley, solved the riddle of the inland sea, penetrated the Tanami Desert, then retreated across the top of Australia to Brisbane. Gregory, that extraordinary horseman, in the saddle for 41 days at one stage, sketched and surveyed as he went, producing maps that are as good as anything that can be bought today. Despite a trip lasting nearly two years and covering 6000 kilometres, Gregory didn't lose a man, reported no serious illnesses, was free of scurvy and lost few of his horses. Through careful management and discipline, he avoided any fatal conflict with Aborigines. The leadership he demonstrated was exemplary. Gregory displayed an ability to motivate and inspire men as diverse as the expedition botanist, Ferdinand Mueller, and the artist, Thomas Baines, on the one hand, and the stockmen, farriers and harness makers who made up the expedition muscle. Gregory saw no difference between officers and men.

The artwork produced by Thomas Baines, 70 pictures in all, gave Europeans and most Australians a look at the *Never Never* for the first time. It now survives in the Royal Geographic Society in London. The botanical collection that Mueller put together is the greatest collection of plants ever assembled in Australia and earned Mueller the distinction of being Australia's greatest nineteenth-century scientist. He attributed his success to Gregory's careful management and the encouragement given to the scientists in his party.

Despite being miffed at losing leadership of the expedition, Charles Sturt best summed up Gregory's achievement: *Unquestionably Mr Gregory's survey . . . has been decisive of the general character of the Australian interior, nor has he left much for any future explorer to hope for, who may hereafter penetrate into it.* The essential climatic and topographic features of Australia were now understood. The flow of Australia's rivers was clarified, disappointing those who hoped for large transcontinental streams or inland seas.

The North Australian Expedition made Gregory a household name in Australia and his expedition was proclaimed around the world. It was then promptly forgotten. He proves that winners, in Australia at least, don't always write history.

Not resting on his laurels, Gus Gregory was back in the saddle two years later in search of Leichhardt, leading a party for 2600 kilometres across southern Queensland and into the waterless hell of South Australia. He didn't find Leichhardt, but he led his party safely through the deserts to Adelaide and opened what we know today as the Birdsville and Strzelecki tracks. This trip allowed stock to be moved from Queensland to Adelaide for the first time and showed the way for Stuart and Burke and Wills, who followed him several years later. That Burke and Wills would soon die in the same area that was traversed successfully by Gregory is a stark comment on the differing skills of the explorers.

As a result of the North Australian and Leichhardt expeditions, Gregory had ridden from the Indian Ocean on the northwest coast of Australia to the Pacific Ocean at Brisbane, then down to the Great Southern Ocean at Adelaide. In total, he rode a distance that was equivalent to travelling from Sydney to Perth three times across the continent, or from London to Beijing, right across central Asia. No explorer since the Venetian, Marco Polo, in the Middle Ages had ridden further, covering such a diverse range of topography and climatic types. Only Stuart covered comparable distances on horseback.

Gregory's explorations had a dramatic impact on the development of Western Australia, the Northern Territory and South Australia. His later activities as Surveyor General of Queensland opened up that state's vast interior and gave it the shape we know today. As a navigator, astronomer and careful leader of men, only James Cook is Gregory's peer. As a horseman, only Stuart came close. As a conciliator of Aborigines, skilled in traversing their country without incident and humane in his treatment of them and in his understanding of their culture, he was years ahead of his time. As an innovator and inventor of saddlery, navigational equipment and exploration technique, he stands alone.

Given these great achievements why are the textbooks silent on Gus Gregory? Macquarie University's Professor Duncan Waterson offered a possible explanation when he told me: 'Australian history has been written by the Left. Gregory, after his exploring career, went on to become a prominent Queensland politician, a conservative associated with the squatters. He is seen as part of the Right and therefore is not considered by some as worthy of study despite his huge exploration achievements.'

I have other theories. One is that he was *too* successful. His entry in the *Australian Dictionary of Biography* alludes to this contradiction, saying of the North Australian Expedition:

It was too successful to be recognised as one of the most significant journeys led by one of the few unquestionably great Australian explorers. Modest, unromantic and resolute in following instructions, he did not dramatise his report, boasted no triumphs and sought no honours despite his admirable aboriginal policy and meticulous organisation. He excelled as a surveyor and manager of men, horses and equipment, and invented improvements for packsaddles and pocket compasses. His seasonal knowledge and bushcraft were unparalleled and he was the first to note the sequence of weather patterns in Australia from west to east.

Another explanation for Gregory's lack of acclaim is simply that he was an Australian and never left this country, while Thomas Mitchell, Charles Sturt and Edward Eyre retired to social acclaim and the clubs of London. Stuart also returned to the old country, and never thought of himself as other than Scottish. The professors and schoolmasters who established the early Australian school curriculums were educated in England. Could these educators have overlooked Gregory in favour of their own countrymen?

Also, much of the Australian history that's taught in schools is dominated by the spectacular, because it's easy to teach. And showing our origins, we seem to have inherited a strong British taste for melodrama. Burke and Wills is our best-known saga – a fiasco of poor management, bad judgment and melancholy death. Leichhardt isn't much better, swallowed up in the lonely outback waving his cutlass. The rest of it is a succession of men staggering into settlements half-dead from starvation and scurvy, survivors of pitched battles with the blacks, eating their boots as a last resort. Is it any wonder that we celebrate the tragic failure of Gallipoli, while the brilliant success of the Charge at Beersheba (now located in southern Israel), executed by Australian cavalrymen in 1917 riding

Australian horses and led by an Australian general, is completely unknown to our children?

Gregory wasn't of this melodramatic tradition. A seasoned
professional, he didn't go into the bush to seek glory or die in
the attempt. Careful, measured in his risk taking, and with the
safety of his men and animals uppermost in his mind, he is as
far from this tradition as it is possible to get. He is like Roald
Amundsen surviving and triumphing in the Antarctic, while
Robert Scott killed himself and everyone in his party. But
which one is taught at school? Bold Captain Scott, of course.

'Imagine what he could have done with camels,' was
Andrew Harper's final comment on Gus Gregory.

My choice of Andrew Harper as a travelling companion was
an inspired one. Skilled and experienced, diligent and organised around the camp, tolerant of my limitations, he proved an
agreeable and reliable partner. His leadership was faultless. I'm
sure there were many times when he was as tired as I was and
never showed it, when he was frustrated at my lack of experience and never let on. When I couldn't lift the green boxes or
couldn't get up to gather firewood, he completed these tasks
without complaint. When the camels strayed, bolted or went
lame, he approached the problem with unshakeable calm and
patience. As a chief executive in a Collins Street company, he
would have been a great success.

In his approach to the outback, Andrew has some of
Stuart's stubbornness and tenacity and some of Gregory's tech-
nical and management skills. He is unusual in that, like
Gregory, he is a good manager of both animals and people.
I had presumed that 21st-century men weren't of the same
calibre as those who had gone before. It was encouraging to
admit my mistake. I think that in another age, Andrew would
have taken his place alongside Kekwick and Thring on Stuart's

expedition, or Henry Gregory and Robert Bowman on Gus Gregory's expedition, or Ben Nicker who accompanied Mike Terry. All were superb bushmen. One day, I might say to an enthralled grandchild, 'I was out in the Tanami with Harper and his camels.'

In Andrew, I met a man at peace with himself and the world. He is confirmation of the proverb that a man who loves his work never works a day in his life. A rare breed of man born in the twentieth century, who has made his love his job, is good at it and content with its rewards. I envy him. As an eighteen-year-old, I went rushing into the kitchen of my parents' country farmhouse with my scholarship papers and proudly announced, 'I'm off to Sydney to go to university. I'm going to be rich.'

My mother wisely replied, 'You'll find it easier to be rich than to be content. There are plenty of rich people in the world, but very few contented ones.' Andrew may never become rich by showing tourists the wonders of the Australian deserts, but he does seem content. On returning to Sydney, I read General Colin Powell's autobiography, *My American Journey*, written on the occasion of his retirement from the US army and from his chairmanship of the Joint Chiefs of Staff, the highest post in the US military. Summing up his life he said: *I had found something to do with my life that was honourable and useful, that I could do well and that I loved doing. That is rare good fortune in anyone's life.* If Andrew sits down one day when his years of desert exploration are past and picks up the pen, his epilogue may be no different. He is indeed fortunate.

The ultimate compliment that I can pay Andrew is that he could have done it without me, but I couldn't have done it without him!

For Andrew, life has returned to its previous course. As 2003 begins, he is reorganising his business following the Australian insurance debacle. He is planning a 2003 tourist expedition starting at Lake Gregory and heading south into the Great Sandy Desert. But it hasn't been easy, as the insurance industry may have done his business irreparable harm. If his business stumbles, it would be a great loss; he is the only operator of long-distance camel treks in the Australian desert. His knowledge of the country and camel-handling skills are irreplaceable.

And me? Every day I join the throng of men in suits queuing on Manly wharf to catch the Jetcat to the city. The desert is now only a memory. But for a moment, for five brief weeks, I walked in the footsteps of giants – Stuart, Terry, Warburton and Gregory.

Would I go back? You bet! But with ongoing family responsibilities, the need to earn a living and the prohibitive cost of mounting expeditions, this is unlikely for some time. The next journey may be years away and it may be riding a camel rather than walking beside one, or it may be in a four-wheel-drive vehicle. But go I must. I am determined to show my family some of the places I have experienced, the view from Mt Wilson being a priority. I would love to take my wife for a swim in Lake Gregory if she could be persuaded.

To sum up my feelings about our expedition, I turn to an earlier Tanami explorer, the formidable Michael Terry, who was as adept with the pen as he was with a camel, and decades ago wrote the lament of the 21st-century male:

> Would to God I had been born fifty years earlier and could have joined those gallant men. The world is so prosaic these days, so fenced and ordinary that one has to be content with detailed examination of the discoveries of the explorers and be denied the larger chance, that wonderful exhilaration of being able to bring back to civilisation some discovery whose magnitude could stir all men to surprise, and if it should be good, then to joy.

Amen!

AUTHOR'S NOTE

After carefully studying John McDouall Stuart's maps and journals, and making daily use of them during part of the Central Australian Expedition 2002, it is clear that he has been done a major disservice. The incorrect naming of the Lander River has already been covered in the text of this book. Mt Esther, which he named, isn't identified on the modern topographic map of the area, although it is easy to find to the west of Central Mt Stuart.

The large mountain that dominates the eastern Tanami plain, which Stuart discovered, named and climbed, and under which we made our Bloodwood Apple Camp, is marked in his charts as Mt Denison and is referred to by that name in many places in his journal. There can be no confusion as to the identity of this mountain, as I was able to check its bearings from Central Mt Stuart and Mt Barkly. Unfortunately, it has for many years been known as Mt Leichhardt. Like Stuart, I was able to take back bearings to this dominant peak until well north of the Studholme Hills. There is no doubt in my mind that it is Stuart's Mt Denison.

Stuart did name a peak in the area Mt Leichhardt, which was south of the large mountain he called Mt Denison. He sent Kekwick there looking for water. This mountain, in the Yundurbulu Range, at about longitude 132° 38' 5" and latitude 21° 58' 9", is the mountain Stuart christened Mt Leichhardt, but on today's maps it's an orphan bearing no name.

Finally, there is a Mt Denison shown on the modern map, a tiny insignificant hill away to the west of both Stuart's route and our own. The Mt Denison of today's maps, at only 885 metres, is so small it is hardly noticeable out on the plain and certainly cannot be used as a landmark in the way that both our expedition and Stuart's used the dominant mountain.

Quite simply, the map makers have got the names right, but they were careless in allocating them to the right mountains. This is an easy task for anyone taking the time to pick up Stuart's journal and maps and a protractor. Geoscience Australia, the Commonwealth government's national mapping agency, produces the Mt Peake map, which contains these errors. It's a shambles of misinformation, confusing for visitors to these historical sites and dangerously misleading to historians. Indeed, the Mt Peake map is a disgrace to the science of cartography and makes me wonder if this is typical of the rest of Australia's maps. However, to make this narrative easy to follow, for anyone with an atlas in hand, I have left the names as they were shown on the modern map, not as shown in Stuart's maps and journals.

ACKNOWLEDGMENTS

To mount an expedition such as this and then write a book about it requires help from a large number of people.

I wish to thank the staff of the Central Land Council in Alice Springs, particularly Michael Prowse and Marah Edwards, for their assistance in obtaining permits to cross Aboriginal land between Central Mt Stuart and the Northern Territory border. Thank you also to the communities of the Central Desert Aboriginal Land Trust for permission to cross your property. Thank you also to Rex Johns and his daughter Julieanne, and the other traditional owners of the Lake Gregory area, for permission to visit Mt Wilson and the lake and for advice on local bush foods.

Mark Sewell and the members of the Mulan and Balgo communities provided memorable hospitality and assistance in loading the camels at journey's end.

To the owners and mangers of Anninge and Tanami Downs stations, thank you for permission to cross your properties. Also Brian Fowler and his staff at the Granites goldmine were very helpful with water and directions for transiting the mine site.

To Ben Ryan in Sydney, who sold me the Alpenaire and Back Country freeze-dried meals, many thanks. They certainly kept us alive. To Trevor Shiell and John Wilkinson, thanks for getting us underway and for resupply and collecting us when it was all over. Thank you to my brothers, Damien and Michael, who joined me for two murderous hikes through the Victoria River country while I screwed up the courage to tackle the Tanami. Barrie Rhodes gave up a weekend to put me through my paces up the Otford escarpment and share his expertise. Sorry I couldn't give you more of a contest, Barrie.

I owe a great debt to Tom Gilliatt, my publisher at Pan Macmillan and my editor Brianne Tunnicliffe for their enthusiastic response to this story and for their professional guidance and encouragement in turning it into a book. Vicki Thurlow has proofread the manuscripts for both my books with an eagle-eyed diligence and skill which is greatly appreciated.

A number of people helped with scientific information for this book and I thank particularly David Gibson for his advice on Tanami fauna, especially the mala; David Albrecht of the Alice Springs Herbarium for information on Tanami plants, especially the desert poplar; and Bruce Monday of the Alice Springs Wildlife Park for advice on the snakes of the central deserts. Any errors are mine, not theirs. Adrian Winwood Smith provided advice on Michael Terry and put me in touch with Michael's sister. Karen Johnson located the Jack Keyser photograph at Thomson's Rockhole among Terry's papers at the National Library of Australia. Thanks for your persistence. Steve Strike, from Alice Springs, allowed me to use one of his photographs to complete the detail of the cuttah in the book's packsaddle sketch.

Finally, to my darling wife Prue, without whom none of this would have been possible. Thanks for once more allowing me to go and visit the wild places. I won't ask again (for a while).

Kieran Kelly
Seaforth
May 2003